Praise for *Æffect*

"In a historical moment plagued by political, economic, and social polarization, Stephen Duncombe provides a useful and engaging manual for understanding and enacting the power of culture to make change. From an analysis of theories of change and their histories, to highly practical questions, examples, and worksheets, *Æffect* delivers a set of important guidelines to consider the impact of artistic activism. Duncombe argues for the need to reach beyond the world of symbols into that of action, while utilizing the pull of emotion to motivate change, detailing an activism that shifts the ways we imagine the world by melding the mystery of art with the clarity of impact, all in an accessible book for anyone seeking social transformation." —**Laura Raicovich, author of *Culture Strike: Art and Museums in an Age of Protest***

"I've lost count of the number of times people working in foundations and nonprofits have asked me and other champions of artistic activism and culture change work, 'but how can we know if it's working?' As Stephen Duncombe shows, the answer to this question is by no means a mystery, but it does require a willingness to answer it. The beauty of Duncombe's approach is that it can be tailored to fit the needs and resources of even the most time- and cash-strapped organizations and activists. *Æffect: The Affect and Effect of Artistic Activism* is one of the most useful attempts to answer the question of impact that I have yet come across, and the next time someone asks about how to measure progress in creative activism, I plan to just hand them a copy of this book." —**Brett Davidson, Founder and Principal, Wingseed, and former Director of Media and Narratives at the Open Society Public Health Program**

"The word 'assessment' makes my skin crawl, but we need to know if what we are doing works and there's no one I trust more to help us figure this out than Stephen Duncombe." —**Andy Bichlbaum, The Yes Men**

"Artists invested in social change often shirk or retreat from the notion of evaluation. Assessment feels daunting, if not entirely out of our skill set. But what happens when we more carefully look at artistic affect when it contributes to a tangible shift and transformation of power in whatever form, duration, or container? Stephen Duncombe's groundbreaking catalog and study offers us not only critical examples of practices in the realm of artistic activism but also illuminate how, when recalibrated toward metrics of social aesthetics, we may better ascertain what is, was, or might be gained in our intentions." —**Shaun Leonardo, artist**

"Grounded in artist-activists' own intentions and observations, Duncombe leads an open-spirited and engaging inquiry into the relationship between *affect* and *effect* in looking at the hybrid practice of artistic activism. Practitioners will find it especially compelling in its wide range of practitioner voices and projects as they reflect upon the *aeffect* of their intertwined aesthetic choices and social intents." —**Pam Korza, former co-director, Animating Democracy, Americans for the Arts**

æffect

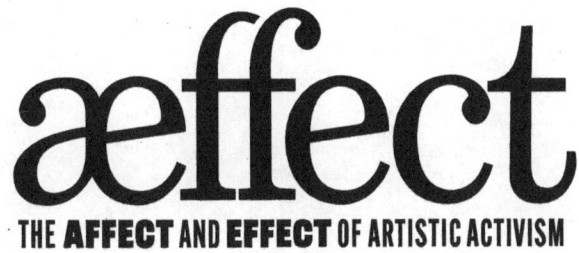

æffect

THE **AFFECT** AND **EFFECT** OF ARTISTIC ACTIVISM

STEPHEN DUNCOMBE

FORDHAM UNIVERSITY PRESS

New York   2024

Fordham University Press has no responsibility for the persistence or accuracy of URLs for external or third-party internet websites referred to in this publication and does not guarantee that any content on such websites is or will remain accurate or appropriate.

Fordham University Press also publishes its books in a variety of electronic formats. Some content that appears in print may not be available in electronic books.

Visit us online at www.fordhampress.com.

Library of Congress Cataloging-in-Publication Data available online at https://catalog. loc.gov.

Printed in the United States of America

26 25 24   5 4 3 2 1

First edition

CONTENTS

If we can somehow observe the process that happens between a work of art and an idea reaching a community and then that community taking a defiant form of action, that's the black box. That's where the great mystery is happening in these beautiful, unbelievable processes of moving from meaning to building relationships, to building power, to taking action. That's where I would love to be able to peer in more clearly.

— GAN GOLAN, ARTISTIC ACTIVIST

What Is Æffect?

SEVERAL YEARS AGO, I HAD the good fortune to ask the world-renowned artist activist Hans Haacke a question:

> How can you know when what you've done works?

It was a seemingly simple and straightforward question and one that Haacke, with more than half a century of experience in the field, is eminently qualified to answer. He pondered my question for a moment, and then replied,

> I've been asked that question many times, and that question requires one to go around it before one really avoids it.

Haacke's response was meant to be funny—and it *is* funny—but beneath his wry humor lies a serious problem: the evasion of, and aversion to, questions concerning the social impact of art and activism and how to assess it.[1] If this reaction was limited to Haacke, it might be excusable as the eccentricity of a singularly brilliant artist, but it's not. It is endemic to the hybrid practice of mixing arts and activism—that is: artistic activism.

I should know. For more than thirty years, I have been a practicing artistic activist, for twenty years I've taught and written about it, and for the past ten, I've traveled the world training artists to strategize more like activists, and activists to create more like artists. I've done this because I have a deep and abiding faith that art can activate people and that there is an art to good activism. I have faith that mixing arts and activism can elevate both and have a powerful impact. And yet it is just that: a faith. For decades, and lately with increasing regularity, a heretical thought haunts my faith. Yes, artistic activism is fun, creative, cutting-edge, and increasingly popular, but a little voice within insists on asking a simple question: *Does it work?*

Like Haacke, I usually go around this question before avoiding it all together. But when I do give it a little thought, it becomes clear that this "simple" question is not simple at all. To answer "does it work?," one also needs to ask, how does artistic activism work? How do we know whether it works? And, what does "working" even mean when dealing with both the affect and effect of a hybrid practice of arts and activism? After more than thirty years of avoidance and circumvention, this book is my effort to honestly and unflinchingly address these questions that lie, or should lie, at the heart of the field of artistic activism. In addressing these questions, I also hope to develop methods and tools that can help artistic activists create projects that work better.

What is Artistic Activism?

Before moving ahead on these questions, we need to back up and address a couple of others: What exactly is artistic activism? Why does it matter whether it works or not? "Artistic activism" is a term first popularized in scholarship by Chantal Mouffe and in the field by the Center for Artistic Activism, but the practice has existed for decades and goes by many names: political art, agit-prop, creative activism, activist art, critical art, artivism, socially engaged arts, social practice arts, aesthetic protest, aesthetic activism, *arte útil*, and so on, with a new term being invented every couple years.[2] For this book, however, I am going to refer to these diverse sets of practices as *artistic activism* and their practitioners as *artistic activists*.[3]

Probably the best way to describe the practice and practitioners is not through more terms, but through examples.[4] What follows is certainly not comprehensive, nor is it meant to signify "best practices." It is merely a handful of examples that I find inspiring (and many of whose creators you will hear from in later chapters) that give a flavor of the field.

Undocubus

In 2012 a group of undocumented immigrant activists living in the United States bought an old bus, painted "No Fear" across its side, and decorated it with images of brightly colored butterflies. They then took the *Undocubus* on a road trip across the country to protest local anti-immigration laws that had created a climate of fear amongst undocumented immigrants and stoked xenophobia in the "native-born."

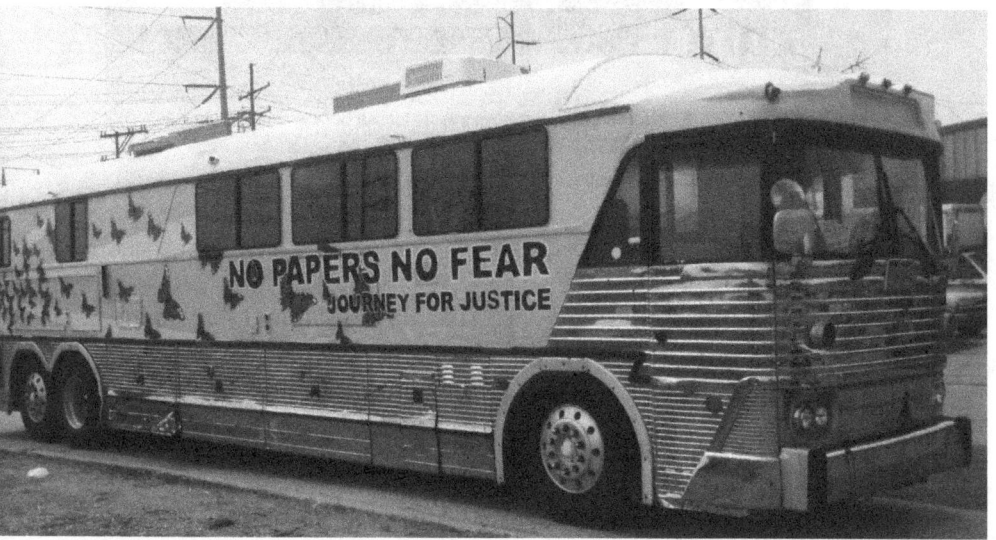

Riding the Undocubus with "No Papers, No Fear," photo: Jobs with Justice.

In addition to adopting and adapting the symbols of previous social movements—their bus was of the same vintage as those used by civil rights "freedom riders" half a century before—they made a symbol of their own: the monarch butterfly, a beautiful creature who annually migrates across North America, from the United States to Mexico and back again. With the help of artistic activist Favianna Rodriguez, this symbol was polished up and reproduced on posters and T-shirts, recreated through do-it-yourself butterfly-making workshops, and joined by the slogan "Migration is Beautiful." The *Undocubus* activists forged an association of human immigration with a natural and majestic migration, reframing the image of a population unjustly feared and routinely degraded. Who, after all, can be fearful of a butterfly?

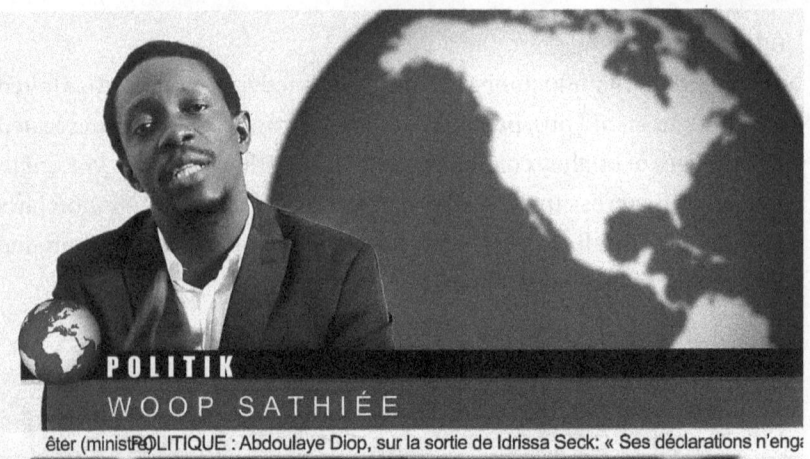

Keyti raps the news on Journal Rappe, courtesy of the artist.

Journal Rappé

Inspired by the "Y'en a Marre," or "We're Fed Up" rap-infused youth movement that started in Senegal in 2011, rappers Cheikh "Keyti" Sène and Makhtar "Xuman" Fall wanted to create a news program to provide information from around their country and across the world that young people needed in order to be effective and aware political citizens.

But the language of politics in Senegal, like in many places, is associated with corruption and the abuse of power and ignored or rejected by many, particularly by youth, who make up 60 percent of the population. So Keyti and Xuman decided that they needed to use a different approach than a conventional news broadcast. Drawing on their talent as rappers, they created *Journal Rappé*, a regular video show where the two artists create a long-form investigative report in the form of a hip-hop mixtape, rapping the current news in French and Wolof (Senegal's dominant local language). The show was so successful that it has been replicated in countries across Africa, and as far away as Jamaica and Vietnam. Through rap, *Journal Rappé* provides political information for young people in a language and through a culture they feel is their own.

I Wish This Was

In 2005 Hurricane Katrina devastated the city of New Orleans, leaving in its wake thousands of damaged residences and stores and the massive job of rebuilding the city. It soon became clear that plans for the redevelopment of New Orleans favored tourist hotels and convention centers while the needs and desires of residents were ignored. In response, Candy Chang made a small and simple intervention.

In the style of greeting tags, she printed thousands of red and white fill-in-the-blank stickers that read: "I wish this was____." She then posted these stickers on vacant buildings and left them in boxes at local businesses all over the city. And like a participatory poem of the community's dreams, people filled them out and posted them up: "I wish this was: *A Community Garden.*" "I wish this was: *A Grocery! Locally Owned!*" "I wish this was: *Fixed.*" "I wish this was: *Heaven.*" By asking people to write their own responses, Chang prompts everyday citizens to imagine what *they* would like for their community and raises the critical question of whose interests are catered to when urban areas are redeveloped.

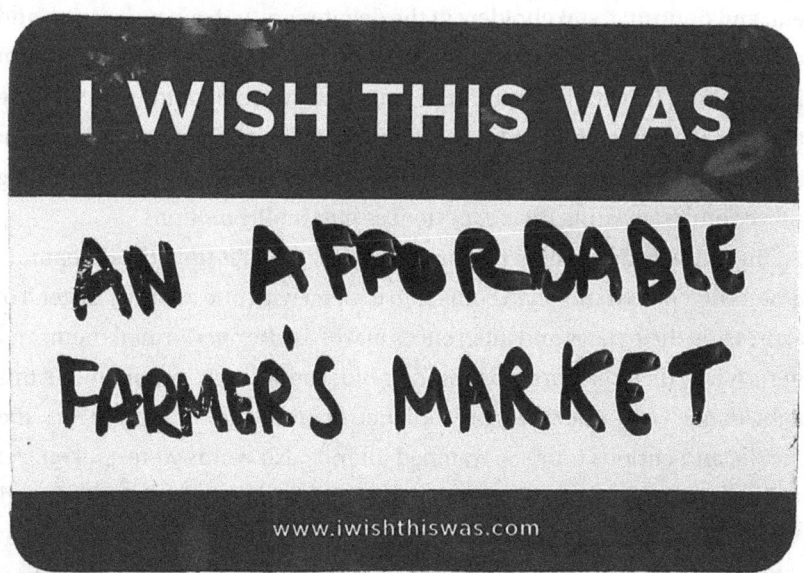

I Wish This Was by Candy Chang, photo: Candy Chang.

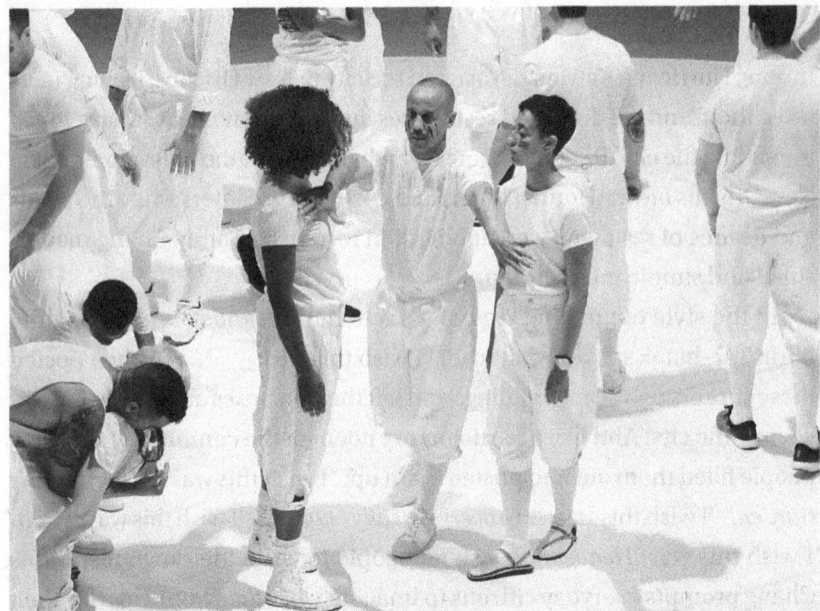

Shaun Leonardo resolving conflict through Primitive Games, video still: Giacomo Francia. Courtesy of the artist and Solomon R. Guggenheim Museum.

Primitive Games

Dressed all in white, four teams of competitors representing four differ-ent, and opposing, stakeholders in the debates around gun possession and control assembled in the airy circular lobby of the Guggenheim Museum in New York City in the autumn of 2018. They were here to wage warfare through an ancient Roman battle game, and for weeks had been training in separate camps, working with the artistic activist Shaun Leonardo, learning moves and translating their experiences into bodily motions.

The culminating public performance was the first time these separate groups of "combatants" had come into contact with one another. Instead of expressing their views and differences in words, they performed them, and in turn had these gestures mirrored or blocked by their opponent. As this fight/dance was performed, an audience of family, friends, art lovers, the media, and curious tourists, watched intently. No words were spoken, yet stories were told and positions articulated, and communication happened. And through this silent mock battle, the divisive ideological identities that divide us were, ideally, undermined, moving us toward more connection and less combat.

War on Smog

Chinese cities are notorious for their pollution. Chinese authorities, wary of a repeat of the Tiananmen Square protests, are equally notorious for being hostile toward street demonstrations. Cleverly responding to this challenging political terrain, artistic activists in the city of Chongqing in southwest China staged a public performance piece in 2014 called *War on Smog*. (The name of the action was "inspired" by the words of Chinese Premier Li Keqiang, who publicly called for a "War on Smog"—then did little). The "war" was waged by a couple in a bridal dress and formal suit being wed in gas masks, a parade of tutu-clad girls, likewise in gas masks, and other "artistic performers" who brought attention to air quality in the city.

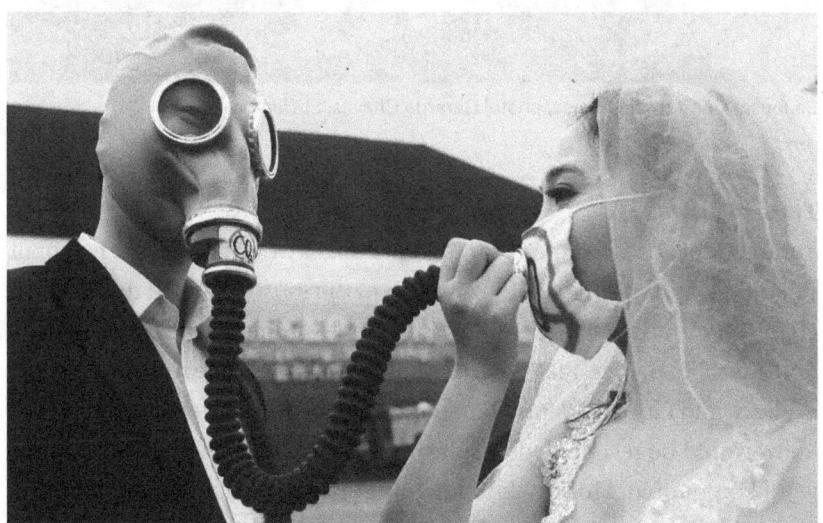

A protest that doesn't look like protest: War on Smog, photo: Imaginechina Limited/ Alamy Stock Photo.

Mixing a street protest with an art piece was a stroke of brilliance. Since it didn't look like a political protest to the authorities, no activists were arrested. But the style and creativity of the War on Smog provided arresting images for both local and world media. By riding the line between politics, which is repressed, and art, which is tolerated and even celebrated in China, these artistic activists found the space to safely protest within an authoritarian regime.

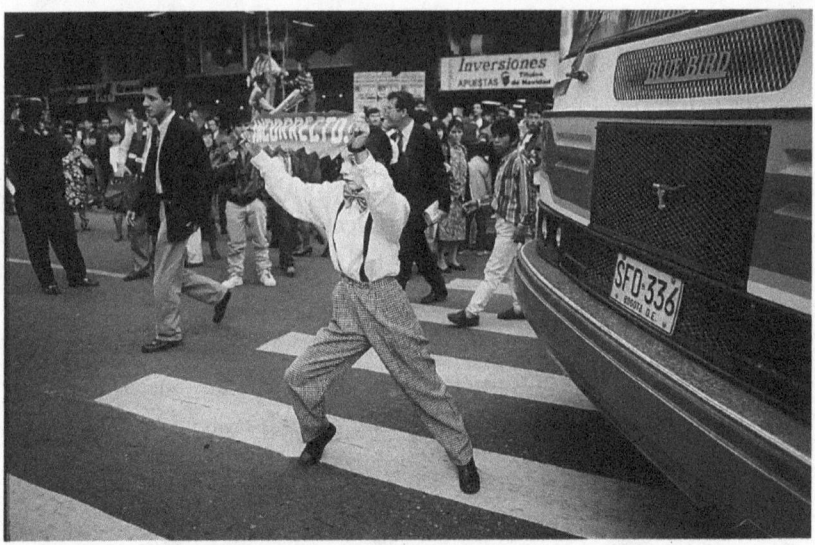

Seriously funny Traffic Mimes, photo: Gerardo Chaves/El Tiempo.

Traffic Mimes

Antanas Mockus faced many serious challenges when he became mayor of Bogotá, Colombia, in 1995. The city, one of the most violent in the Western Hemisphere, also had a seemingly intractable problem with traffic congestion. Cars and people alike ignored signs and laws, and the result was chaos: gridlock and fatal accidents. Rather than imposing heavier fines, which he knew would be resented, or displaying more traffic signs, which he knew would be ignored, Mockus did something artistic: he hired 420 mimes (yes, mimes) to direct traffic.

These traffic mimes roamed the streets of the capital in brightly colored clothes and painted faces, mocking and shaming pedestrians and drivers using the centuries-old art of pantomime. The shock value of the mimes' presence, along with their appeal to citizens' sense of humor (and their fear of ridicule), was impressively effective. Because of the mimes and other creative tactics used by the municipal authorities, traffic fatalities dropped in Bogotá by over 50 percent.

Intention

These practices of artistic activism cover a wide range. *Primitive Games* and *I Wish This Was* have their roots in the art world; the creators of *Journal Rappé* are pop-culture musicians. *Undocubus* and the *War on Smog* are the productions of groups of activists, and the *Traffic Mimes* are a project of a municipal government. All these interventions, however, have a couple of things in common.

The first is that all the interventions are *intentionally change-oriented*. People create art for all sorts of reasons, but when a person engages in artistic activism, no matter what name they call it, they are making a claim, whether explicit or implicit, that the intention of their work is to help bring about some sort of social change. This change can be material: lowering traffic deaths, as in the case of the traffic mimes. It can be perceptual: changing attitudes about migration through butterflies and a bus tour. Or even communicative: developing visceral connections between ideological combatants through an ancient game. What change looks like differs according to specific objectives and overall context, but an intention of change is a constant in artistic activism.

Intending change through one's artistic activism, however, does not necessarily mean that change happens. Many projects—maybe most projects—don't result in the impact the artistic activist intends. Either little or no social change occurs, or it happens in surprising and unintended ways. Conversely, there are instances in which an artist has no desire to bring about social change through their work yet it happens anyway.[5] And then there are those artists who use social change, or the need for it, as subject matter for their art with little real intention of creating actual social change, the result being art *about* politics, but not art that necessarily works politically.[6] Defining artistic activism by its subject matter or even its results is not productive. Change is something often outside the control of the artistic activist; the intention of change, however, is not. As a defining feature of artistic activism, intent allows us to distinguish artistic activism from other forms of artistic expression; it also provides, as we'll see later, an Archimedean point from which to leverage a useful method of assessment.

The second thing these interventions all have in common is that *they combine the aesthetic, expressive, and affective concerns of the arts with*

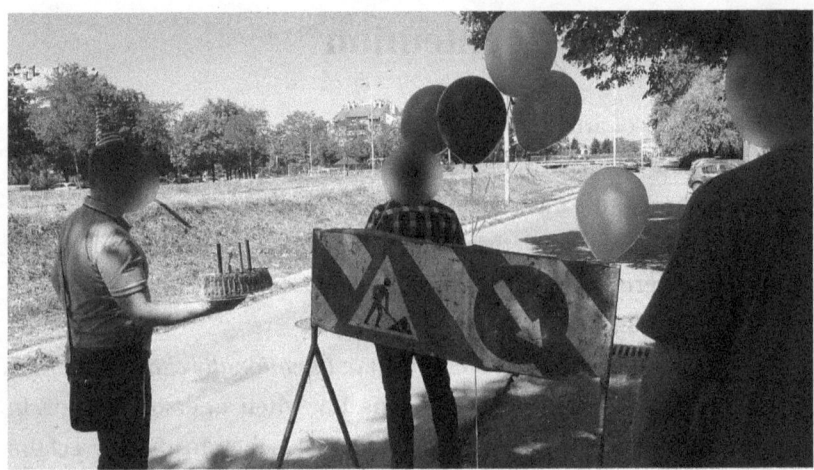

Throwing a birthday party for a pothole with the Contemporary Arts Center, courtesy of CAC and Nikola Pisarev.

the more instrumental, and effect-oriented, goals of activism. The aesthetic, expressive, and affective distinguish *artistic* activism from other forms of activism; instrumental and effect-oriented goals distinguish artistic *activism* from other forms of art. The examples above occupy different places on the spectrum between art and activism, with Leonardo's aestheticized approach (as well as the museum setting) pushing his project closer to the art side, and Rodriguez's work with immigration activists as part of a larger campaign moving closer to the activism end. There is a lot of space, however, between these poles, and a lot of slippage even within one project or the work of one artistic activist. Take, for example, the work of the North Macedonian artistic activist group the Contemporary Arts Center (Центар за современа уметност), or CAC for short. The innocuous name of the group (necessary cover when they formed under a repressive political regime) belies their deep commitment to social change, and their approaches to artistic activism range across the art–activism axis.

What the CAC call *creative activism* are interventions meant to have a focused, demonstrable, and often immediate impact. What sort of an impact? "Potholes!" That's how the co-founder of the group, Nikola Pisarev, responded when asked that question, and then went on to tell me the story about the genesis of his group. A decade or so previously, as part of a group of idealistic artists from the capital city of Skopje, Pisarev traveled to the countryside with the noble objective of bringing art to the people. But when they got to these towns, the people didn't want to talk about art. They wanted

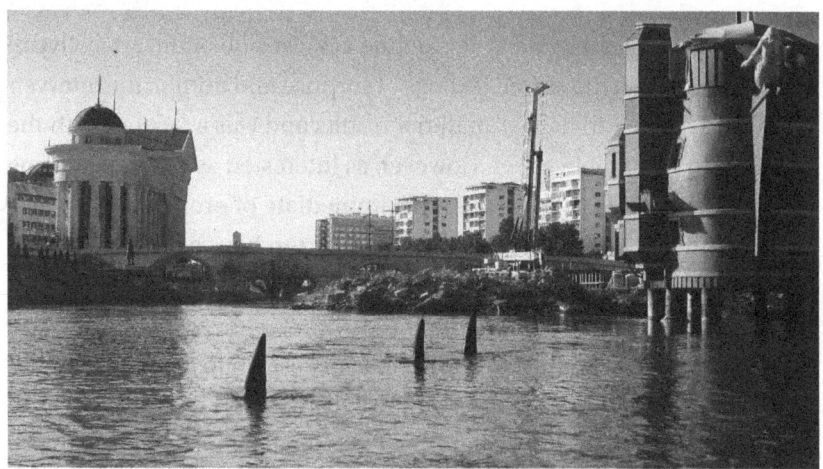

Sharks in Skopje, courtesy of CAC and Nikola Pisarev.

to talk about potholes. Big, gaping, potholes in the main streets of town that were deep enough to break a car's axle and create a small lake when it rained. Potholes that hadn't been fixed by municipal authorities for years and were symbols of the ineptitude and corruption of the current governing regime. Meetings had been held, politicians confronted, and petitions delivered, but still the potholes remained. So instead of bringing art to the people, they decided to bring their artistry to the people's problems.

Upon hearing that it was coming up on two years that one particularly large hole had not been fixed, the CAC decided to throw the pothole a birthday party.[7] Pisarev describes the preparation: "We buy one cake, it costs ten dollars. At the supermarket we buy flags, candles, and everything and we call the media. But we don't call it a protest, we call it a celebration of the birthday of the hole in the road." And people, many of whom would have been too apprehensive or apathetic to show up at a protest, came to the party. The news media, promised a new and entertaining angle on an old and dull concern, also came. "The trick," as Pisarev puts it, worked.

> We were the main topic on the news. For two days, it was the only important news in Macedonia. And all of the media started asking the ministry what would happen. . . . "Will you fix the road?" and they have to do something. And in three days . . . they found the money, and they started fixing the problem immediately.

The pothole birthday party lies on the activist side of the art–activism spectrum. While it mobilized feelings of surprise and humor, the intervention was designed to deliver material results and was executed with the activist aim of tangible effect. However, as interested as CAC are in using their artistic talents to solve the most immediate of problems, they also understand and appreciate the capacity of art to have a longer, larger, if less discernible impact. This is the aim of their "urban art actions," the best known of which is *The Sharks*.

In order to appreciate *The Sharks*, it is necessary to understand a bit about the country and its recent political history. The Republic of North Macedonia, as it is now formally named, is a small nation on the southern edge of the Western Balkans, situated right above Greece. Created as an independent political entity with the breakup of Yugoslavia, the country was run by a nationalist, conservative, and notoriously corrupt regime from 2006 until 2016. While in power, the regime expended massive amounts of public resources (those they didn't pocket) on immense monuments to mythologized heroes of the Macedonian people. A thirty-meter-high, gold-plated statue of Alexander the Great astride a horse still dominates the capital city's main square, and hundreds more statues were erected around the city as part of the ruling party's controversial "Skopje 2014" development plan. As part of this plan, three sailing ships were constructed on the banks of the Vardar River, which runs through the center of the capital. They were monstrous, ugly things, created to house gambling casinos and restaurants. They were also ridiculous. Land-locked Macedonia has no seafaring tradition, and just like the resurrection of Alexander the Great and the adoption of Greco, Roman, and Baroque style for all newly built public buildings, the ships were an absurd nationalist fantasy.

And so the CAC decided to amplify the absurdity. They crafted several very large shark fins and, when no one was looking, anchored them in the middle of the river surrounding the ships. It was simple, and silly, and having pulled their stunt, the members of CAC put up a Facebook page about it and left town for a holiday, assuming that the sharks would elicit a chuckle or two and then get quickly removed. Instead, the sharks created an uproar. Security officials were sent to the Vardar river to terminate the sharks with sniper rifles. Pictures of the sharks were on the front page of national newspapers and even picked up by the BBC. Within days, the sharks' Facebook page garnered two hundred thousand hits. *The Sharks* struck an affective chord, perfectly capturing the absurdity of all the faux history and the faux reality of the nation-building plans of the government.

What was the point? What did it change? As Pisarev explains, the purpose of *The Sharks,* like the other "urban art actions" the CAC does, is "not to change particular things, but to use more creative actions to change people's minds." Asked to elaborate, he says: "It is just liberating, . . . making fun of Skopje 2014. Because fun liberates people, humor liberates people, to start to speak, to start to publish." There *is* an effective element to the CAC's urban art actions—changing minds and prompting others to speak and publish—but these effects are not at the concrete and immediate level of fixing potholes. The primary purpose of these projects is affective: to create an emotional charge and stimulate feelings of fun and liberation. This is not to say that artistic affect has no activist effect. In 2016, what was called the "colorful revolution" broke out in North Macedonia. Citizens protested in the streets and, joined by the members of the CAC, splashed the monuments and buildings built by the corrupt government with bright daubs of paint. In this public explosion of fun and liberation the repressive regime was finally brought down.[8]

Affect, Effect, and *Æffect*

You may have noticed that I have been using two words with increasing frequency: *affect* and *effect.* These words are often used interchangeably in the English language but their meaning differs subtly—and critically. *Effect,* as the *Oxford English Dictionary* tells us, is to "bring about (an event, a result); to accomplish (an intention, a desire)." To have an effect, then, is to cause a demonstrable, often physical and material, change. *Affect,* the same source informs, is to "have an effect on the mind or feelings of (a person); to impress or influence emotionally; to move, touch."[9] As such, to generate affect is to stimulate feelings, or create an emotional state in a person or group of people.

When we think of activism, we often think in terms of its *effect.* This makes sense. Activism, as the name implies, is the activity of challenging and changing power relations, what the political scientist Harold Lasswell once famously defined as "who gets what, when, how."[10] There are, of course, many ways of doing activism. Activism does not necessarily mean holding a protest to condemn the powers that be and demand more resources; it can just as easily be organizing a childcare collective amongst parents in one's neighborhood, thereby creating new resources by empowering the community. But the common element is an activity targeted toward a tangible end. Simply put, the goal of activism is *action* to generate an *effect*.

Affect, however, is a term we usually use when speaking of the arts. Art tends not to have such an instrumental use. It is hard to say what art is for or against; its value often lies in showing us new perspectives and new ways to see our world. Its impact is often subtle and hard to measure, and confusing or contradictory messages can be layered into the work. Indeed, good art always contains a surplus of meaning: something we can't quite describe, or put our finger on, but has an impact upon us nonetheless. Its goal, if we can even use that word, is to spur us emotionally, stimulate a feeling, or alter our perception. Art *moves* us.

Stripped down to its essentials, one might say that *activism*'s goal is *effect* and *art*'s aim is *affect*. At first, these intentions seem at odds with one another. Activism moves the material world, while art moves the heart, body, and soul. The scope of the former is social change, while the latter is an individual impression. But effect and affect are often complementary.

The social is not some mere abstraction: society is composed of individual people. And change doesn't just happen: it happens because people make change. As such, the individual and the social are intertwined. This is obvious. Less obvious, perhaps, is *why* people make change (or prefer stasis). Classical democratic and economic theory would have us believe that people enact change because they have been "enlightened" to do so through a process of reasoned deliberation and rational choices. As any seasoned activist can tell you, however, people don't just soberly decide to change their mind and act accordingly, they are moved to do so by emotionally powerful stimuli, be it love, hate, fear, hope, or compassion.[11] And, as recent developments in cognitive science suggest, we understand our world less through reasoned deliberation of facts, and more through stories and symbols and metaphors that allow us to "make sense" of the information we receive.[12] As such, when it comes to stimulating social change, effect and affect are intertwined.

While marking out distinct theaters of operation, with *effect* most often referring to a material force and *affect* an emotional one, both are concerned with change and transformation. However, they approach the challenge from different directions. What is special—and potentially powerful—about the hybrid practice of artistic activism is that it works on the registers of affect and effect simultaneously. As such, artistic activism is considering, at all times, parallel concerns: What changes in the material world—practices, policies, structures—are brought about? What is the *effect* of the practice? And what mental, moral, spiritual, emotional, and even bodily feelings are engendered; what is the *affect* of the practice? If we chart a line with *affect* on one side and *effect* on another, we can imagine that some practices more traditionally activist in nature will be pulled toward the effective pole, while others that are more artistic might side toward the affective. The practices with the most potential world-changing impact might reside somewhere in the middle, resonating with both poles:

$$\text{Affect}-----\text{X}-----\text{Effect}$$

Artistic activism strives towards this X: *affective effect;* or if you prefer, *effective affect.* Or even simpler, a hybrid word for a hybrid practice: *Æffect.*[13] Keeping the *æ*ffective dimension of artistic activism in mind reminds us that thinking about art and activism needn't be an either/or proposition. Changes in ideas, emotions, *and* material conditions are necessary in order for social change to happen, and artistic activism, if it is to be *æffective*, must work on multiple levels.

Why Working Matters

Artistic activism, no matter who practices it and whatever name it goes by, has received a great deal of attention lately. A cursory search on Amazon .com under "art and activism" at the time of this writing returned a staggering two-thousand-plus results, art schools have devoted whole programs to the practice,[14] mixing arts and activism has become a commonplace theme for art exhibits[15] and an accepted approach for advocacy organizations.[16] This recent surge in interest in artistic activism is understandable.

The first rule of guerrilla warfare is to "know your terrain and use it to your advantage." Today, we live in a highly mediated world where the political topography is characterized by signs and symbols, stories and spectacles. To operate successfully in this new world, a fusion of art and activism simply makes sense.

Even a cursory look back into history, however, reminds us that activism has always employed creative strategies reliant upon cultural resources. Considering U.S. history alone, we might think of the self-conscious "strategic dramaturgy" of the civil rights protests that rendered the invisibility of white supremacist violence visible in front of international news media.[17] Or, further back, the pageantry of suffragette marches that not only drew upon but also overturned traditional signs of femininity. Or the public theater of the Boston Tea Party, which drew attention to the unfair taxes levied by the British colonial power. Reaching even further back, and casting our gaze wider, we might imagine the poetry of the Prophet Mohammed, the prefigurative performances of Jesus, and the spectacles of Moses as artistic activist strategies to capture attention and change hearts and minds.[18] One might plausibly argue that all successful activism has also been artistic activism.[19]

It is also worth remembering that art, from its first recorded appearance forty thousand years ago in caves in Indonesia, has often served a change-making (or retarding) function. Whether it was to curry favor with a god, to ensure fertility, or secure a successful hunt, art was supposed to *do something*. As the powers of church and state grew, art and artists kept pace, creating magnificent expressions of religious and secular power through the architecture of monuments, stone temple carvings, stained-glass windows, and images of deities, saints and rulers. Art, at times, also served the other side of power: reflecting and valorizing the experiences and perspectives of the poor and downtrodden. The idea and ideal of art not having a social function, of *l'art pour l'art*, is only a blip in the long history of art.[20] Just as activism has often had an artistic component, art has often had what one could call an "activist" aim.

Despite the surge in the popularity of artistic activism, there is plenty of art that makes no claims to being activist. As someone who enjoys non-activist art a great deal, I think this is a good thing. Yet I expect *all* art, if it is any good, to have some sort of affective impact on me. Likewise, there are plenty of forms of activism that make no claims to being artistic, and I've participated in many of these myself, yet if these practices had no effect, I certainly wouldn't consider them good activism. In other words: art should generate affect and activism should have an effect, and if they don't deliver on these, they are missing something essential. When art and activism come together, therefore, both sets of claims must be applied. Taking artistic activism seriously demands an honest accounting of the affects and effects, or rather, the *æffect* of the practice. To do anything else under the name of artistic activism is a form of misrepresentation.

Worse, it is a lost opportunity. The combination of arts and activism can do what neither can on its own. Art and activism often conform to expectations—and for many people those expectations are, unfortunately, negative. Art is elitist and obtuse, while activism is self-righteous and predictable. Artistic activism, however, is activism that doesn't look like activism and art that doesn't look like art. The ability of artistic activism to surprise us—to show up in unlikely places (e.g., not a gallery) or take on unfamiliar forms (e.g., not a protest march)—provides an opportunity to disrupt people's preconceived notions of art and activism, and their predetermined ideas about the messages we are trying to communicate. Artistic activism creates an opportunity to bypass seemingly fixed political ideas and moral ideals and remap cognitive patterns. This surprise is a moment when hearts can be touched and minds reached, and both changed.

Artistic activism's ability to escape easy categorization is a benefit in societies where protest is commonplace. Whereas traditional forms of protest, like marches, need to constantly increase in size or scope or descend into violence to become noticed and newsworthy, the creative innovation at the heart of artistic activism provides something uncommon or out of place that can attract attention and become memorable. And, as we saw with the *War on Smog*, the boundary slippage of artistic activism works equally well in repressive regimes where overt political protest is prohibited yet artistic practices are tolerated. Slipping under the radar, artistic activism is not identified as "politics" to authorities while still being able to communicate a social message to the public. Our current "post-truth" environment also provides fertile ground for artistic activism. Even for those committed to telling the truth, it has become clear that the simple presentation of facts falls upon deaf ears, and if facts are to be heard and heeded, they need to be made into engaging stories and compelling images that capture attention and resonate with ways people make sense of their world. People need to be moved to feel, think, and act in new ways, and artistic activism can do this.

But Does It Work?

Does artistic activism deliver on its potential? As mentioned previously, there has been an explosion of interest in, and writing on, arts and activism in recent years. A great deal of it, however, has been focused either on the *theoretical*, a broad view of how artistic activism could or should work, or on the *tactical*, with descriptive focus on what happened with a particular intervention. What is missing is in the middle: an empirical exploration of what happens in the space between intention and outcome. To draw from the epigraph of this book, in the words of the artistic activist Gan Golan:

> If we can somehow observe the process that happens between a work of art and an idea reaching a community and then that community taking a defiant form of action, that's the black box. That's where the great mystery is happening.

As long as the relationship between tactics and outcomes is not understood, artistic activism will remain a mystery, a black box, and our conceptions of its practice will be akin to magic.

Literally. Magical thinking is characterized by a lack of knowledge, or even concern, about the relationship between cause and effect. One casts a spell, and *poof!*—something happens. Science, on the other hand, demands causality: a link between the action and its effect.[21] In order for artistic activism to be anything more than magical thinking, we need to explore *how* it works and then come up with some criteria for assessment so we can answer how we know *whether* it worked. None of this is to say that we can, or should, create a science of artistic activism. As I raised earlier, questions of "how it works" and "how we know it works" immediately bring up a thornier question: What do we even mean by "working" in the context of the marriage of arts and activism? There will always be magic and mystery in the practice. There will always be unintended consequences and unexplainable results, and actions guided more by feelings and hunches than rational considerations and reasoned plans. Understanding the forces at play may not allow us to predict exactly what will happen, but it helps us make sure that *something* happens, and then, once we've determined what has happened, *refocus* our efforts. To do this, we need a basic understanding of impact and criteria of assessment. We need *metrics*.

Metrics is an ugly word for many artistic activists. But it means simply a method for measuring, and although many might argue that metrics—like questions of æffect—have no place in creative work, the art world is already beholden to metrics. There are measurements of *commercial success*, gauged in terms of prices fetched for a work of art, gallery representation, and attendance at and length of run for a show; *institutional success*, determined by grants received, museum shows and collections; and *critical success*, judged by approval by critics and peers, shows reviewed, mentions in scholarship, and ultimately, place within "the tradition." As artistic activism has grown in popularity, it too has become subject to metrics. In parts of the world where such artistic activists rely upon funding by nongovernmental organizations, metrics are determined by program officers and governing boards, resulting in what artists Alex Nikolic and Sam Hopkins have called the "NGO Aesthetic."[22]

For artistic activism to be æffective, it too needs criteria to gauge success. But—and this is an important but—these must be the *appropriate* objectives and evaluations. Metrics used by the art world, or measurements that are of interest to NGOs, may not be appropriate for determining the æfficacy of artistic activism.[23] Activist artists can learn from these sources, borrow from them, but we must never forget that the measures used to gauge success in getting voters to the polls or building paying audiences were created for those purposes. Artistic activists need their own metrics.

My Intention

My intention in this book is to explore how artistic activism works in order to develop a methodology to assess whether it is doing the work we want it to do. The hardest part of this exploration, however, may be overcoming our resistance to wanting to know the answer. The distinguished Cuban American artistic activist Tania Bruguera once confided in me after a museum panel discussion that, "The reason why so many artists don't measure their impact is because they are afraid they might not have any." When we interrogate what works and how we know if it works, we risk being confronted by our worst fear: that maybe what we are doing doesn't really work, or at least not in the ways we want it to. Avoiding this dark place, artistic activists opt instead to simply make work, get it out there in the world, and hope that something happens. Or the opposite: get discouraged by the possibility that it's not working and quit, or come up with excuses why not to go out and do it in the first place. Embracing assessment also raises the fear of furthering the growth of an evaluation society already run amok, and by concentrating solely on those things we can measure, losing sight of the important things we can't.

But I believe there is a productive space between the magic of creation and the science of assessment. The purpose of this book is to point toward that place. My goal here is not to dictate the definitive set of metrics for assessment that can be handed down and applied mechanically across a range of practices. Rather, it is to develop a flexible but robust methodology to be used as a tool by practitioners (and their supporters) to see more clearly what it is they are doing (and supporting), reflect upon their practices more productively, and do them with greater social impact.

My approach is grounded in three sets of concerns. The first is a *theory of change*. Upon what theory of change, or theories, is artistic activism based? The second set of concerns has to do with *intention*. What do we hope and expect artistic activism to do? And how does it do this? The final concern has to do with *evaluation*. What actually happens as the result of an artistic activist intervention? How do we know? Can it be measured?

Some readers may be disappointed, though others I am sure will be pleased, to find that this is not a book of theory. The ideas here are certainly theoretically informed, and you will find plenty of theorists in my footnotes and even a few scattered across the pages. While *affect* is in the title of my book, and at the core of my analysis, if you are looking for the latest contribution to the field of affect theory, you should look elsewhere.[24] (Though you may find my etymology of *affect* and *effect* in the third appendix enlightening.) Where I do go deeper into theory—as I do in chapter one—it is because the theories I am presenting have had a shaping influence on the ideas and beliefs of practitioners, and because my own theorizing is necessary to create a practical theory of change. This book is also not an ethnographic account of examples of artistic activism. I do describe specific interventions in the following pages, but only to give context to what I am really after: the ideas of artistic activists about what they believe their interventions are doing, and how they assess the outcomes.

As important as such scholarly theories and academic studies are, I believe that critical knowledge is often generated from the bottom up. Artistic activists themselves act upon implicit and explicit ideas of what works and what doesn't, and in this way, they are constantly creating and reflecting upon theories of change and methodologies of assessment. This is why the primary sources for this study are the words and ideas of artistic activists themselves. For this book, more than one hundred in-depth interviews were conducted by myself or by researchers I supervised or collaborated with. Of these interviews, about one fifth are with "field leaders" who, in addition to being practitioners, have some institutional standing, such as running centers, training institutes, or assessment programs devoted explicitly to artistic activism. The remaining artistic activists run the gamut from the world-famous to the work-a-day practitioner; from the more expressive to the more instrumental; from those who see themselves primarily as artists, to those who see themselves as activists, to the majority who see themselves somewhere in between and often feel uncomfortable with any labels at all. Solely due to proximity, more than half of the individuals interviewed are from the United States, but about 40 percent live and work elsewhere: West and South Africa, across western and eastern Europe and the Balkans, as well as in countries like China and Guatemala. Nearly half those interviewed identify as women and a third as people of color, and while the question was not posed in the interviews, a significant number of respondents self-identified as queer, trans, or non-binary. This sample is not representative, nor is it scientific, but I do think it provides a diverse and robust reflection of thought—or rather, thoughts—in the field.

This focus on practitioners' knowledge is crucial, and not only for the political reasons of recognizing and valorizing the ideas and expertise of those who practice. It is also essential for practical reasons: this book is meant to be applied. I want this book to be read and appreciated by scholars, arts administrators, and program officers, who I hope will find in these pages new ways of thinking about the import and impact of artistic activism. But most of all I want this book to be useful to artistic activists, and therefore it needs to start from where they are and respect the experience and wisdom (and acknowledge the gaps and omissions) they possess. There are too many fine reports and pamphlets and guides in the field that are not read and not used solely because they don't speak to and from the experiences of artistic activists. I don't want this book to be one of those. Unless it works for artistic activists, it isn't really working at all. Finally, I privilege the ideas of practitioners because it is what they think their artistic activism is or could be doing—their *intent*—that will be the cornerstone of the "bottom-up" methodology of assessment I'll be developing in the pages to come.

In 1995, Nina Felshin edited a foundational book in the field of artistic activism called *But is it Art?*[25] The overarching concern of her book was to understand creative activist practices as a valid form of art. Now, twenty-five years later, Felshin's battle has largely been won. Artistic activism is now a field in the academy, a concentration in art schools, and a presence in museums and art shows. There will always be some stuffy art critic, or strident activist, sniffling that arts and activism are incommensurate, but they are fighting a rearguard action. It is time now to ask a different question of artistic activism. It is no longer sufficient to ask the question *But is it Art?* Or even *But is it Activism?* If the practice is going to evolve and mature, take itself seriously, and possess the social impact it promises, we need to interrogate the affect and effect, the *æffect,* of the practice. We need to ask: *But Does It Work?*

CHAPTER ONE

How Artistic Activism Works

TO UNDERSTAND THE ÆFFECT OF artistic activism, we must first explore how it works, specifically how it brings about the social change it promises. In short, we need a theory of change. A theory of change, for all its formidable sounding name, is actually quite simple: it is a proposition that change happens and it happens for a reason. Underlying any practice aiming to have an impact is a theory of change. Some theories are explicit, such as when a program officer for an nongovernmental organization is drafting an official report and needs to explain exactly how a certain program will bring about a desired outcome. But sometimes theories of change are more implicit, which is often the case in a field like artistic activism, where so much is done by feel and through practice, rather than theorized and articulated.

Many "theory of change" models, however, are not really theories at all, but rather concrete applications of larger theories that remain unstated and unexamined. This is not to say these applications are wrong, but they are right (or wrong) only in a particular instance and don't work as generalizable theories to guide future work. My goal in this chapter is to develop a general theory of change for artistic activism that can then be applied within, and adapted for, specific circumstances and particular contexts. To create such a theory we need to step back in order to move forward, exploring multiple theories — both explicit and implicit — of how and why change happens, and how artistic activism can contribute to that change.

Theories of Change

There are numerous theories of change, stretching back for millennia, and at the risk of oversimplification, they tend to fall into two camps: *natural* theories and *social* theories. Natural theories suggest there are "natural" forces that guide development, while social theories stress the importance of human intervention in bringing about change. The current debate around climate change is a place where we can see a conflict between natural and social theories of change play out. Are the undeniable rise in global temperatures and ensuing climate instability part of a natural cycle as climate-change skeptics and carbon-fuel companies argue, or is all of this change the result of human activity? While science is firmly on the side of a social change in this instance, there is no denying that sometimes natural interventions have massive impacts, such as the extinction of dinosaurs from an asteroid falling from the sky. But given that both arts and activism are decidedly human activities, it is *social* theories of change that concern us.

Traditionally, there are also two schools of thought when it comes to social theories of change: *idealist* and *materialist* (to which I will be adding a third, *affectist*, later). In common parlance, an idealist is someone whose head is in the clouds, a dreamer with little concern for the practicalities of life, whereas a materialist is someone obsessed with the things of the world, often money, property, and possessions. The terms *idealist* and *realist*, however, take on specific meanings — although not unrelated — when it comes to theories of change. An idealist theory of change contends that humans act to bring about change through the power of ideas. People develop an idea of what is wrong with society as it is, an idea of what a better society might look like, and an idea of what must be done to bring it about. A materialist notion of change flips this theory on its head. Instead of ideas prompting people, it is the material conditions in which people find themselves that move them toward change. Humans respond to their environment and through this activity generate ideas, including ideas about social change.

With these basics out of the way, it's time to dig a bit deeper, and to help with this excavation, I want to turn to the ideas of three influential theorists of social change: Mathew Arnold, Karl Marx, and Gustave Le Bon. One conservative, one radical, one reactionary — and all white men, living and writing in northwest Europe in the latter half of the nineteenth century. One could, and should, ask why, in a book that explicitly foregrounds the experiences, ideas, and words of a diverse group of contemporary artistic activists, I am privileging the ideas of a group of dead white men from a small corner of the world at one brief moment in history?

Part of the answer has to do with what was happening in Europe at the moment when these men were writing. It was, as historian Eric Hobsbawm coined it, the "Age of Revolution." From the French, Haitian, and American Revolutions in the late eighteenth century, then the uprisings in Ireland and Greece and across Latin America, through the radical upheaval across Europe in 1848 and the Indian Mutiny of 1857, to the final crushing of the Paris Commune in 1870, intellectuals, activists, and artists at the center of Empire were forced to confront and grapple with the fact that humans can transform society on a massive scale. Some applauded such changes, while others were horrified, but all were forced to confront and explain it, and Arnold, Marx, and Le Bon were three of the most influential.

It is the enduring influence of the ideas of these three that explains why they are present here. Eurocentric theories of social change have, for good or ill, colonized the world, and these ideas frame how people, be they avid boosters or fierce critics, think about social change. They are, in a word: *foundational*. Does the contemporary Kenyan playwright and theorist Ngũgũ wa Thiong'o do a better job describing the power of art to serve as both an agent of social and mental control and also a vehicle to valorize indigenous thought and experience than, say, Marx, who wrote very little on culture and next to nothing on the arts? Of course, he does. Yet it's also important to recognize that Ngũgũ's trenchant analysis of the power of colonial language and culture to alienate the colonized from their own material existence *self-consciously* builds upon and extends Marx's ideas.[1]

As Judith Butler argues (borrowing another concept from Marx), we live within "the historical present."[2] What we do with what we are given is not predetermined: ideas and practices inherited from the past can be adopted, adapted, rejected, or refuted, but they influence us nonetheless. To adapt Marx's observation about revolutionaries in *The Eighteenth Brumaire* to the current setting: artistic activists make their own history, but they do not make it purely as they please; their thoughts and actions in the present are forever influenced by the traditions of the past. Millennia of ideas and arguments about how art works have shaped the contours of the political and artistic traditions in which artistic activists find themselves today. Whether they like it or not, or whether they are conscious of it or not, "the tradition of all the dead generations weighs like a nightmare on the brain of the living," as Marx explains.[3] Like all foundations, the theories and theorists offered below can be built upon in all sorts of ways, creating new sorts of structures that the originators never dreamt of. They can also be deconstructed and replaced. But they offer us someplace solid to start.

Idealism
Idealism has a long intellectual lineage. Religion is probably the clearest exposition of an idealist conception of social change. Amongst the Abrahamic religions, God may be the creator of all that exists, but God's plan for action is transmitted through a set of ideas. "In the beginning was the Word, and the Word was with God, and the Word was God" begins the Christian Gospel of John.[4] It is then the role of prophets and priests to deliver these ideas to the people: delivered through carved commandments in the case of Moses, taught as cryptic parables by Jesus, or transmitted as poetry through Muhammad. As these ideas spread and achieve sufficient popularity, a new world order is born (or an old world order reinforced). As we pass from a religious age to an ostensibly more secular one, prophets are replaced by rulers and revolutionaries, professors and policy wonks, artists and activists; yet the idea that ideas create change remains constant.

Matthew Arnold is a good example of a secular proponent of idealism: good for our purposes because his idealism takes on a decidedly political (or anti-political) mission, and good because Arnold believes that ideas are best expressed through the arts, or what he calls "culture." Arnold was a solid member of the nineteenth-century British elite: the son of the headmaster at Rugby School (birthplace of the game), educated at Oxford University, and appointed as one of Her Majesty's Inspectors of Schools, where he helped set the standards of what he — and people who attend schools like Rugby and Oxford — thought best for the young minds of Britain.

Arnold was also an artist, probably best known for his 1851 poem "Dover Beach," whose last lines read: "And we are here as on a darkling plain/ Swept with confused alarms of struggle and flight,/Where ignorant armies clash by night."[5] The "darkling plain" of which Arnold writes is mid-nineteenth-century Britain at the height of industrialization, empire, and dissent. Workers' revolutions, and their brutal suppression by the forces of order, have shaken Europe. At home in England, the Chartists are holding demonstrations and demanding the vote for all people. Rebellions are breaking out across the Empire. Arnold's poem is a conservative's requiem. The "confused alarms" are the clashing ideologies and interests of "ignorant armies" of new political actors. The old patterns, traditions, and faith that once gave order are in decline, and the barbarians are at the gates. Now that God is dead as a singular guiding and controlling force, what will take his place?

By 1869 Arnold believes he has found the solution: Culture. No mere reactionary, Arnold wants to move forward, he believes in change, but there must be a force that will motivate and guide this transformation. In his book *Culture and Anarchy*, he lays out his theory of change:

> The whole scope of this essay is to recommend culture as the great help out of our present difficulties; culture being the pursuit of our total perfection by means of getting to know, on all the matters which most concern us, the best that has been thought and said in the world.[6]

Against what Arnold perceives as the anarchy of political and economic life, he holds out the promise of the timeless and universal appeal of culture. Culture provides the beacon to lead society out of the rancorous social divisions of the industrialist, imperialist, and class-torn England of his time. And culture, for Arnold, is the "best that has been thought and said in the world." For Arnold, the "best" could be found in the Bible (the King James Version, of course) and Shakespeare, but was generalizable to any great art form. Art, in Arnold's theory of change, provides a model of how we should live or an ideal vision to which we should aspire, "culture being the pursuit of our total perfection."[7] For Arnold, *ideas* and *culture* are transcendent, as they rise above the world, yet he is interested in culture precisely because of its transformative power in the world: "the passion for making [sweetness and light] prevail" in the struggle over the shape of society.[8]

In sum, the theory of change that Arnold proposes is this: Ideas, expressed through culture and manifested in great art, provide the critical perspectives and visionary ideals necessary to motivate and guide people to transform the chaos of industrial society and usher in a new world of "sweetness and light." In visual form, this *idealist theory of change* might look something like FIGURE 1.

FIG. 1

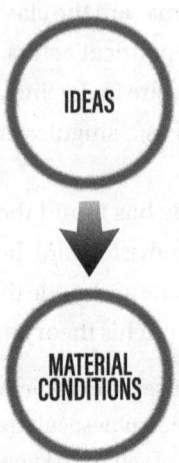

Changes in ideas lead to changes in the material world.

However, because it is a *social* theory of change that we are interested in, we need to add in the element of human agency, recognizing that human thought and action are the motor forces in transformation. As such, the abstract category of "idea" is manifested as human *ideas*: religion, philosophy, and in our case, arts and culture. Similarly, "material" should be thought of as the human-made *conditions*, be they political structures, economic systems, or physical environments, within which we live and interact (for example, the British schools that Arnold supervised). A sketch that takes into account these social aspects of an idealist theory of change might look something like FIGURE 2.

FIG. 2

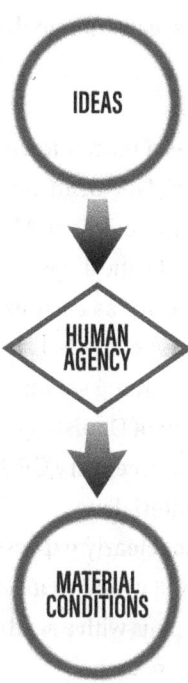

Ideas influence people who act upon and transform their material conditions.

It is fashionable these days to read Arnold, if he is read at all, as the cultural elitist he most certainly was. There is an obvious question never asked in his work: who is going to determine "the best that has been thought and said in the world"? Arnold didn't need to ask that question because he believed that great culture was self-evident. Today we are rightly skeptical of such claims. Defining what is "great" and "best" has traditionally been done by elite, white men like Arnold and tends to reflect and reproduce their ideas and experiences. To create a guiding culture upon these ideals is to code a certain race, sex, and class supremacy into society, and this "solution" does not sit very well for many of us today.

But before we dismiss Arnold with righteous disgust, we need to acknowl-edge that the theory of change of this cultural conservative is the very same employed, consciously or not, by many artistic activists who locate themselves on the opposite end of the political spectrum. Yes, their ends are different: Arnold's mission was to restore the superiority of elite ideas, and many artistic activists work to undermine the very same, but the theory of change employed is remarkably similar — art, by providing critical perspectives and/or alternative ideals, can change the world.

Materialism

The next theory of change has a more radical lineage. If Matthew Arnold can be held up as an exemplar of idealism, it is his contemporary Karl Marx who best represents modern materialism. Materialism, as a philosophical tradition, predates Marx. Kanada, the ancient Indian philosopher and scientist, devised a theory of "atomism" as early as the sixth century BCE when he argued that all matter could be divided and subdivided until it reached an indivisible core, and Wang Chong set his naturalist theory of the world against the traditional idealism of Daoism and the dominant moral philosophy of Confucianism in the first century CE. It is Marx, however, who fully develops the idea of *social* materialism.

Marx's materialism is most clearly expressed in *The German Ideology*, a long essay written between 1845 and 1846 with his frequent collaborator Frederick Engels.[9] The essay opens with a scathing attack on radical German Idealists (of whom Marx was once one):

> As we heard from German Ideologists, Germany has in the last few years gone through an unparalleled revolution.... Mighty empires have arisen only to meet with immediate doom. ... Principles ousted one another, heroes of the mind overthrew each other with unheard-of rapidity, and in the three years 1842 – 45 more of the past was swept away in Germany than at other times in three centuries.

And then, with their concluding sentence, Marx and Engels deliver the kicker: "All this is supposed to have taken place in the realm of pure thought."[10] Beneath their caustic wit, the authors are leveling a serious charge: all this sound and fury in the realm of ideas has signified nothing in terms of material transformation. Germany in the mid-nineteenth century, with its radical ideas and reactionary political and economic structures, is a test case for the failure of idealism as a theory of change. Yet if ideas don't create change, then what does?

"The first historical act . . is the production of material life itself," Marx and Engels write, laying out their countertheory of change.[11] For Marx, change — including changing ideas — comes about through our relationship with our material environment. But again, Marx's materialism is a *social* materialism. Unlike the natural materialists who understood humans as just another part of nature to be acted upon by the material world, Marx argues that the very thing that makes humans human is that they act upon the material world that surrounds them. To survive, we work, we build, we transform, and it is through this creative process of interaction with our environment that we develop our ideas. To quote from *The German Ideology* again: "Men, developing their material production and their material intercourse, alter, along with this their real existence, their thinking and the products of their thinking. *Life is not determined by consciousness, but consciousness by life.*"[12] Through interaction with, first, a natural material environment and, then, human-built conditions like institutions, laws, policies, and other social, political, and economic structures, we develop our ideas about the world and our place within it.[13]

At its simplest, a social-materialist theory of change looks something like FIGURE 3.

FIG. 3

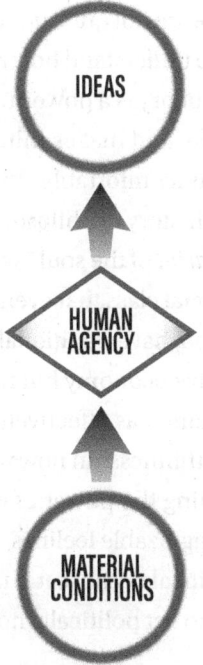

Material conditions shape people who go on to create ideas.

What is the role of art in such a theory of change? Art, as an expression of ideas, does not arrive from the sky as a gift of the muse, as an idealist might think, but comes from below, forged out of the material conditions through which we live our lives. That is: life determines consciousness. A simplistic reading of Marx's materialism ends here. Following this dogma, to bring about change one first changes material conditions, and from this, a change in ideas, and art, will follow. All artists must report to the factories! But, again, it's important to remember that, for Marx, material conditions include things that we as humans create: cities and factories, yes, but also language, culture, and the arts. This human creation — all of it — then makes up the environment in which we live. Today, arts and culture are an important product of the global economy, and so in an economic sense, they are a form of matter.[14] Therefore, a shift in the culture is not a mere shift in a superstructure — as it might have been in Marx's time — but a shift in the material base. Culture is also a material form of power.

Affectism

So far we have explored two major theories of change, idealism and materialism, through the words of their most prominent proponents, Matthew Arnold and Karl Marx, but we are not quite done yet. There is another theory we must entertain in order to understand how artistic activism brings about change. At the heart of this theory is a powerful force that lurks in the shadows of political respectability and makes thinkers, from the conservative Arnold to the radical Marx, uncomfortable. The specter of emotion.

"Throughout much of the history of philosophy, the emotions have been treated as the *lumpenproletariat* of the soul," writes the philosopher Robert Solomon, referring to the social class that even Marx disparaged as useless. Emotions, continues Solomon, have traditionally been understood as "playing little role in the productive economy but nonetheless to be feared as a cost and danger, to be contained as effectively as possible."[15] The result of this neglect, he argues, is a "thinness" in how we understand, among other things, politics. Understanding the power of visceral emotions, and their mental manifestation as recognizable feelings, is critical to any understanding of social change.[16] It is critical because it is now increasingly recognized that humans are motivated to act politically not merely through reason, or in some sort of reaction to material circumstances, but because they *feel* the need for change. As social-movement scholar Deborah Gould notes: "Ideas about the need for change and movement toward bringing it about often begin with an inarticulate and inarticulable sensation that something in the established order is not quite right; . . . affective states can inspire challenges to the social order."[17] Recognizing the social power of "affective states" is even more important when we are dealing with *artistic* activism. The power of art, it has even longer been recognized, is to stimulate emotions, generating feelings that we often can't quite comprehend or explain. We simply say art *moves* us. This is art's emotional power.

Gustave Le Bon, a French social scientist living and writing at the end of the nineteenth century, was one of the first social theorists to recognize and analyze the power of emotions and feelings in struggles for social change. Le Bon, politically far to the right, was neither a fan of social change nor a friend of "the crowd" of which he wrote, but he had noticed — and at the time it was impossible not to — that collective mobilizations had substantial social and political influence. But what motivated the crowd? Why did they act as they did? What drove their demands? In his masterwork *The Crowd*, Le Bon argued that it was neither ideas that were the influence nor were material conditions to blame. Instead, the crowd was governed by something else. As individuals, people might use reason and react rationally, but when they banded together as a "psychological crowd" (as Le Bon referred to social mobilizations) they were animated by their "unconscious."

In thrall to its unconscious, the crowd is ruled by "impulsiveness, irritability, incapacity to reason, the absence of judgment and of the critical spirit, [and] the exaggeration of the sentiment."[18] In other words, the crowd is ruled by emotion. This is their power. As Le Bon explains, "Crowds, doubtless, are always unconscious, but this very unconsciousness is perhaps one of the secrets of their strength." For, he continues, "The part played by the unconscious *in all our acts* is immense, and that played by reason very small."[19] It is precisely the fact that the crowd taps into this potent source of motivation, following their unconscious emotions rather than listening to conscious reason, that makes them an active force for change.

Today, Le Bon has largely been consigned to the ash heap of social change history. His hoary elitism is out of step with our democratic age, and the fact that both Hitler and Mussolini read *The Crowd* and applied his theory doesn't help his cause. Yet his basic insights into the power of unconscious emotion to move people to bring about social change are still useful. And, if the phrase "unconscious emotion" makes a modern audience uncomfortable, merely swap in the word *affect*.

"The primary motivational system in human beings," the psychologist Silvan Tomkins asserts, "is the affect system."[20] Again, I have no intention of wading into the deep pools of affect theory here, but for Tomkins, the progenitor of modern affect theory, affect is what precedes our conscious awareness of a feeling, which is then categorized through past experience and social convention into an emotion. In other words, affect is the feeling we feel before we know what it is we have felt. It is the sense one has before it is made sensible by naming, defining, and assigning it to a recognizable emotion. (This is why I believe LeBon's "unconscious emotion" grafts so well onto our contemporary understanding of affect.) Affect can be triggered by a material stimulus, like a workplace condition or a painting, and we "make sense" of this sense through feelings like "anger" or "awe," which we then abstract into ideals like "injustice" or "beauty." This process happens so quickly that we come to believe that a certain feeling is *created* by an object and *becomes* the idea we use to describe it, but affect is not reducible to these things.[21] What contemporary philosopher Brian Massumi calls the "autonomy of affect" is precisely its unconscious, emotional character.[22] There is much more to say about affect, but here we are dealing with theories of social change, and we owe a debt to the unpleasant Mr. Le Bon for pointing out that affect is not merely an individual sensation, but can also be a collective force for social change. What Le Bon usefully describes is how people, swept up in emotions, generate ideas and transform material reality. And while Le Bon is concerned only with riot, rebellion, and revolution, peaceful change through public pressure or nonviolent creative action is also motivated by emotion.

So what might an affectist theory of social change look like? Something like FIGURE 4.

FIG. 4

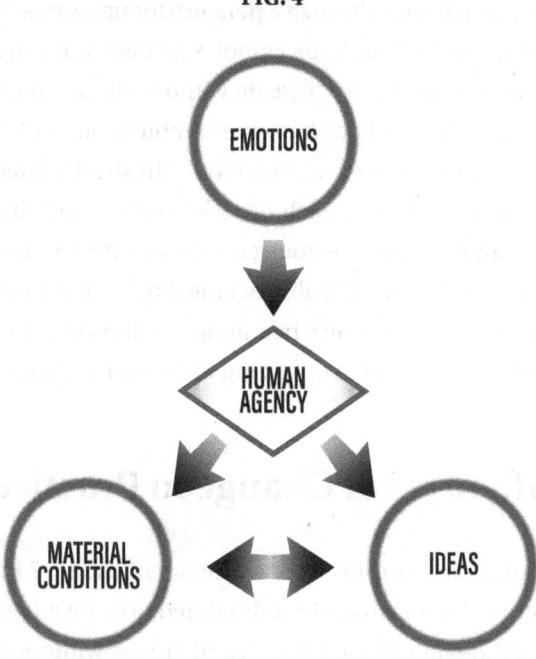

Emotions *move* people, who then generate ideas *and* transform their environment.

Idealist, Materialist, and Affectist

These theories of social change are what social scientists call "ideal types": analytic categories used to separate and categorize the messiness of the real world. In the mess of life, however, idealists acknowledge the power of the material.[23] The value of ideas, ultimately, is the power these ideas have to transform material reality. "On Earth as it is in Heaven," as the idealist Christian church reminds its believers through the Lord's Prayer. And even the staunchest materialist believes that humans don't merely react to material conditions; they *interact* with material conditions, and this is a conscious and creative activity. As Marx writes in volume 1 of his *Capital*: "What distinguishes the worst architect from the best of bees is this, that the architect raises his structure in imagination before he erects it in reality."[24] Finally, the "autonomy" of affect is a misleading term when it comes to affective change. While affect is not predetermined by its stimulus, it is generated as a response to *something* — material or ideal — and affect goes on to have an effect, ideal or material, through a person's thoughts or actions. Furthermore, as Tomkins notes, people are complex beings who both *feel* and *think*, and we need both to act freely: "Reason without affect would be impotent, affect without reason would be blind. The combination of affect and reason guarantees man's high degree of freedom."[25] In short, ideas, matter, and emotions are all mixed up in each other's business, coming together to create what I named in the previous chapter as *æffect*. Categorizing theories of change into discrete and abstract ideal types, however, affords us a degree of useful clarity as we dive headlong into the ideas and actions and motivations of artistic activists operating in the real and messy world.

Theories of Change in Practice

What do artistic activists think about a theory of change? In the abstract, not all that much. No one interviewed claimed to be an adherent of one of the schools of thought outlined above, and almost without exception, no one used the term "theory of change" unless prompted. However, when it came to discussing ideas about *their* own practices, it became very clear that they are thinking of and acting upon theories of how change happens, and generating theories regarding the role of artistic activism in bringing about that change. In other words, they are theorizing change.

Shifting Culture

Being artistic *activists*, it's not surprising that most practitioners interviewed believe that through activity people can bring about social change. And as *artistic* activists, it's equally predictable that they felt that arts and culture are powerful means to create that change. As Matthew Arnold proposed: change happens when the culture is shifted.

"Culture shifting is the most valuable and important thing [for] socially transforming the world," explains Terry Marshall, co-founder of the artistic activist group Intelligent Mischief: "The culture is the glue between everything else." This theory of social change is mirrored by the The Culture Group, an influential collective of activist artists and kindred researchers. "Culture is the field on which change occurs," they write, explaining that: "Public sentiment is gathered and swayed through cultural means. Political change is the lagging indicator demonstrating that cultural change has already arrived at new coordinates."[26] Culture plays a dual role in this theory of change. It is the wider set of ideas, beliefs, and norms within which all change is articulated, made sense of, and acted upon: that is, the cultural field. And it is also a means to intervene within that terrain via the creative manifestation of an alternative set of signs, symbols, and stories: that is, art. Or, as The Culture Group succinctly states, "culture is both the *agent* of change and the *object* of change."[27] I'll expand upon this dual role of culture later, but for now, let's see how artistic activists theorize how culture shifts and the role of artistic activism in making this happen.

Creating a New Culture

"Art is the space of ideas and myth-making and culture-making," says Favianna Rodriguez, the artist who collaborated with the *Undocubus* activists, mentioned in the introduction, who mobi-lizedthe symbol of a monarch butterfly to re-frame migration as both natural and beautiful.[28] Rodriguez explains: "In order to win, we need to have a vision of where we're going. And," she continues, "that is what art is to me. I mean art is really our imagination."

Ibrahima "Ibou" Niang is a Senegalese artist who also works for an international social-change NGO in West Africa. With these dual alliances (and a PhD in political science), Ibou has given theories of change a great deal of thought. His first insight: "Social change is very, very slow."

He continues:

> Now, how does it happen? It happens when people accept that the ideas, or the behaviors, that they were practicing up to that very specific point are no more relevant, and that there will be added value to their lives if they adapt to the situation. If they adopt new ways of thinking, new ways of being, and new ways of doing things.

For Niang, this is where the role of arts in social change comes in:

> And I think for people to get to that stage, they need to see, to envision the situation that they are being led towards. They need to see the picture. They need to see the vision. They need the vision to be materialized, before they get there, which is very difficult. But that is one of the things that arts do. They help people see the final state to which they

are aspiring, if they make the necessary moves and sacrifices together. Because they can see the colors, they can see the shapes, they can feel it, even before being there.

Implicit in this cultural theory of change is a critique of an overly materialistic theory of change that *begins* with political and economic structures and then moves out to cultural meaning. Here's Rodriguez again:

> I think that in the social justice world we have overwhelmingly concentrated our efforts on policy change. I think that's a huge mistake because cultural change precedes political change. And culture has to change before policy does, in fact, policy is like the final manifestation of an idea.

Coco Fusco, an established artistic activist, takes up the refrain, articulating why culture is as important as matter in creating change or maintaining the status quo:

> To have an understanding of politics that is limited to organized electoral politics is not to understand how political formations work in the present. I think politicians understand that very well. That's why religious organizations are so important to politicians. And why the Nazis were so interested in film and radio. Because they understand there's a way in which culture, and particularly the culture of the image, works on people that direct political discourse doesn't.

This is not the first, nor is it the last time that a historically minded artistic activist raised the example of the Nazi party to describe how radical social change can happen. All the artistic activists interviewed are vehemently opposed to the politics and policies of the Nazis, but they also recognize that the Nazi rise to power, and their ability to bring about radical social change, horrific as it was, was due in part to their ability to create a new culture through their mastery of the arts of symbol, story, style, and spectacle.

Art is understood as having an important role in creating culture. "Art is part of creating the culture that creates our society," sums up Eric Gottesman, co-founder of For Freedoms, a U.S.-based organization that organizes and funds nation-wide public-arts campaigns around a range of social justice issues. Explaining the rationale for For Freedoms' projects like commissioning dozens of artistic activists to create a series of politically provocative billboards across the United States, Gottesman takes a step further by draw-

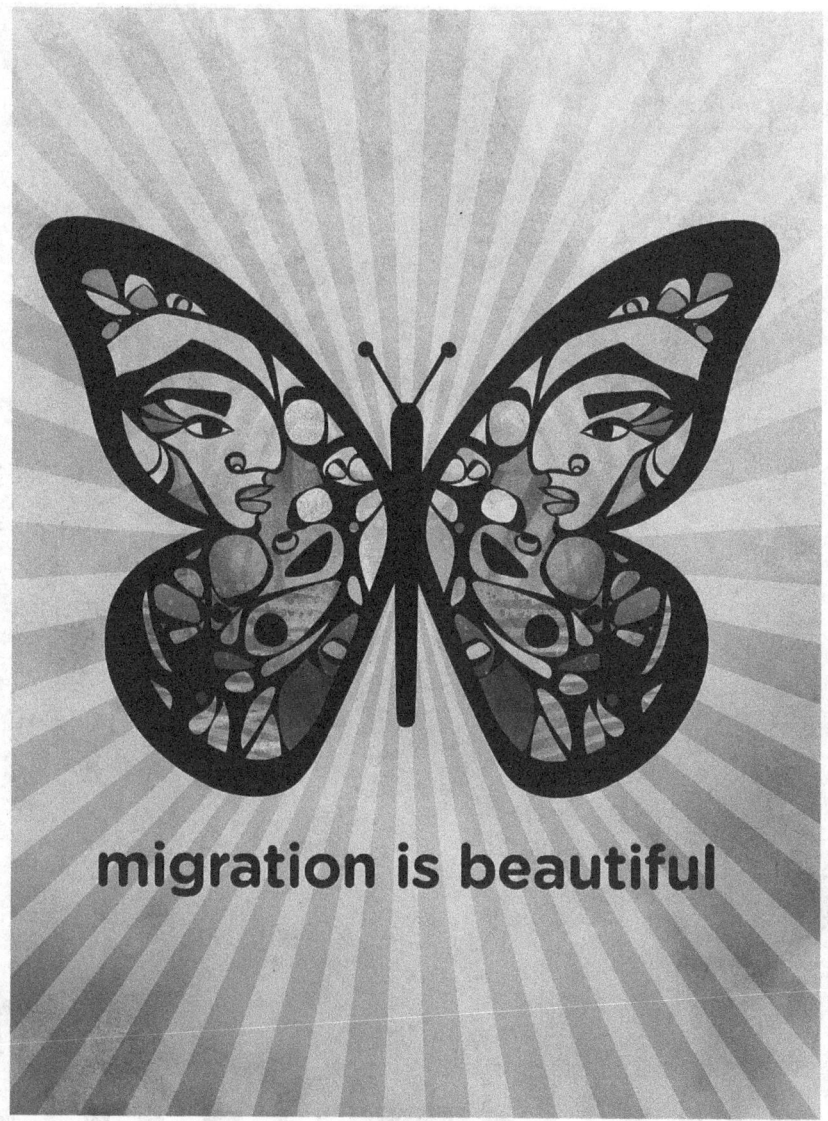

Favianna Rodriguez making migration beautiful, courtesy of the artist.

ing explicit lines between art, culture, and material transformation. "All art is political," he argues, "and public policy is a product of our culture that art helps create."

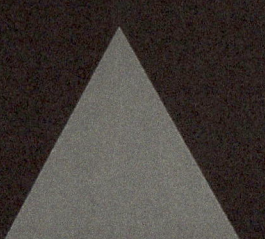

Turning symbols upside down with ACT-UP's Silence = Death Triangle Poster, courtesy of the Avram Finkelstein Archive.

Modeling an Alternative

"I'm a man of actions, I don't have so many theories, I don't have a big theory of social change," Spanish artistic activist Sergio Galen insists. "But," he then says, "if I'm interested in issues or changing things, what I do is talk about those issues in new ways." For all his insistence, Galen does have a theory of change: reframing issues or things "in new ways." Alfredo Jaar, the Chilean-born, world-renowned artistic activist, describes it this way: "I create models of thinking, models of thinking the world." Jaar then uses his art to articulate and disseminate these "models" so they have social impact. As he explains, "hopefully these models of thinking, if other people and enough people apply them, confronting certain situations, the world will change."

"Models of thinking" is a pretty good definition of culture, and other artistic activists see their role as creating these alternative cultures. Fernando García-Dory is another Spanish artistic activist who, among other things, once facilitated a meeting of traditional shepherds at the international art show Documenta 12. Expanding Jaar's "models of thinking" to include patterns of living, García-Dory says that, "I think social change happens through creating visible, alternative forms of life that have enough critical mass and interest." As García-Dory elaborates, he articulates a theory of social stasis: "Our current cultural values of competition, accumulation, capitalism — these are just part of a cultural setting created through mass media and culture." This insight leads him to his theory of change: "If we can somehow develop and embody other values and other forms of life, and make them visible, then people might be able to unplug from the current system and start to work for the creation of other, better systems." The role of the artistic activist is to make visible — and attractive — an alternative culture.

Queering Culture

Instead of creating an entirely new culture, some artistic activists think the best opportunity to shift culture is in hijacking cultures already in existence. "I think we should put more emphasis on effecting popular culture as activists, as militants," says Paolo Pedercini, contending that "this kind of superstructure is more flexible, especially in late capitalism where everyone has a niche, there is space for everyone or room for everybody." The cultural "superstructure" that Pedercini exploits is video games, using his skill as a programmer and his talents as an artist to create games with subversive ends. In his popular McDonald's game, for instance, he invites players into a world where human exploitation and ecological destruction are necessary to win. The result, he hopes, is an immersive experience of the brutality of capitalism and the fast-food industry through the comfortable familiarity of popular entertainment.

Other artistic activists use the art form of capitalist persuasion: advertising, as a means to gain attention, capture market share, and sell their message of change. Avram Finkelstein helped design ACT UP's "SILENCE=DEATH" poster that used the infamous Nazi symbol of the triangle for marking homosexuals and flipped it on its head and colored it pink, transforming a symbol of oppression into a call to action. Finkelstein is acutely aware of the power of appropriating and subverting dominant symbols, including, in today's world, the symbols of commerce. He speaks of "utiliz[ing] the language of capitalism as a sleight-of-hand to create the illusion that we were more organized than we were." Gran Fury, the arts-and-propaganda wing of ACT UP, frequently drew upon mainstream commercial aesthetics and "queered" them for alternate ideologies, once famously pirating a Benetton advertisement and swapping out the kissing heterosexual couples with homosexual ones while changing the tagline to "Kissing Doesn't Kill. Greed and Indifference Do."

In addition to queering contemporary commercial culture, artistic activists also usurp older, traditional cultures. Jordi Claramonte, of the Spanish artistic activist group Las Agencias, tells a story of an intervention to save a public garden.

> Here in Madrid, there was a huge space, which was supposed to be a garden, a public garden for the neighbors. Suddenly the Partido Popular, the right-wing government, gave it to the bishop for him to do some office building. So the neighbors tried to organize, and it was very difficult because the neighbors were completely disorganized, and the city council was very powerful, and they had the police, and they had everything. So we had to develop very creative ways to interfere in the whole thing.

Traditional culture was their creative way to interfere. "In the South of Spain," Claramonte explains, "there is this flamenco singing [*cante flamenco*], which is where some young *gitana* [Romani] comes out of a balcony and starts singing a song, which is very sentimental about the Virgin and about religion."

Las Agencias' borrowed the form of the *cante*, "but the lyrics were changed. It was about the political situation in the barrio. But it was sung by a young *gitana* who's a very fine singer, so it was very fine formally." On the day of the intervention, Claramonte describes,

> We had the mayor. We had all the media. So the [*cantaora*] appeared in the balcony and started singing and everybody was silent, listening, and the young *gitana* said the Virgin of the Paloma was very sad because in her barrio the only empty space left was going to be used to build offices on a garden. So, everybody was really emotional because it was very subtle and very clear, and it didn't break at all the code of the procession, of the parade, because it was exactly in style. The neighbors got angry against the mayor at that moment. They started insulting him. It changed [the situation] because it made a big number of neighbors know what was going on, there was a group organized and they joined. It was a big thing. ... Finally, we won.

Instead of creating new cultures, Claramonte and Las Agencias drew upon signs and symbols of preexisting traditional culture, and the attending memories and feelings they evoke, to shift the political culture to their advantage.

Working Through Culture

Whether to appropriate preexisting cultures or create them anew is a tactical decision within a larger strategy of "shifting culture." But for any new set of ideas and meanings to become accepted, or even understood, they need to be made sense of *within and through* the cultures in which people are already living. This is a delicate balance. Play it too safe and the intervention doesn't challenge and change the status quo, but if an artistic activist creates something too far outside the common cultures of their audience, their intervention risks illegibility and their message not being understood. This line between legibility and illegibility is what avant-garde art often plays with. Displaying a urinal in an art gallery, as Marcel Duchamp did in 1917, struck the right balance: a familiar object given new meaning in an unlikely setting.

In order to subvert the dominant culture, therefore, an artistic activist has to be a careful student of it. Favianna Rodriguez, who earlier spoke about the power of art as a tool of imagination to create new myths and new visions — that is, *new* cultures — is also well attuned to the culture of the here and now. "I follow the news, I follow social media, I see what people are talking about. I'm participating in culture. ... I care about culture, I care about pop culture," Rodriguez freely admits. Part of the reason she "cares" about culture is so she can spot what she calls "openings." As she explains:

> Right now we're in a #MeToo wave. And that to me means that this is the time to talk about a bunch of stories around sexual abuse, it's a completely different landscape than last year. Or when the [forest] fires happened, I'm like, okay, let's talk about climate policy. Now that the migrant caravan is happening, I am pushing out the butterfly again. ...Much of my time is [spent] in actually understanding. ... What is the narrative? What are people saying, and where is there some friction? Where are there some openings?

"It's very simple," Jacques Servin (a.k.a. Andy Bichlbaum), one of the founders of the Yes Men, a group who ridicules the powerful through impersonation, adds:

> I mean we live in democracies. The way to change is through mass attention to things. One avenue to that is through the mainstream media. So we basically hop on issues that have a certain momentum and we just try to add some more attention to it.

If Rodriguez and Servin sound opportunistic, it is because they are. They are looking for opportunities within the existing dominant culture to push for the new culture they want.

Transforming Everyday Culture

No matter what tactics are used in the short term, there's a general understanding that shifting culture is a long term strategy that reaches deep into the way people make meaning in their lives. "We're mostly putting out fires," Diana Arce, a Berlin-based African American artistic activist explains.

But the change has to come from socialization. It's the way that people are being taught to interact with other people. I don't think it's something that's going to come quickly; I think it's a generational issue. If we do enough right things now and teach these younger generations of people what's up, get them on board early, then a generation or two from now, something can happen.

In other words, change doesn't happen instantly with the introduction of new ideas, but occurs only when those ideas become deeply embedded in the everyday, lived culture of a people. Art is seen as an affective means to do this. Andrew Boyd, the creator of the protest troupe *Billionaires for Bush* and, more recently, the book-cum-organization *Beautiful Trouble*, recalls "a quote … from one of the Irish revolutionaries: 'The movement isn't really real until the people take it up in song.' This," Boyd argues, "is how people take it into their hearts."

Affective Change

"People take it into their hearts" is how many artistic activists understand change. Ideas matter, but it is not the rational, cognitive understanding of ideas that changes society; instead it is ideas as they are felt and experienced. Social change is more a matter of hearts than minds, and artistic activism is a strategy of *affective* change. Igor Illievski, a journalist turned artistic activist from the Republic of North Macedonia, underscores the limits of cognitive experienced information when he explains: "There are so many whitepapers and NGOS proclaiming their positions, but at this stage, they are really limited in their impact. … Everyone has heard about climate change, the danger of extremism and radicalism, etc., but after a while they are just buzzwords." The key phrase here is "at this stage." Trained as a journalist, Illievski is not interested in jettisoning ideas — instead he wants to animate them.

"I have been exploring different ways to engage the public," Illievski continues, "to provoke a reaction and make people do something." Having read that a significant number of children did not have the resources to attend school during the COVID-19 pandemic, Illievski partnered with a women's social justice group in 2020 to create a "virtual classroom" — complete with blackboard, chairs and books — in the central square of the capital city of Skopje. They labeled it "The Classroom for 8,000 Students" (who lost access to schooling) and set up a station for people to write letters to the Ministry of Education. In animating an abstract statistic through a public installation, Igor Illievski hoped to move ideas from the stage of feelings to actions, moving from merely affective to æffective.

Extending Illievsk's distinction between (journalistic) information you know and (artistic) information you feel is Vanessa Carr, a former member of the San Francisco Print Collective, a group of artists that produces visual material for social movements. "People are so saturated with things like letters to the editor and there is just information overload in a lot of ways," Carr laments, and the way to get past information overload, she believes, is through art:

> Art can draw people's attention in a way — even someone who's already sort of tuned out or checked off — you know, "I don't have time for this" or "I'm too busy" or "I already know about this." . . . There is something about the aesthetic pathway of cognition or something that I feel like bypasses a lot of normal people's defenses in a way.

Underlying this tactical choice for Carr is a deeper understanding of what creates change. As she continues:

> The basis for any action is really a feeling, and I think if you can inspire that feeling in someone, which I think often is not necessarily a fully reasoned thing, someone might be inspired to act on a feeling even if they're not fully sure.

As Le Bon understood: ideas move people to action when they are *felt*, not just thought.

It is not surprising that the arts are seen as a natural medium for generating these feelings. "The arts have an incredible way of getting to people's heart chakra, making people feel things and question things," explains Sade Lythcott, the head of the National Black Theater of Harlem. And, for Lythcott, "getting to people's hearts" is connected to other forms of social change: "I believe that if you can change the hearts and minds of people, policy will follow." Referring specifically to *Lyrics on Lockdown*, a performance piece of spoken word poetry done in collaboration with incarcerated young people and staged in front of an audience of politicians and public officials, Lythcott describes how:

> In the audience, you can hear gasps, and you could hear people get a different perspective to something that was totally policy-driven [and] totally inhumane. Perhaps, if you are looking at the dollars and cents of programs, or who your constituency is, you don't see the beating heart of these stories. That's what art can do uniquely. Humanizing the stories of these policies is a really effective way of creating systemic change.[29]

Or was "affective" the word Lythcott used? Listening to my recording now, I'm not quite sure. But it really doesn't matter, because, for many artistic activists, to be effective is to be affective, and vice versa.

Intimate Connections

We tend to think of emotions, and the feelings they generate, as a personal affair. And so, when attempting to have an affective impact, it makes sense to forge intimate connections. This is what Federico Hewson strives to do. Hewson, whose work is concerned with the economic interconnections and injustices of the flower industry, staged an action on International Women's Day in which he gave out roses with information about where the flowers came from and the labor conditions of the people that grew them. Nothing new here: the dissemination of ideas in the form of facts. But Hewson also attached poems and excerpts from the voices of the flower farmers, because, as he believed, "There's something very intimate and vulnerable about a poetic statement that you know is coming from someone that wrote it just for you as a consumer. That can be quite moving."

Poems are also an integral part of the *Transborder Immigrant Tool*, an otherwise utilitarian project that guides undocumented migrants safely across the U.S.–Mexico border. At first glance, it's hard to see the art in this activism: the *Transborder Immigrant Tool* is a phone with a GPS system and a map. But the "tool" provides more than directions to stashes of water in the hot desert. Periodically a poem addressed to the person crossing the border pops up on the screen. Asked what the point of this was, Ricardo Dominguez, one of the creators of this "Geo-Poetic-System" as he calls it, explains that, once they had solved the technical challenges of creating a geolocation device for a cheap cell phone, "it was important to me that experimental poetry be a part of it." Why? Wasn't the function of the project to guide migrants to water stashes and a safe path across the border? Yes, Dominguez responded, but people are more than biological beings,

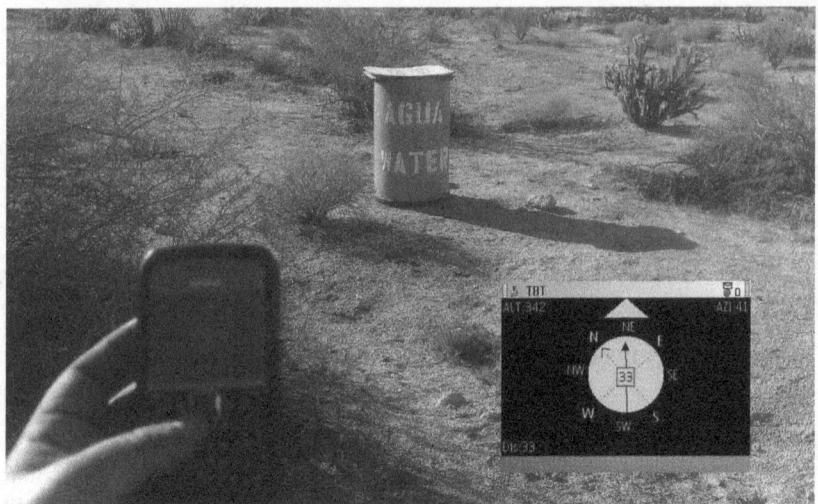

Aiding migrants with water and poetry, the Transborder Immigrant Tool, courtesy of Electronic Disturbance Theater 2.0.

and he wanted the tool to respond to that too: "We often want to think of undocumented immigrants as being 'bare life,' here to take our jobs, but not as culturally intelligent human beings. And so I thought the most radical poetry possible would be useful as a type of sustenance." For both Hewson and Dominguez, the power of the poem is its intimacy in addressing the individual, as a whole person, for it is through these small and intimate bonds that changes can be made.

Eve Mosher, an environmental artistic activist, describes her frustration with the lack of intimacy and individual connection she witnessed in campaigns for the environment: "The organizations were going out and giving lectures to people. I felt we needed to really have conversations and the most powerful way to make change happen was in a one-on-one conversation." Mosher's response to the challenge was the *High Water Line*. To draw attention to the future effects of climate change, she navigated the streets and sidewalks of New York City pushing a wheeled machine used to paint stripes on ballfields, leaving a bold line behind her showing where the shoreline will be with continued global warming, handing out flyers with factual information on the climate crisis as she went. When asked about the project's impact, it was not the spectacle or the facts that Mosher mentioned, but the one-on-one conversations — prompted by the spectacle and backed up by the facts — that she had with people along the way: "The project idea was to go out and do something that would spark a conversation," person by person.

One at a Time

In *Domestic Tension* (a.k.a. Shoot an Iraqi), Iraqi-born Wafaa Bilal lived alone in a small room in a gallery for a month with a remote-controlled paintball gun trained on him. Visitors to the gallery and the accompanying internet website could view Bilal, aim the gun, and shoot him... or refuse to do so. It was a personal — and of course political and moral — choice on the part of his audience. Having to make the choice, Bilal hoped, would change how the person thought, felt and acted when confronted with the first imperative of war: to dehumanize the Other. "Change does not come very easy. And everyone who is in art and activism understands that," Bilal explains. His solution is to scale down and focus on touching individuals: "I'm not going in there and saying, 'Okay, I wanted to change people's lives and how they behave.' I am hoping just to touch one person's life. And that person might touch another person."

"How do you change the world?," Joey Juschka, a transgender artistic activist from Berlin muses. "People think that you can't really do anything.... But if one person sees a flyer on the street, and starts to think about an issue in a different way, then great — you changed something socially, even if the laws are still the same." "Everything I'm making is an attempt to change people's minds about things," fellow Berliner Diana Arce adds, then qualifies "people" by explaining that, "I don't ever really think about the work that I make in the sense of trying to change the system as a whole, but it's about: How can you change the ideas of actual, individual people?"

This emphasis on intimate connections leads to an intimate understanding of politics and what constitutes change. "If my art makes somebody, even one person, think about justice, that's success," explains An Wei Lu Li, who paints large public murals raising social and political issues on billboards, the sides of buildings, and once across much of the surface of a public square. Even though his public art is big and grand, An Wei thinks of social impact on a far more intimate scale: "I'm not a politician, I'm just an artist. I'm trying to translate the life I see in my point of view. If I make even one person think, for example, about the subject, that is a success. Even if it's one person. When that happens, you change a bit of your surroundings."

Change happens, it seems, when individuals are moved to change by being touched by other individuals. The valorization of the affected individual as change-maker by artistic activists is understandable. This, after all, is how artists have largely been taught to think of themselves: as individuals who, through their art, will have an impact on another individual. When An Wei says, "I'm not a politician, I'm just an artist," he's not merely asserting an identity, but a way of thinking about change. "I'm dealing with lowercase politics," Sam Gould declares. Sam's work often involves creating spaces and places for collective creativity, but when asked what sort of social change this makes, he too stresses the small, intimate, and personal: "Politics doesn't end outside of the Capitol Rotunda, or outside of the Oval Office. It exists in the space between you and I."

It Takes a Movement

As much as artistic activists may talk about the power of reaching one individual and changing their ideas, most are not as naïve as to believe that social change is only one mind or heart away. While Sam Gould, quoted above, wants to extend politics beyond the walls of the Capitol Rotunda or Oval Office, his response implicitly recognizes that politics also happens in those institutional places of power as well. In order to bring about change at this level, it takes more than an individual; it takes a movement. This social understanding of agency, however, often rubs against the modern tradition of artistic individualism. "There is this kind of bizarre, romantic modernist throwback idea that art students have, and I see it in the classroom all the time," Coco Fusco explains.

> That you, as an individual, have to do something that effects millions of people. What kind of egotism does that speak about, right? The choice is not either "I as an individual change this" or do nothing about it. The choice is what can I do along with many others to keep on making it clear, publicly, that there's opposition to things that happen in the world. And that's a group effort, that's an ongoing thing. ... That's how things happen.

Fusco is acknowledging small "intimate" change efforts, but she's putting them within a collective vision: millions of small changes together make a big change.

Ummi Yakubu is an artistic activist from Nigeria who, among other things, makes films revealing the impact of police violence on women and designs video games to encourage civic participation across West Africa. Like Fusco, Yakubu takes a distributed approach to the "huge responsibility" that comes with figuring out how social change happens and how her artistic activism might — or might not — contribute to that process. When asked whether she had a theory of change, Yakubu sat silent for a moment, then replied:

> I know this can sound very cliche. It's just my grandma has this thing she says that I feel really embodies it and I hope I don't butcher it in the translation. So, if you are in a room that's flooded, and you are on your own, you cannot get rid of all the water before it brings damage. But if everybody takes one corner of the room and starts getting rid of the water, we can get that down in no time.

Yakubu then links this parable to her theory of change:

> I feel like that's how social change happens. You need people from different perspectives, different parts of the community, different views and different formats of activism. Whether it's the white-paper report or the documentary film or the really fun video game or whatever. You need people from all over to tackle these problems. You need all people from the society to grab a cup and get rid of the water before it causes damage.

"I look at the cultural side of the movement as just one wing of the movement," explains Larry Bogad, a theorist and performance artist who trains traditional activists in the techniques of performance art. "You know, you have combined operations, in military terms. You can have air power and land power and sea power." As Bogad concludes: "A movement without a cultural aspect is not going to do so well, but the movement can't be only cultural workers. That's not enough."

More Than Hearts and Minds
Ummi Yakubu and Larry Bogad's call for "combined operations" is an assessment that social change requires a collective effort. It is also a recognition that social change may require more than just "cultural work." The work of artistic activism, up until this point, has largely been defined as having a cultural effect on people at the level of ideas and feelings. This is not enough

for some artistic activists, who hold that social change necessitates change at the level of both actions and institutions.

One problem is the common assumption that changed ideas lead inexorably to social change. "It's just way more complex than that," insists Dara Greenwald, whose work often calls attention to hidden histories of historically marginalized peoples. "We have our consciousness raised about a lot of things and it hasn't changed the world." Greenwald even wonders whether critical ideas, by themselves, might actually hinder social change. "Expressing a critique is allowed in this particular society. And it's allowed for a reason. Actually, I think…that it's a release valve that allows for the system and status quo to maintain itself."

Artistic activists, of course, go beyond merely raising consciousness. By making people feel and experience ideas, they are engaging in what might be called "unconsciousness raising." But there is skepticism with this affective strategy as well. "The risk, the huge risk," worries Paolo Pedercini, the video game designer we met earlier,

> is to create a system, a software that has some kind of cathartic effect.…
> I mean, okay, you're, like, an activist, and you are changing things, and
> you play your game, and at the end, you are kind of relieved. "Oh, wow,
> that was easy!"…I mean, there is this danger effect to make the people
> think, or give the illusion of, empowerment.

Aware of these dangers, a number of artistic activists interviewed, while stressing the importance of changing hearts and minds to bring about social change, mentioned a next step: linking ideas to material action.

Andrea Polli, whose work imagines both real and speculative environmental solutions, begins by telling us, "I've tried to think about art as being effective in terms of changing the way people think." But, pressed on what she means by this, she clarifies: 'When I say "change the way you think," it has to do with agency. It's having the attitude that you can come up with new ideas and they can be implemented." This, she summarizes, means "changing people from taking a passive point of view to an active point of view." Polli is not rejecting the importance of ideas, but she is suggesting that ideas need to be implemented for change to happen. Likewise, she is not discounting the power of "changing the way [people] think," but she identifies the primary thinking that needs changing as having less to do with awareness about something that should be changed, and more to do with changing people's attitudes about change itself: moving people from "a passive point of view to an active point of view."

Neither Dara Greenwald nor Paolo Pedercini nor Andrea Polli is rejecting the role of culture as a driving force for social change. Instead, they are expanding culture to include notions of *agency*. The dominant culture they worry about, and the culture that must be changed, is one where radical arts and even activism itself can become objects of personal contemplation and public celebration yet be divorced from any material activity in the world that might bring about structural or institutional change. This, of course, is the problem identified by Marx and Engels in the opening pages of *The German Ideology*. One answer to this challenge is to apply "cultural work" directly to the institutions and structures of power themselves, beginning with institutions of cultural power.

Institutional Change

Institutional critique is a critical art practice that calls attention to the power of cultural institutions. In the early 1970s, when Hans Haacke detailed the business connections of the board of trustees of the Guggenheim Museum, his show was canceled. Today, *institutional critique* is an accepted, almost respectable, art practice. Artistic activists, however, while still drawing upon this tradition, push critique into change. They aim past the target of "raising awareness" about the myriad contradictions and hypocrisies of institutional power and set their sights on the transformation of those structures themselves.

Nato Thompson is well situated to recognize the power of cultural institutions. As the former artistic director of Creative Time, one of the largest U.S. funders and supporters of arts for social change, he organized annual "summits" to bring together the most prominent artistic activists from around the world before audiences that numbered in the hundreds, if not thousands. From their inception, these summits had been controversial in the world of artistic activism. Held in fancy venues, recognizing the "best" of artistic activism, and conforming to traditional — that is, *elitist* — art-world standards, Creative Time faced the predictable charges of "selling out" the practice. Upon attending the first Creative Time summit, held in a majestic hall of the New York Public Library on 42nd Street and opened by the scion of one of the city's most renowned — and wealthiest — philanthropic families, I must admit that I harbored suspicions too. But Thompson sees the function of the summits differently: as tactics in a long-term strategy to shift the organizations and practices of the art world.

"I have kind of a materialist relationship to culture, which is to say I believe ideas are produced through physical spaces and structures," Thompson explains. "So, for example, the New York Public Library isn't just an idea, it's a place, and *Art Forum* magazine is both: it's a physical object that's distributed from a place." Through his access and power, Thompson leverages the institutional power of dominant structures, bringing artistic activism into mainstream places in order to give it legitimacy. "You set the terms of the debate," he proposes, and "now everyone's arguing within your terms."

"I can only tell you what I have seen change, and one thing is the art world," says Greg Sholette, a scholar and artist who has been at the center of the marginal practice of artistic activism for decades. When asked about making change, he immediately answered in terms of the place of artistic activism within the art world:

> Now almost all artists are making social claims for their art. You'll have an artist painting blue squares in a purely formalist gesture, and they'll say it's blue because the sky was the same color over Tahrir Square during the Arab Spring. Now that's bullshit, but I think it's good that it becomes acceptable, even expected, for art to engage with the social. I've been doing this since the mid-1970s and it wasn't like that back then. That's social change.

The change that Thompson and Sholette point to here is at the level of discourse: what is and is not deemed acceptable for inclusion within the institutional canon. Beka Economopoulos and Jason Jones, through their latest project, *The Natural History Museum*, set their sights on a different target: changing the policies and practices of the institutions themselves. The way to do this, as they see it, is to concentrate on the material aspects of institutions: funding, governance, and above all their workforce. Instead of "just shaking our fist from the outside and mobilizing actions," Economopoulos explains, they created a pseudo institution to identify and infiltrate the field, "being sympathetic players inside the sector that can collectivize and give agency to people on the inside who want to make change."

Nathan Santry also targets institutions, but not cultural ones. As the art-school-trained former director of Greenpeace's famed Actions Team, the institutions he goes after are in industries like resource extraction and manufacturing. His strategy is not to change the institutions in order to change culture, but use culture in order to change the institution. One particularly ingenious intervention involved having the actor William Shatner — Captain Kirk of Star Trek — robo-call every employee at the tech giant Hewlett Packard. Shatner left a message asking the employees to ask their bosses why their company had reneged on the environmental deal regarding their production process that they had struck with Greenpeace. The objective was to disrupt employee morale as workers wondered why their company had backtracked on the environment, and occupy work time as they asked one another whether it was *really* William Shatner calling them up. As Santry explains, "If you can tie up middle management anywhere, you kind of got people by the short and curlies, right? 'Cause the world doesn't work without middle managers spending their time doing something." After the Kirk Call and other creative tactics by Greenpeace, Hewlitt Packard honored their original agreement and changed their manufacturing operations.

"The people in the streets are not important, people in the institutions are," insists Nikola Pisarev of the North Macedonian artist activist organization Contemporary Arts Center. Pisarev is being provocative when he says this, but his reply to our question about the intended audience for his interventions is also instructive, for it says something about how he believes change happens. "The audience is part of the action, like they are actors, they are performers," Pisarev explains. "You want people to laugh, you want people to interact and talk. But the real thing you want is to get on the news and embarrass the politicians, so they feel pressure." For Pisarev, the public audience — their thoughts, feelings, and perspectives — are important, but only insofar as they have an impact on structures of power.

There's No One Logic to Change

Most artistic activists, including the ones staking out claims above, do not see themselves as just activists, concerned only with structures, organizations, and material change. Nor do they see themselves as only artists, interested solely in ideas, feelings, and culture. Instead, they see themselves as, well, *artistic activists*, and have reasoned their way through to an understanding of how the material, the ideal, and the emotional are interdependent. They are not interested simply in affect or in effect, but rather in how they combine in producing *æffect*. The complexity of these interrelationships makes it hard to recognize any simple, singular theory of change. As Servin (a.k.a. Bichlbaum) of Yes Men concludes: "A lot of it is quite mysterious. Change happens, [and] some things happen in very unexpected ways that nobody predicts."

Servin is not alone in not seeing a clear theory of change for artistic activism. "There's no logic," Cheikh "Keyti" Sène, one half of the popular Senegalese rapping news webcast *Journal Rappé*, declares. "And if we agree on that, then you don't control social change." Keyti's seemingly fatalist response, however, is far more nuanced than it might initially seem. As an artistic activist who has worked around the world, he is acutely aware that any theory of change — at least at the level of application — is necessarily contextual: "One theory may be valid for the U.S. and not for Africa," Keyti says, "and one theory may be valid for Senegal, for the Senegalese population, with their background, the history background, the economic background, but not valid to our Malian neighbors." As an experienced artistic activist Keyti is also well aware that the message he conveys, the meaning it accrues, and the impact it has are often out of his control: "We have to propose things to society," he explains. "But once society snatches [an idea], it molds it in its own way. It develops. It goes out of your hands. And probably when it comes back to you years, or decades later, ... it will be very different from what you thought of."

"So [social change] is not in our control," he concludes. With all the unknowables when it comes to change, it might make sense to simply not intervene. Keyti, however, draws the opposite conclusion: "We don't know when [change] is going to happen, we don't know how it will manifest, but we can't just sit back and think that nature will do its thing. We have to be proactive. We have to do things." Not knowing definitively how change happens does not stop Keyti — or any other artistic activist I have met — from creating with a hope for change.

An Artistic Activist Theory of Change

While there is no consensus among artistic activists regarding a theory of change, and even a bit of resistance and skepticism to thinking in these terms at all, there are general areas of agreement about how change happens:

1. Humans can create change.
2. Culture, as a social system of meaning, must be changed to bring about social change.
3. Culture, as an art form, can change culture, as a meaning system.
4. Culture works when it is felt, not just thought.
5. Affect is necessary for effect.

And some artistic activists go further to argue that:

6. Cultural "awareness" is not enough and must be linked to action.
7. Change is a collective endeavor and should be an integral part of social movements.
8. Institutions, organizations, laws, and other tangible structures, as well as cultural expressions and meanings, must be changed for social change to happen.

And, of course,

9. Change, when generated through arts and activism and expressed through ideas, emotions, and actions, within different contexts and acknowledging uncontrollability, is exceedingly complicated.

In sum, the *aeffect* of artistic activism is complex and difficult to theorize.

With the daunting complexity of the task acknowledged, and drawing upon foundational theories of change outlined previously and the practical insights of the artistic activists above, we are finally ready to develop an artistic activist theory of change. This theory will need to account for the power of ideas to transform material reality. It must also recognize that ideas are created by people who live and create within a material world. It needs to acknowledge that people are moved to act in the world by emotions and feelings as much as they are by ideas and material circumstances. And such a theory should incorporate the importance of culture, both as individual artistic expression and a social system of meanings. A lot of balls in the air.

Like any good juggler, I want to start by limiting the number of objects I handle, adding each new element slowly. I'll start with just idealist and materialist theories of change. On top, we put Arnold's "best that has been thought and said in the world," or *ideas*, and on the bottom, we have Marx's "production of material life itself," *material condition*s, as in FIGURE 5.

FIG. 5

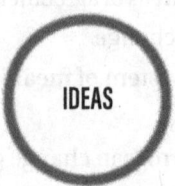

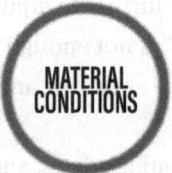

Instead of drawing unidirectional arrows linking the two and giving one dominance over the other as done earlier, we can make the arrows circular in order to recognize their interdependence, as in FIGURE 6.

FIG. 6

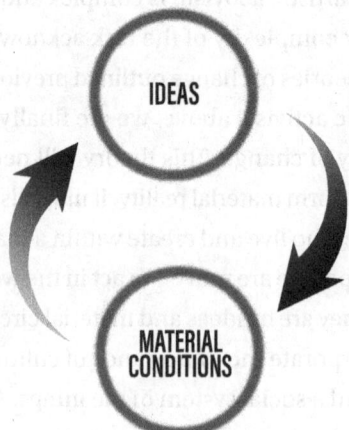

Replacing a directional theory of change with a cyclical one resolves the
questions "which comes first, chicken or the egg? Material or ideal?" Ideas
and material conditions are each shaped by the other.

Now we can reintroduce the social component of this theory of change,
not as the abstraction "human agency" as before, but with a description
of the type of human activities that are shaping, and being shaped by, the
ideal and the material. These are thinking and doing, shown in FIGURE 7.

FIG. 7

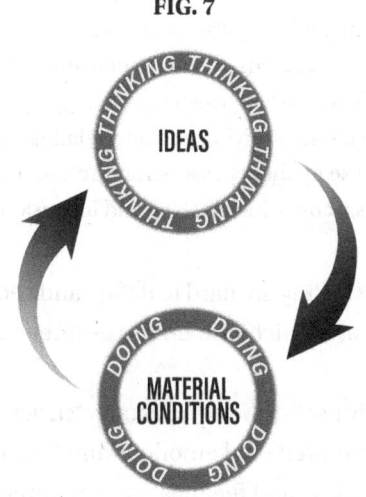

FIGURE 6 might now be read like this: People, by what they do in and
with their material environment (and recall Marx's expanded notion of the
material here), *think* up ideas and ideals. This *thinking* then guides what
they end up *doing* and how they do it. This doing then shapes what they
think, the thinking shapes what they do, and so on, ad infinitum. We will
later need to return to this cycle in order to determine how best to intervene
in order to create change, but for the time being it is enough to have a better
understanding of the process we need to intervene within.

We are now ready to introduce the affective element of change. But
before we do, we need to rescue emotions and feelings from the way they
are usually defined: as individual experience — *I* feel, *you* feel, and so on.
Feeling is personal; of course it is. You always experience emotions as an
individual, and the feeling that generates is intensely personal, but feeling
is also *social* and historical, every bit as much as Marx's "historical epochs."

It was, after all, the social aspect of feeling, the collective emotions of the crowd, that so worried Le Bon.

Raymond Williams, a cultural historian and one of the founders of the academic discipline of cultural studies, developed the term "structures of feeling" as a way to think about social and historical affect. Williams was trying to draw attention to the fact that material conditions, as lived by humans, generated not only formal sets of ideas and ideals, in the form of official ideology, but also,

> characteristic elements of impulse, restraint and tone: specifically affective elements of consciousness and relationships: not feeling against thought, but thought as felt and feeling as thought: practical consciousness of a present kind, in a living and interrelating continuity. We are then defining these elements as a "structure": as a set, with specific internal relations, at once interlocking and in tension.[30]

These structures of feeling are hard to define and spot. They can, however, manifest in works of art, which function as aesthetic reflections of certain sets of feelings.

What is particularly useful about Williams's "structures of feeling" is that they open up a way to understand emotions and feelings as both *structured* and *structuring*. Emotions and feelings are structured in so far as they are in response to, and shaped by, given conditions, be they material or ideal. But they are also structuring in that they shape the thinking or doing that follows.[31] But it is more than shaping, or influencing, or molding that feelings do. Feelings *animate*. Without human feeling, our actions are drudgery and ideas mere abstractions. Without engaging the senses, thinking and doing are senseless. Since it is a theory of *change* I am exploring here, this animation of thought and action through emotion is essential.[32]

But where to place the emotions ball? Here I want to make a bold, but hopefully not too controversial, statement: *Feeling* is as much a part of what constitutes and directs human agency as *thinking* and *doing*. Materialists argue that the first human act is to produce our means of survival, but we build a house or plant our crops because we *feel* cold or hungry. Idealists may argue that in the beginning was the Word, but we listen because we *feel* it has something to say to us. That is to say, both material conditions and ideas are experienced affectively, as well as bodily and cognitively. As such, we need to think of emotion as a sort of intermediary stage between the ideal and the material. Something like FIGURE 8.

FIG. 8

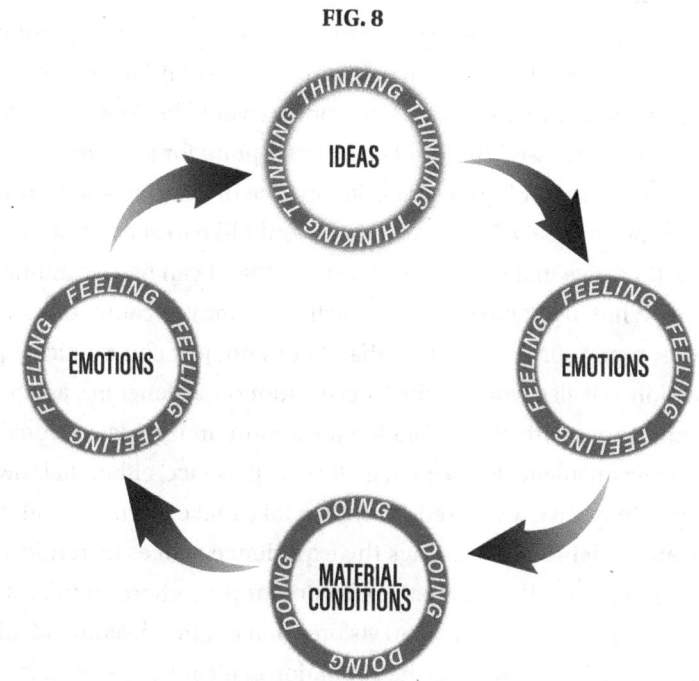

We now have a model that accounts for the *material*, the *ideal*, and the *emotional*. It also incorporates the full range of human agency — our capacity to *think*, *do*, and *feel* — without giving primacy to any one. Translated into words, the diagram might read like this: In the course of living and acting within material conditions, we experience emotions and develop feelings. We then learn to think these feelings as ideas and represent them through arts, philosophy, religion, and so on. These abstract ideas, now animated into forms where they can be represented, communicated, encountered, and felt as ideals motivate us into doing, which in turn shapes our material conditions, and the circle goes round again.

So far we have created a model that accounts for the three primary forces of change and their interrelationship. But it is not yet a useful theory of social change. In order for it to become useful for the study and practice of artistic activism, we need to locate the pressure points: where to intervene in order to generate (or retard) change. This was the advantage of the unidirectional materialist, idealist, and affective models — they gave clear direction. If one holds to a materialist theory of social change, then the point of intervention is at the level of material conditions: seize the means of production! An idealist, on the other hand, would emphasize the production and dissemination of ideas: take control of the media! An affectist would privilege emotions, and any such intervention would be done solely at this level: stir up the masses! But what is the entry point for an artistic activist?

An artistic activist often begins with an idea of what they see wrong in the world or an ideal of the world they would like to see. Through their practice, they give that idea or ideal form so that it can be communicated to others. What distinguishes artistic activist communication from a written thesis, report, or law statute is that it does not just communicate pure information — it also works at the level of emotion. It generates affect, and these emotions motivate people to take action on the idea or ideal. An artistic activism might also begin with lived experience, either their own or something they have witnessed. They then take that experience and distill, define, and heighten the feelings the experience evokes by rendering it into aesthetic form. This aesthetic reflection or projection stimulates new understandings, perspectives, and visions: that is, new ideas and ideals. In other words, artistic activism is the animation of ideas by emotions in order to motivate action and change material conditions, and/or the animation of experience through emotion in order to generate ideas and ideals. In brief: artistic activism makes ideas and experiences more effective by making them affective.

With this in mind, we can think about the intervention of the artistic activist somewhere between ideas and emotions, and emotions and material conditions, as in FIGURE 9.

This space between is the space of *culture*. Culture, as you'll remember, is a word and concept employed frequently by the artistic activists we interviewed when discussing what makes change: "culture shifting," "culture making," and so on. Whether the artistic activist believed that changing consciousness was sufficient to bring about change, or whether there needed to be more institutional and structural change, they all agreed, in the words of The Culture Group, that "culture is the field on which change

FIG. 9

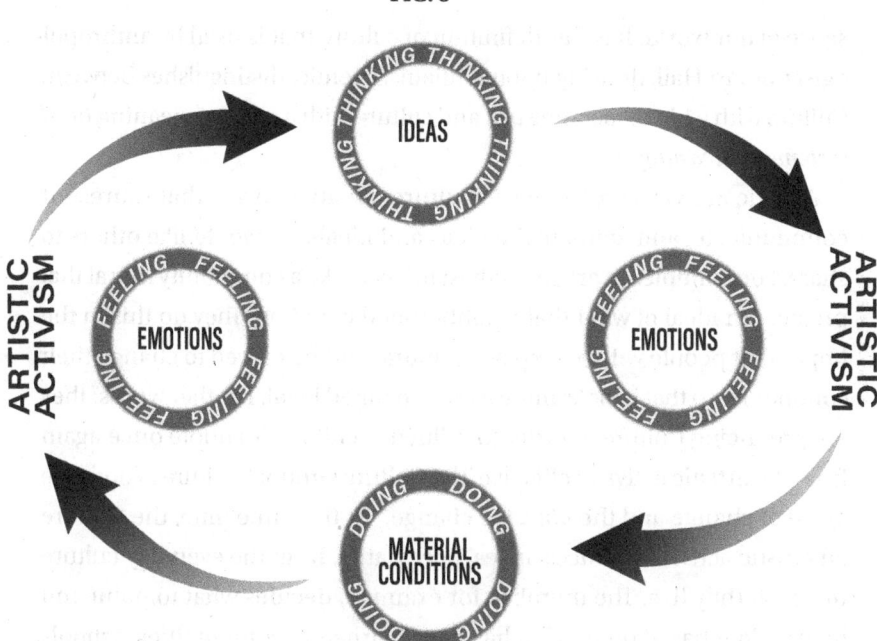

occurs." Or, as Terry Marshall put it so aptly, "culture is the glue between everything."

If one is a legal activist, then the law is the material with which you work. If one is a sculptor, your medium might be stone or metal. Culture is the medium of artistic activism. But culture is a complicated medium. It is one of those words used all the time without giving much thought to what it actually means. This slipperiness is okay in day-to-day use, but because it is a fundamental building block of artistic activism, we need to be more rigorous. So, first we need to define what is meant when we use the word *culture*.

The first definition might go like this: Culture is what society creates in order to represent itself or express its ideals. This is the definition of culture that an art historian, a museum curator, or Matthew Arnold is likely thinking of when they use the term. Art is culture in this sense. But there's another way of understanding culture, a definition much broader and inclusive. This is culture as the patterns and byproducts of everyday life: the languages we use, the rituals we perform, and the unspoken rules we abide by. It's what is created and recreated through work, play, conversations, and everyday interactions in our homes, schools, jobs, and places of worship. This culture surrounds us: it is the material from which we create our lives and make sense of our world. It is this definition of culture that is used by anthropologists. Stuart Hall, drawing upon Williams, usefully distinguishes between Culture with a big *C*, meaning *art*, and culture with a small *c*, meaning *lived systems of meaning*.[33]

Artistic activists create big-*C* Culture: creative forms that represent, communicate, and animate the ideas and ideals we would like others to share. For example, an artistic activist might make a community mural that projects an ideal of what that neighborhood could be. They do this in the hopes that people will look up at the mural and be moved to change their community so that it looks more like the painted ideal. In other words: they are producing Culture in order to influence culture. To quote once again from the artistic activist collective The Culture Group: "Culture is both the *agent* of change and the *object* of change." At the same time, the Culture an artistic activist produces arises, necessarily, from the everyday culture in which they live. The muralist, for example, decides what to paint and how to do it based upon what has been learned in communities, schools, political associations, and so forth. In addition, this big-*C* mural is interpreted and acted upon by an audience through their own small-*c* systems of meaning. Put together, it goes something like this: Big-*C* Culture works as a representation of and reinforcement for small-*c* culture, and small-*c* culture shapes, and is shaped by, big-*C* Culture. This cyclical relationship might be pictured as in FIGURE 10.

FIG. 10

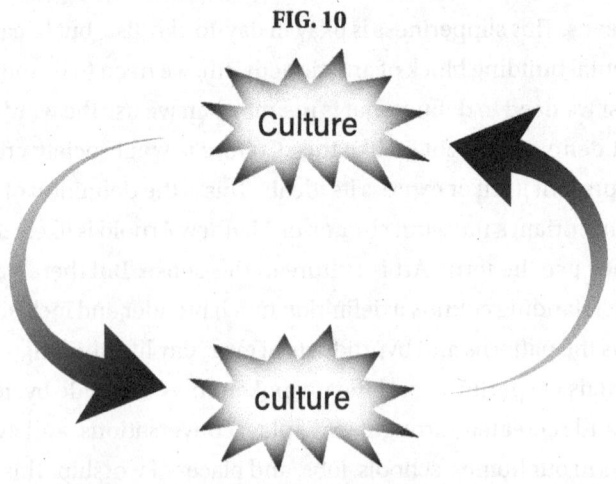

We are made by culture, but through Culture we also remake it. Culture is our point of artistic activist intervention.

We are now at the moment where we can put all these variables in play with one another, and out of this complexity generate a coherent theory of change. So far we have a cyclical model of social change that incorporates ideas, material conditions, and emotions as forces driving change. This change does not happen mechanically, but through the human agency of people thinking, feeling, and doing. We then set this model into motion by positing that what artistic activism does is intervene to animate ideas with emotions — charge them with affect — in order to motivate action and change material conditions. Artistic activism, however, also animates lived experience through emotions and, through its representation, gives rise to ideas and ideals. Finally, we added in the medium through and upon which artistic activism operates: culture. By "culture," again, we are describing small-c culture: the "webs of significance" that give meaning and direction to our actions, feelings, and thoughts, but also big-C Culture as the creative expression of actions, thoughts, and feelings.[34]

If we put all of this together, our theory of change for artistic activism might look something like FIGURE 11.

FIG. 11

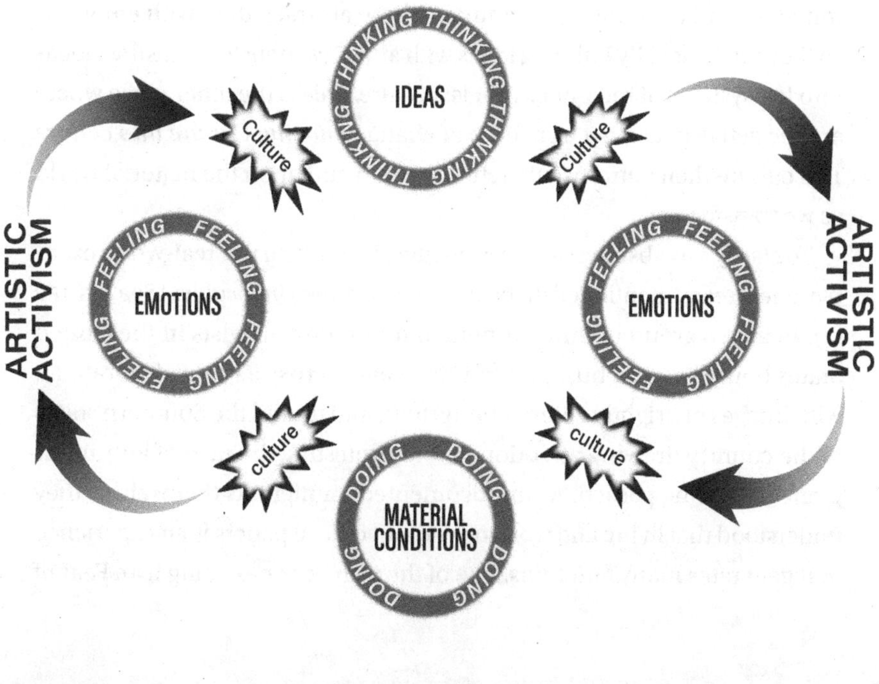

Because this model is complex and its visual representation can be as confusing as it is clarifying, let's try moving through the model, starting at the bottom and continuing clockwise. We start with our environment, including both natural and human-made elements: mountains, plains, and rivers, but also skyscrapers, shopping malls, and service call centers. These are the "material conditions" in which we live. Living is active — it's doing — and, because we are emotional beings, living is also our feelings about what we are doing and what is being done to us. This is one of the points where artistic activism can make an intervention. Artistic activism can crystallize our feelings that arise from material experience into an art form so they can be represented, recognized, and generalized.[35] This is the process of *making culture into Culture*. This Culture, in crystallizing feelings (or structuring them, as Williams would have it), enables their abstraction into ideas and ideals, things we can think about and eventually act upon.

At this point, we've made it to the top, the realm of ideas, and we are ready to introduce another point where artistic activism might intervene. Humans are doers and feelers, but we are also very much thinkers. We reflect upon what we do and feel, and think up new ways (or justify old ones) of ordering our world and our place within it. In other words, we create ideas. Sliding down and to the right, we express these ideas and ideals through Culture — performances, paintings, pop songs, video games, community murals — and in doing so, we animate these abstract ideas with emotions so they can be felt. By imbuing ideas with affect, we transform abstract ideas into felt systems of meaning. That is: culture. This is the other place where artistic activism can act as a force of change: *making Culture into culture*. This culture then patterns our actions within and upon the material world as we transform it.

To clarify this abstract theory of change, let me turn to a real-world example, one already mentioned in the introduction: the *Undocubus*. (See FIGURE 12). In 2012 a group of undocumented immigrant activists in the United States bought an old bus, painted "No Fear" across its side, decorated it with images of brightly colored butterflies, and toured the Southern states of the country drawing attention to and protesting the rash of anti-immigrant laws being passed. As undocumented immigrants themselves, they understood that living and working without official papers is an experience that generates many emotions, one of the primary ones being fear. Fear of being stopped by the police for the most routine of reasons, fear of being detained, fear of being deported, fear of being separated from the ones you love. Responding to this "culture of fear" in the United States, they named their campaign "No Papers, No Fear" and used a vintage bus reminiscent of those used by "freedom riders" in the 1960s in order recall an older, well-established — and successful — campaign against unjust laws and fear: the U.S. civil rights movement. With assistance from the artist Favianna Rodriguez, they also designed a visual symbol for the campaign: a monarch butterfly, a creature of dramatic beauty that migrates across the U.S.-Mexico border freely. The campaign slogan, the bus, and the butterfly distilled, structured, and reflected the lived experience of undocumented immigrants, transforming a felt negative into a positive representation. The artistic activists turned culture into Culture.

Their work was not done. The purpose of their campaign was twofold: to challenge anti-immigration laws being debated in the states where the bus visited, and to shift the consciousness, among immigrants and non-immigrants alike, from an idea of migrants and migration in negative terms — "aliens," "illegals," "invasion," "replacement" — to a positive idea: "Migration is Beautiful." For that idea to come alive, to move from an abstraction to a felt reality, the idea needed to be made visible and charged with

FIG. 12

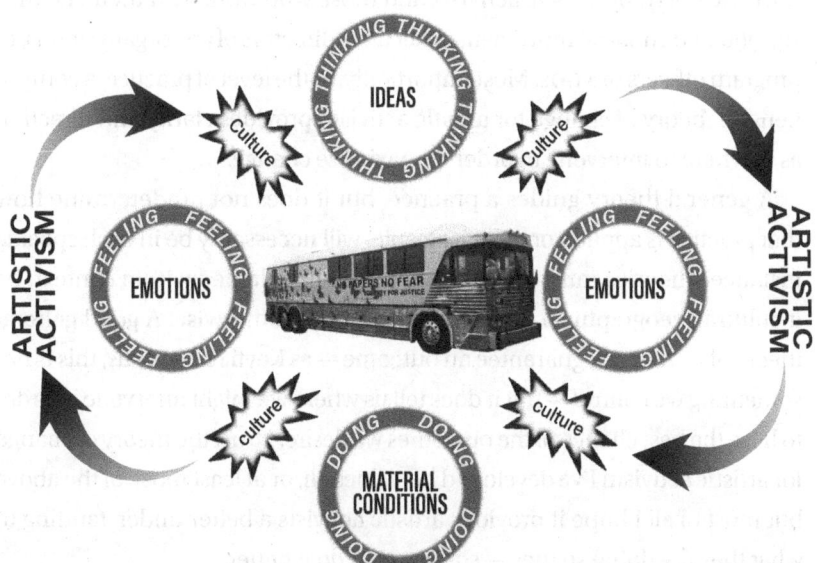

emotion. This was the role of the nostalgic vintage bus, the beautiful butter-fly, the stirring slogans, and the reproduction of the symbol and slogans on posters and T-shirts. All this was done to animate the idea and insert it into the way people "make sense" of migration, turning Culture into culture in the hope that they would then act upon this understanding and demand changes in immigration law, policy, and practice.

Compelled to sum up and simplify this rather complex theory of change for artistic activism into one sentence, it might read like this:

> Turning culture into Culture and Culture into culture, artistic activ-ism animates lived experiences into felt ideas that change the way people think, and animates ideas into felt experiences that change what people do.

Is such a general theory of change for artistic activism useful? I think so. It provides a model to think through and reflect upon artistic activism as a complex practice that combines the affective power of the arts with the effective aims of activism, allowing us to better understand, and thus maxi-mize, the æffect of artistic activism. It also gives us a wide-angle lens through which to see how artistic activism might create change. Such a macro view is helpful when thinking through and assessing more specific and neces-sarily contextual micro theories of change that are applied, consciously or unconsciously, by artistic activists and those who work with them, be they stakeholders in social movements, executive directors of arts organizations, or program officers of NGOs. Most importantly, at the level of practice, a compre-hensive theory of change for artistic activism provides clarity and direction as to where to intervene in order to maximize change.

A general theory guides a practice, but it does not predetermine how that practice is applied or what its results will necessarily be in each specific instance. Theories must always be applied and adapted within context, be it cultural, geographical, political, historical, or otherwise. A good general theory also does not guarantee an outcome — as Keyti reminds us, this is not something we control — but it does tell us where we might intervene in order to have the best chance of the outcomes we desire. I trust the theory of change for artistic activism I've developed here does all, or at least most, of the above, but most of all I hope it provides artistic activists a better understanding of what they are doing so they — so we — can do it better.

CHAPTER TWO

What Artistic Activism Does

THEORIES OF CHANGE PROVIDE A necessary framework for understanding how artistic activism *might* bring about social change, but if we are to assess how artistic activism actually *does* generate change, we need to take a step down from a general theory of change and ask how artistic activism actually works in practice: what it does, or aims to do.

Defining what it is that artistic activism does, or aims to do, is not an easy question to answer, and unfortunately, turning to art and social theory does not offer much clarity. Intellectuals and artists have theorized the role of art as an active agent of change for thousands of years and have generated nearly as many ideas as to how this works. For some (like the jealous God of the Abrahamic tradition), art's capacity for representation and the artist's power to create pose a powerful threat to (divine) authority.[1] For others, art's suspect power lies in its capacity to falsely emulate reality and trigger improper emotions in response.[2] Conversely, art's power may reside in its ability, through identification and catharsis, to diffuse those emotions.[3] Art may also be a way to capture and communicate the essence of reality, that is more than its mere physical representation.[4] Or art may be a representation of a certain reality, often that of those in power, which then becomes a "way of seeing" for us all.[5] But art can also be a means with which to overthrow those dominant ways of seeing reality and replace it with others.[6] Art can generate new forms of knowledge,[7] "alienate" what we already know,[8] or disrupt, defunctionalize, or agonize dominant systems of thought and structures of power.[9] Art is a means to create new, and as of yet unspoken, languages, visions, and perceptions, or unlock those that have been buried or repressed.[10] Or perhaps the power of art is not the reality it creates, but its ability to create new creators,[11] make spaces to have new conversations amongst new peoples,[12] or provide a stage to rehearse revolutionary actions.[13] Some theorists argue that it is the autonomy of art from society that engenders its critical function,[14] while still others make a case for recognizing the embeddedness of art in everyday life.[15] And then there are those who hold that art does not, and should not, have any activist function at all: *l'art pour l'art* — art for art's sake.[16]

Not surprisingly, there is no historical consensus on what art as activism can do — other than it does something (even if that something is nothing). Eleonora Belfiore and Oliver Bennett, in their article and then book on *The Social Impact of the Arts*, identify three major traditions of thinking about art's æffect: (1) Negative, or art as corruption; (2) Positive, or art as physically and morally uplifting; (3) Autonomous, or art as anti-instrumental.[17] Such simplification allows us to step back and see patterns that help us better understand what artistic activism can do, and therefore how we might measure it. Yet it also risks ignoring the elephant in the room of theoretical multitude, and as we hear what practitioners have to say about how artistic activism works, the theories are just going to multiply.

While perspectives of theorists and philosophers are important, it is also essential to recognize that artistic activists are forever theorizing the function of their own work and, in doing so, ruminating philosophically on the question of how artistic activism works. To listen to their words and take them seriously, again, takes on political and practical significance. Politically, it acknowledges that practitioners think and these thoughts are just as perceptive as, and likely more relevant than, those of professional theorists and scholars. Practically speaking, any methodology of evaluation that one hopes to be accepted and used by artistic activists needs to understand what they are doing and what they are thinking. Some of what the artistic activists say below overlaps with what was said in the last chapter about theories of change. This makes sense. It is, after all, through discussions of actual practices that many artistic activists are able to abstract a theory of change. In addition, every theory of social change suggests certain practical approaches on how to bring it about. As was the case with a theory of change, the artistic activists interviewed rarely articulated a clearly defined theory in response to the question of how their artistic activism works. Instead, they tell stories: stories about their practice, their intention, and what happened as a result of their interventions. Listening to these stories, I noted similarities and dissimilarities, patterns and groupings, and then organized these into the following broad, and not always exclusive, analytic categories of what artistic activists believe their artistic activism does.

Artistic Activism Makes Ideas Affective

Artistic activists often stress the importance of communicating ideas. Not just any ideas, but critical ideas that challenge conventional positions and structures, and not just factual communication, but creative forms of communication that attract, interest, and above all *move* the public to bring about change. Sim Chi Yin began her professional life as a traditional journalist and photojournalist. Currently based in China, she now creates haunting, "artistic" photos that explore the ecology and politics of geographies like nuclear sites and artificial landmasses. When asked what prompted her move in a more artistic direction, Sim explains, "I'm really looking for new ways of expressing and telling stories." When asked why, she elaborates:

> I'm currently more interested in having someone have a deep experience of the work than reaching a lot of people which I could have by being published in the *New York Times*. I'm experimenting with different ways of making things and making exhibitions that reach, that hit people, maybe not a lot of people, but hit them in a deeper way.

The way that Sim uses the word "reach" here is telling. She begins by using it to describe the breadth of her audience, but then ends by using it to describe the depth to which her message affects her audience. What her move toward artistic activism may sacrifice in the former, it makes up for in the latter, as the affective intensity of her new photos and the stories they tell "hits" people "in a deeper way," not just cognitively but emotionally.[18]

Rebecca Bray shares her experience of trying to tell the story of factory farming while working at a nonprofit nongovernmental organization dedicated to food issues. She understood the importance of facts in making persuasive arguments, but she became increasingly aware that these facts were frequently ignored. She recalls how she and her collaborators "were telling people how horrible the [conditions of factory farming] were and nobody really wanted to hear it. Everybody was disturbed and they didn't want to listen. So, we realized that we needed another angle." The other angle was to embed facts in a short flash-animation story starring cartoon farm animals who learn about the hidden truths behind factory farming. Based on the hit movie *The Matrix*, it was called *The Meatrix*. Jettisoning what Bray describes as the "how many facts can we get in?" focus of a more conventional advocacy pamphlet or documentary, she and her collaborators worked to "bring characters into it, and some sort of personality and humor," quite literally animating facts through a pop culture narrative. Recognizing that stories are an affective way to reach people (in terms of depth), Bray was also able to effectively extend the reach (in terms of the breadth) of the information she wanted to convey. *The Meatrix* and its sequels have been translated into thirty languages and viewed by more than thirty million people.

For Prince Afful, a spoken-word and performance artist from Ghana's capital city of Accra, reaching people with information means presenting it through cultural mediums they connect with. "What creates that feeling of connection?," he muses, describing an event he hosted where he invited artists to present their thoughts and feelings on mental health and care in a range of mediums.

> So, okay, those who are around who like rap — they're hearing rap about mental health. Those who are around who like singing — they're hearing someone else singing about mental health. This is what they connect to the most. Those who like poetry are hearing poetry talking about mental health. Those who like painting and drawing, or people who draw there, that was their relation to mental health. It was a way of making sure people understand it in a language they are very familiar with. That was the whole idea, to speak to them in their very own language.

Marisa Morán Jahn, who earned her university degree from the elite Massachusetts Institute of Technology yet works with domestic workers in the United States and rural villagers in Honduras, speaks of the importance of reaching people where they are, in a language that belongs to them. Her father is from China, her mother is from Ecuador and never attended college,

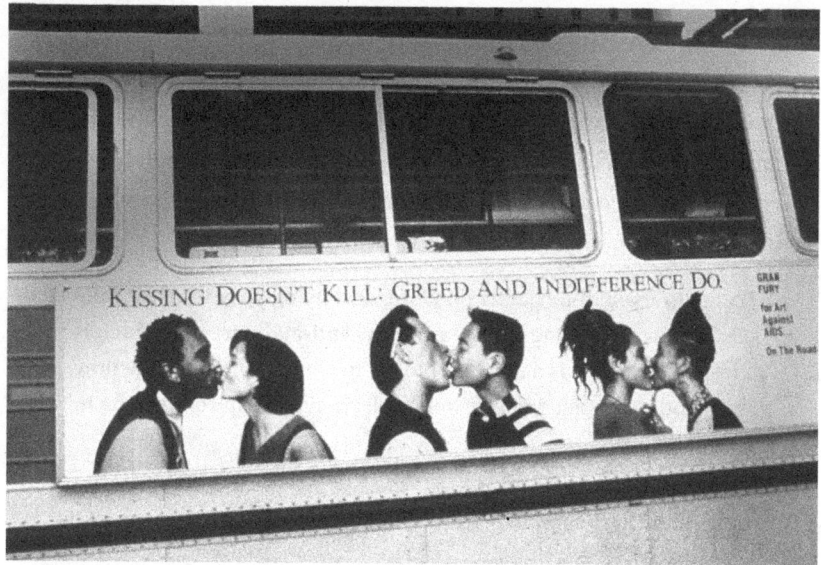

Queering culture with Gran Fury's Kissing Doesn't Kill "advertisement,"
photo: Creative Time.

and many in her family work in the garment and restaurant industries. "So I'm just very mindful," she says, "I think about my parents when I'm making work. '"Would my mom get this? Would my dad get this?' That's always in the back of my mind." In practice, "being mindful" for Jahn takes the form of teaching Honduran kids the value of literacy by acting out the fanciful character of a masked, story-eating villain called the Bibliobandido. It means reaching out to domestic workers through faux fortune tellers, dramatic audio-novellas, and a tricked-out NannyVan vehicle to inform them of laws that protect their rights as workers. The medium needs to be welcoming if the message is to be received.

It's not just reliance on sober scientific fact and the language of NGO expertise that gets in the way of æffective communication; artistic activists point the finger at the esotericism and elitism of the art world as well.[19] "Vernaculars are essential," says Avram Finkelstein, one of the designers of ACT UP's famous "SILENCE=DEATH" poster. He elaborates:

> I think that art that isn't about communication; [it] is about class. So, if you're an activist who's making art and what you're trying to do or say is not clear, you're no better than being in a Gagosian Gallery [a global chain of high-end art galleries]. It's not activism if it's not understandable.

It's no surprise that Finkelstein, as well as others in Gran Fury, ACT UP's artist collective, draw their inspiration from the visual languages of advertising and commercial design, as much, if not more, than from the art world. In an inventive (and humorous) analogy, the street artist Posterchild — who also employs the vernacular of pop culture in his work — compares the esotericism of art languages to masturbation:

> Trying to make it perfectly obscure, and using your idiosyncratic symbolism, that to me is masturbatory, anti-audience art. Which is fine, masturbation is a great way to get to know yourself, it's healthy, it's a good way to get practice, but it will always pale in comparison to the interaction of sex.

Æffective artistic activism, like good sex, requires good communication.

Artistic Activism Creates Conversations

Political and artistic communication is frequently unidirectional, with the activist or artist transmitting their ideas to be received, more or less passively, by an audience. A number of artistic activists interviewed were striving after something more: more dynamic, more interactive, more multidirectional. They wanted conversations.

The conversations they are looking for are not within the worlds of art and activism, but conversations with people outside these enclaves, often total strangers. "Often it's a very one-way experience within certain art sectors," says Phoebe Davies, a London-based artistic activist whose work facilitates conversations that occur in pop-up "feminist nail salons" or amongst people lounging about on white duvets in "sex re-education" soirees.

"For me," Davies says, "some of the most interesting moments happen when there's things that can be discussed or unpacked, . . . with those you wouldn't normally have conversations with." Kenneth Tin-Kin Hung, whose work combines a pop-art sensibility with political subject matter, takes the novel step of putting his name, address, and telephone number on his work so he can talk to people about it, "because this connects me with the real people." Hung describes an encounter with a person who saw one of his works on the attacks of 9/11 and the U.S. response:

I was sleeping and this guy from New York called me, I was in San Francisco at the time, and then said, 'What the fuck are you doing, why the fuck'd you put the Twin Towers as a firework [in your artwork]?' blah blah blah blah blah. "Do you know 2,000 people died there," blah blah blah blah blah. "One of my friends died there." ... I'm not really good in English, but I just start talking and speaking with him, I just say these are the facts: Saddam Hussein, Al-Qaeda — we trained them. Basically, just all these things that I read and I know, and I just had a really good, direct conversation with him.

While Hung's approach of providing contact information and talking to anyone who follows up is extraordinary, "creating conversations," "stimulating dialogue," or "provoking discussion" is a familiar objective in the world of arts and activism.[20] Conversation itself can be seen as a world-changing activity: the creation of knowledge through a collaborative interchange of ideas as opposed to passively abiding by received wisdom. Adelaide Damoah, a founding member of the Black British Female Artist Collective, explained that "people have their own interpretation" of her work, but that's a "good thing," in that "it provokes discussion, it provokes conversation, and that to me is a massive compliment." This æffect is not accidental. As Damoah goes on to state: "There has definitely been an intention behind my practice to provoke conversations and discussions — I'm just not actively going outside and holding public debates."

A critic might argue that simply provoking discussion, whether through art or on a street corner, does little to bring about change. Indeed, the practice of creating conversations might be seen as a way for the artistic activist to refuse the responsibility that comes with committing to a point of view. Most artistic activists we talked to, however, framed their interest in conversation in more pointed terms. Far from evading politics by refusing to take a stand, and not content with conversation for conversation's sake, they were interested in creating spaces for dialogue in order to activate particular ideas and make their public reception more æffective. In the case of Damoah, she isn't interested in just any old discussion; she is interested in provoking an *intentional* discussion about Black female bodies through her artistic activism.

"It was a conversation starter," says Finkelstein when describing the objective of the famous ACT UP image of an upside-down pink triangle. "Stories are told one sentence at a time, or one word at a time," he explains, "so, all we're going to do today is come up with the first sentence. And that's exactly what SILENCE=DEATH was doing." It is not some abstract "conversation" that artistic activists like Finkelstein are interested in, nor is it the monologic presentation of a set of one's own ideas — it is someplace in between. They see their work as setting the stage for specific conversations about particular issues that they, through their intervention, can then help frame. The Illuminator, at first glance, is an artistic activist project as far away from conversation as one might imagine. It is pure spectacle: the projection of words and images ten stories high on the sides of buildings. But Rachel Brown, a member of The Illuminator collective, told us that the function of their spectacle is not just to get people watching, but to get them talking. "We go into physical public space, intervene there, and make a spectacle," she explains, "and contribute to that conversation, kind of turning, changing the story."

Some artistic activists are less interested in the direction that conversations take and more interested in directing whom they are between, creating conversations between audiences who might otherwise not speak to one another, about topics they might not usually talk about.[21] Elaine Forde lives and works in Northern Ireland where distrust between Catholic youth and the predominantly Protestant police force runs high. Since 2012 she's been running a project called Street Talk, where young people in trouble with the law take weekly workshops with DJs, graffiti artists, musicians, filmmakers, and theater practitioners. The workshops provide the setting for conversations around crime and criminal behavior and allow the kids to express their thoughts, feelings, and experiences through art. Forde, however, invited another set of interlocutors to the conversation: the police, so that the youth "can tell the police officers the experiences that they've had and how they think it could be better or different; share their own perspective." These conversations have "been quite powerful," Forde says, claiming to have "seen a number of police officers and teams changing how they work with young people as a result of the voices of the young people that I work with."

Shaun Leonardo's artistic activism is built around creating opportunities for "conversations" between people who intersect the same spaces but never connect with one another. His interventions can range from staging a spectacular Roman-era combat game amongst people with differing positions around gun control (as described in the introduction) to quieter, more intimate, online workshops, where incarcerated youth, prison guards, legal advocates, and jail administrators explore and share their experiences and beliefs. These "conversations," however, don't take place through words — they happen through bodies.[22] In his work with people on opposing sides of issues, Leonardo found that words can separate and alienate, because, as he explains, "it's in that language that you start to create difference.... Especially when you start identifying oneself as opposition, or when you are identifying the storyteller as opposition."[23] In response, Leonardo began facilitating what he calls "body stories," where people communicate through their posture and movement. Stripped of their ready-made verbal expressions and ready-made responses, people found other ways to really communicate. As Leonardo describes it, "in our body language something else, some other type of common ground might possibly be found." Conversations can be had, and connections can be felt, even if words fail us.

Artistic Activism Encourages Participation

One of the possible liabilities of activist art is that it can reinforce the division between those who do (the artistic activist) and those that have things done for them (the audience). Turning the audience into actors, watchers into doers, is something that artistic activism can do.[24] The group Radical Joy for Hard Times brings people to devastated natural environments to engage in purely expressive acts of artistic creation. Why? "Because it's a way of doing something," says Trebbe Johnson, the founder of the group. She justifies this seemingly non-instrumental practice by pointing out that the real "change" is with the participants themselves:

> It's a simple action, but it's very powerful because so often people feel powerless. They feel that the problems that confront them in their communities and in the world are so huge and so technical that, "How can I possibly have any influence at all?" But making something together and giving it, leaving it there, is a first action. It is an action that you can see.

In a world where most people are encouraged to be consumers of what others have created, and political activity is left up to professionals, moving people to action, no matter what the material effects of that action are, is seen as the most important work of all: "a first action . . . an action you can see."[25]

While shifting public opinion and changing policies might be the primary work that Beautiful Trouble's Andrew Boyd wants his creative actions to do, he also discusses at length the "secondary aspects" of "bringing people in who were previously turned off of politics, who didn't feel there was an outlet for them [because] they were too creative and most politics was too straightforward and lockstep and boring." When he was planning *Billionaires for Bush*, an ironic campaign crafted with an advocacy group to draw attention to campaign financing corruption, Boyd made a decision to maximize participation by creating downloadable do-it-yourself instructions on how to create your own chapters and stage your own demonstrations, even though it cost him a certain amount of creative control. He explains: "It just wouldn't do to just have some huge event that I controlled and just do it. That wouldn't achieve anything like the results that we wanted to achieve" of creating an "expanding mutating participatory artistic project." Reaching this objective, Boyd explains, "required an open architecture that required us to let go of some control to a certain degree." By emphasizing the "open architecture" of his work, Boyd challenged not only the division of creative labor, but also creative ownership. He describes how:

> People would take ownership of it, see it as their own, reinvent it in small or large ways and then stay through the whole year and sustain that interest and enthusiasm. It became one of the most beautiful aspects for me: to see this set in motion, [to see] that I was sort of the prime mover of getting it to mutate and grow in ways that I previously hadn't imagined.

Billionaires for Bush "worked" when it took on a life of its own, and when the lines between artist and audience, or activist and "the people" blurred, and everyday people became artistic activists themselves.

"A lot of people are copying these actions," Nikola Pisarev notes, referring to his North Macedonian group's creative interventions aimed at fixing practical problems, "some are asking [for permission], some are not asking. Nevermind." What is important to Pisarev is that the practice is spreading, and as it spreads, it leaps from the property of the individual artist to the expression of anyone, and potentially everyone: "meeting kings [in disguise], Superman. All the heroes we know, you never know who is behind them. . . . It's me, it's you, it's all of us, *it's we*." Sam Gould of Red 76, when asked what he wanted people who participated in his interventions to experience, replies simply: "I want them to feel like: (1) they could do this, (2) they can get involved, and (3) they don't need us. They can just do it by themselves."

Artistic Activism Reveals Reality

Communicating ideas to audiences, creating conversations, and encouraging participation are all important functions of artistic activism. But before people will listen, talk, or participate, they need, in contemporary activist parlance, their awareness raised. "Everyone has a million things to worry about. They concern themselves with other things, they think they're masters of their own journeys. . . . It's all an illusion," says Amin Husain, co-founder of Decolonize This Place, a project devoted to revealing the racist and imperialist realities that lie behind the facades of many cultural institutions. For the illusion to be broken, Hussein believes, people need to see what remains hidden. A number of artistic activists talked about how they intended their interventions to reveal hidden, overlooked, or uncomfortable realities. Artistic activism can *make the invisible visible.*[26]

Many of the most pressing social issues are largely invisible. How does one *see* climate change? Structural racism? Capitalist exploitation? In order for these long-term, deep-seated processes to become actionable, they need to be made visible, and visceral. This is nothing new. It's what Martin Luther King and the Southern Christian Leadership Conference were doing when they wagered that "Bull" Connor, the commissioner of public safety of Birmingham, Alabama, would overreact to their peaceful demonstration and reveal the everyday, but often hidden, brutality of white supremacy in front of the world's news cameras. It's also what Pablo Picasso did when he recreated the horror and chaos of the fascist bombing of Guernica in a painting as a wakeup call for an indifferent world public at the 1937 Paris International Exposition. Through their activism and their art, King and Picasso made the invisible visible.[27]

"It's not easy to represent corruption visually," states Edisa Demi, a long-time activist from Bosnia and Herzegovina. To do this, she turned to artistic activism, working with a local artist to paint a public mural about corruption using a local symbol, the "old bridge" of Mostar. Demi used her mural to visualize the corruption endemic in waste collection and disposal services in Mostar, and also to envision the equally hard-to-represent ideal of citizen solidarity. "We showed the sewage system dumping bribes into the river, and the bridge representing people uniting to stay above it." Taking on the invisibility of social problems more directly, Demi's group then performed in front of municipal buildings while wearing masks and chains. "Corruption is hidden in plain sight — like being behind a mask," Demi says, explaining the symbolism; "it's up to the public to work together to take off the mask and break the chains."

"How could we make what was happening real to people?," asks Ron Goldberg, the "chant queen" of ACT UP, as he describes the challenge of building bridges into reality at a time of AIDS denial. "As [famed LGBTQ activist] Vito Russo said, it was like living in an alternate universe where we were the only ones who could hear the bombs dropping. So, how do you make other people hear the bombs dropping?"

"Bombs dropping" is the exact reality that Aaron Hughes, an artist and organizer with Iraq Veterans Against War (IVAW) aims to reveal. Exposing the gap between the reality he experienced as a soldier in Iraq and how war was represented back home is a theme Hughes explores in his individual creative work and the interventions he helps create with his group. Explaining the function of a series of performances staged on the streets of cities across the United States in which veterans, wearing battle fatigues, acted out combat maneuvers learned from their experience occupying Iraq, Hughes says: "We were trying to bring an occupation home."

> People [at home] do not understand what it's like to be terrorized. To have a military patrolling your streets every single day..... The whole idea was to share that because there was no way — in our minds — that people in the United States could think that an occupation was "moving towards a democracy" if they understood what an occupation was.

The goal of *Operation First Casualty*, as the intervention was called (truth being the first casualty of war) was to have U.S. civilians feel the horrible truth of war as a "real" experience, albeit through a staged performance.

"Reality" in an age of public relations, political spectacle, and image consultants is often itself staged. And a function of artistic activism, explains

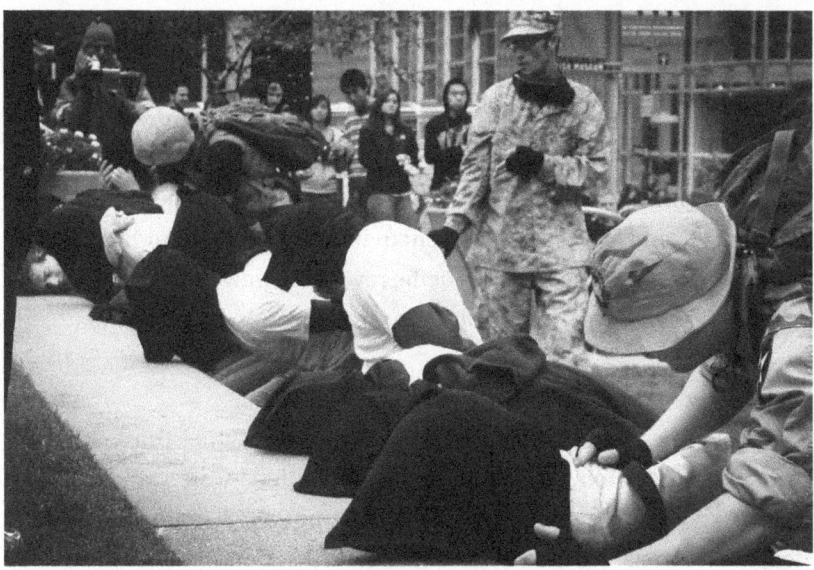

Bringing the war home with the IVAW, photo: Ian Paul/Indybay.

Eric Triantafillou of the San Francisco Print Collective, is "to expose the relationship between appearance and reality. It's to try to pull away the veil and ask questions: Is what you're seeing, what you're interacting with, is it really real?" Because they are not acting as investigative journalists, the way artistic activists "pull away the veil" is often through creative means — staging, story, spectacle — that one normally associates with creating illusions in the first place.[28] Here, however, these techniques are used to upset the illusions of everyday reality. There is "a scenery which is built up by the politicians, by the media. They are playing theater, too, with our lives and with our destinies," explains André Leipold of the German artistic activist group Center for Political Beauty. "So, by poking holes in the scenery, we are trying to get a look at the truth, to see what's under the surface. It's about building bridges into the real reality."

The truth-teller who reveals reality and changes the world is a familiar story. He is the young child in Hans Christian Andersen's fairytale *The Emperor's New Clothes* who announces to the crowd, "The King has nothing on!," exposing the world as it is and ensuring that they all lived happily ever after. This belief in the simple revelatory power of the truth can be naive. It presupposes that people will want to know what reality is, yet as Husain stated at the beginning of this section, there are millions of distractions from reality and plenty of reasons to prefer our illusions. Artistic activists, however, recognize that making the invisible visible is as much an emotional appeal as it is a cognitive reveal. To be compelled to leave the comforts of our illusions, to see the truth and act upon it, we need to be *moved* to see, to know, and to act. This is where artistic activism can help: reality needs help to be heard, seen, and felt. It is no accident that Hans Christian Andersen chose to convey his enduring message of the revelatory power of truth through a compelling story: it's what made his communication æffective.

Artistic Activism Generates Affect and Empathy

Cognitive scientists suggest that people feel as much as think their way through information, especially when confronted by an overabundance of facts and data.[29] For artistic activists, it's not just a matter of reaching people's hearts and minds, but reaching minds through hearts. Marlène Ramírez-Cancio is one of the founders of the Latina satire collective Fulana and also develops the craft of other artistic activists through her work in various nonprofit arts organizations in New York City. Asked about what artistic activism does, Ramírez-Cancio speaks about the necessity to "make people feel something first, and then they get to think about it." Her approach is rooted in her theories of how art itself works:

> A lot of art is not necessarily thinking first. You might think about it later, but it impacts you somehow, whether it makes you laugh or whether it's something that makes you sad. You have empathy, those are all feelings. And then you might reflect and think about the issue, but it's not like reading an essay. It's a different form of expression.

Generating emotions in others, particularly strong feelings of connection to social issues or other people, is what many artistic activists hope to accomplish through their interventions. Affect is their desired effect.

During the economic crisis of 2008, which hit Spain particularly hard, Barcelona-based artistic activist Leónidas Martin Saura organized joyful occupations in dispiriting places. In one intervention, Martin and his group Enmedio threw a dance party inside an unemployment office; in another action, they celebrated a customer shutting down her bank account with a public surprise party. Asked, "What was the point?," Martin replies simply, "to break the fear." Pushed to elaborate, he explains: "We thought a lot of people are not really suffering the crisis right now, but they are suffering the fear about it. So we wanted to do something about breaking that fear somehow." For Martin the impact of the economic crisis in Spain was as much emotional as it was material, and even those who did not yet suffer economically were suffering psychically. Channeling Franklin Delano Roosevelt's famous declaration, during a previous economic depression, that the "only thing we have to fear is fear itself," Martin held out the hope that his action could, if maybe only for a moment, change the way everyday Spaniards felt, turning fear into joy and laughter.

Artistic activists also mobilize affect for a different effect: to generate empathy, particularly empathy with people who might otherwise be ignored or even demonized. "I don't know [if] you saw *Fiddler on the Roof* growing up, in some middle school or high school production?," asks Ari Edelson, the director of *Building the Wall*, a contemporary dystopian play on immigration. Then Edelson makes his point: "That's the first time most Americans meet a Jew." Generalizing from this, he explains that:

> Whether at a museum, or in a theater, it's [through the arts] where we all meet people we never met before, and hear stories we've never heard before, ... they are physically present. You are in that room with those people, you are not just watching them through a flaneur's lens — you are seeing them there in front of you.

What Edelson is pointing out here is the power of the arts to build emotional bonds between the audience and the subject of the artwork, making otherness familiar, even intimate.[30] Be it a Jew in a Shtetl in Russia in the first decade of the twentieth century or an undocumented immigrant today, art — and by extension, art in the service of activism — allows us "to see each other three dimensionally," Jan Cohen-Cruz, A Blade of Grass's field researcher and evaluator remarks.

Diana Arce stages what she calls *Politaoke*, a participatory Karaoke-style engagement where, instead of singing along to popular pop songs, audience members recite current political speeches. These speeches are not from political heroes, but often from contemporary politicians whose political positions the audience may not agree with, or even understand. The problem with political discourse, as Arce understands it, is that, "whenever you talk about politics in a mixed room of people, all they do is get caught up in language and stereotypes, ... and then they don't actually have a real conversation." By mouthing the words of a political Other, Arce hopes to build empathetic bridges between people who have stopped understanding — much less talking to — one another because of ideological divides. "For me," she says, "it's about finding a way to talk about politics without actually talking about politics."

Artistic Activism Circumvents Barriers

Artistic activists often describe the function of their creative work as reaching people with ideas in ways that circumvent people's usual barriers.[31] As Arce concluded above, the purpose of her Politaoke was to "talk about politics without actually talking about politics." For Nana Akosua Hanson, the creator of *Moongirls*, a Ghanaian graphic novel that follows the adventures of queer superheroes fighting for an Africa free from corruption, patriarchy, and legacies of slavery and colonialism, the biggest obstacle to change is how fiercely people hold on to what they already believe. "Artistic activism," Hanson explains,

> allows you to play with those parts of the mind where you are often trapped by prejudices that were given to you from birth, ... where someone's beliefs, which are actually not facts, are made facts. Art gives you an opportunity to dislodge that; it shakes you a little bit. And if it shakes you a little bit, that's all you need, because it tells you that this is shakable: "This is not a fact, this is a belief, this is programming."

Hanson's comics do this shaking. They are "politics without actually talking about politics," as Arce put it, and circumvent the "political" positions and prejudices that people hold on to.

"I think a lot of it is thinking under people's radar," the Canadian street artist Posterchild explains when asked how artistic activism works. "When we see a protester," he elaborates, "there's automatically a connotation depending on your political outlook of either a wackjob or a hero. Either way, we know and are familiar with that method of delivering a message. ... We're very good at filtering information." To reach people with their messages, artistic activists need to get through, or around, the filters that people use in order to screen out unwanted intrusions. As Posterchild points out, one of the things that people sometimes want to filter out is anything that looks like politics.

"If you are from a political party or you represent a certain dogma," people know what to expect — and reject — explains Maja Kalafati, an artistic activist working in Serbia and Slovenia. Conversely, "creative activism helps you to invite people in, engage them, and connect over an issue. We have a clear goal, but we can also use humor or approach the idea from 'around the corner.'" In the poetic words of Mahamadou Cellou Diallo, an investigative journalist from the West African nation of Guinea-Conakry who has embraced artistic activism as a way to æffect his audiences, "with art people come to see what is happening, and not speeches or someone speaking. There it is real, it speaks, it communicates, it communicates without speaking."

In more democratic "free" societies, the obstacles that need to be circumvented are largely within the minds of the audience, but in societies that suppress activism, the obstacles are more material: arrest and imprisonment. Artistic activism is used to circumvent these as well. Recall the Chinese ecological activists mentioned in the introduction who staged an "artistic" *War on Smog* as a way to outwit the official ban on political protests. Passersby, and even authorities, knew that it was a protest against the lack of official action on the environment, but as "art" it was allowed to happen and people were unafraid to watch it. "This is one aspect of 'artistic license,'" says Greg Sholette when explaining why artistic activists are sometimes allowed to get away with things that activists cannot.

Sholette, in addition to being a scholar, teacher, and practitioner of artistic activism, works with Gulf Labor, a group of artistic activists interested in exposing and rectifying the connections between elite art institutions in the United States and exploitative labor practices used to build satellite cultural institutions in the oil-rich states of the Persian Gulf. His experience with Gulf Labor, and their ability to do "activism" in the Gulf Region that routinely gets human rights NGOs banned, prompted him to speculate on how traditional ideas about the arts — namely their autonomy from politics — can, and is, mobilized for political advantage. "Basically artists have the right to represent other things," Sholette explains, and because of this, "artists are able to speculate about their identity in a certain way, to take the place of, or mimic, an NGO or activists and do things they would not be able to do."[32] In other words, artists can represent the functions of activism without being recognized, or repressed, as activists. Ironically, one of the reasons for this is that authorities — and everyday people — don't expect the arts to work politically. Sholette continues:

> We are leaning on all that long tradition of the idea of art being free from the burden of utility....Whether that is true, whether it has ever been true, it is this little thin crust of deterrence we can still call upon to do certain things. A weird utilitarianization of what is anti-utilitarian.

That is to say: the "artistic" part of artistic activism allows for a level of acceptance that otherwise would be denied to the "activist." Tina Orbán, a Hungarian trans-rights organizer working inside Prime Minister Viktor Orbán's far-right "illiberal democracy," has increasingly turned to more artistic forms of activism. When asked, "Why this creative turn?," they are frank: "We are not really engaging in politics. That would be a suicidal act in Hungary at this point."

Whether resistance to activism comes from a weary audience or a repressive state, the ambiguity of a hybrid of art and activism allows radical ideas and actions to slip and slither past the barriers erected against them. "Art is like a snake," concludes Beatrice Glow, whose own practice broaches social ideas through a wide range of sensory experiences. "It moves through different sectors. It can come off as innocuous in certain societies where art isn't seen as anything that can affect change."

Artistic Activism Surprises

The obstacle artistic activists face the most, however, may not be suspicion or oppression, but the public indifference that comes with preconceived notions of activism and art. These conceptions may be negative, or they may be positive, but because they have already been decided, there are few openings for new ideas and experiences.

The "hegemonologue" is what Larry Bogad calls the "hegemonic monologue of the dominant ideology" that closes down thought. When asked how he circumvented the hegemonologue with groups like the Clandestine Insurgent Rebel Clown Army, an "army" of absurd clown protesters that confront riot police with ridicule at large protests in Europe, Bogad explains that, "there is an emphasis in activism on occupying space. 'We're taking this over and we're going to chant our slogan, and now this space is about our slogans. And you're not in here and we are.' And that sometimes is totally appropriate." But there's another model of activism, Bogad explains, that instead of occupying space, upsets conventions by opening it up. "Opening a space is like, 'Wow!' It's not predictable." For Bogad, the key to "opening space" is surprise. As he elaborates, "surprise can open up a temporal, experiential space where anything can come in." Like clowns confronting riot police, for instance.

Packard Jennings, an artist based in San Francisco's Bay Area, drops what he calls "thought bombs." He creates little pamphlets that provide directions for trashing shopping malls, wrecking workplaces, usurping bosses, overthrowing capitalism, and returning to an idyllic state of agrarian communism — all illustrated in a friendly, step-by-step cartoon style used by airlines to instruct passengers what to do in case of an emergency. Jennings then leaves these guides to insurrection laying around in shopping malls or he posts them back to corporate mailrooms in free-reply envelopes. He doesn't really expect anyone to take action on his directions, but he does want to create a little explosion in the "hegemonologue," a surprise that pushes people to think and reflect.

Mystery, Jennings believes, helps with this: "As soon as people can nail something down, they can catalog it, dismiss it." Unlike those artistic activists trying to engage in conversation with their audience, Jennings doesn't sign his work and leaves no contact information, believing that, "any kind of authorship or signage connection immediately corrupts the experience.... When you don't have that on it, it expands the experience, which is where all the power lies to affect someone." What sort of experience? "Processing of the content," Jennings replies,

> trying to figure out what it is, and where it came from, the only clues you have is the thing itself, so you have to figure out maybe what it's saying, what the imagery is. I think it just provides more time on the thing in a more experiential moment. Which...you could say is a more transcendent movement. Moments of transcendence are powerful.

Whereas Packard's work is small, private and intimate, the murals and portraits of An Wei Lu Li, which often occupy whole public squares, are grand and public. Yet An Wei is also reluctant to explain his work to his audiences. "I want people to reflect upon it. If I make somebody reflect, or think, that's good," he says, then adds: "And I think when people are curious they get involved."

Improv Everywhere is a comedy collective based in New York City that "stages unexpected performances in public places." Some of their more famous stunts include flooding a Best Buy electronics store with one hundred additional blue-shirted, khaki-clad people; stopping time in the busy Grand Central train station lobby with a flash-mob freeze; and having a group of performers board a subway train wearing nothing but underwear from the waist down only to have another member of the troupe board at the next stop and distribute pants to put on. My favorite Improv Everywhere intervention involves a long escalator and a guy named Rob. It begins with an unsuspecting crowd of commuters on their way to work in the financial center of the city who pile off the subway and move up the escalator to street level. As they start their grim-faced ascent, they are greeted by a person holding up a sign with the words: "Rob Wants." A few steps up the adjacent steps another person holds up a sign saying: "To Give You," followed by another: "A High Five." A few feet higher up is a sign reading: "Get Ready." Finally, a person holds aloft a sign with just the word "Rob" and an arrow pointing down. Sure enough, underneath the arrow is Rob, an innocuous white man in his mid-thirties dressed in khakis and a polo shirt, who offers up his palm to a steady stream of smiling, high-fiving (and a bit bemused)

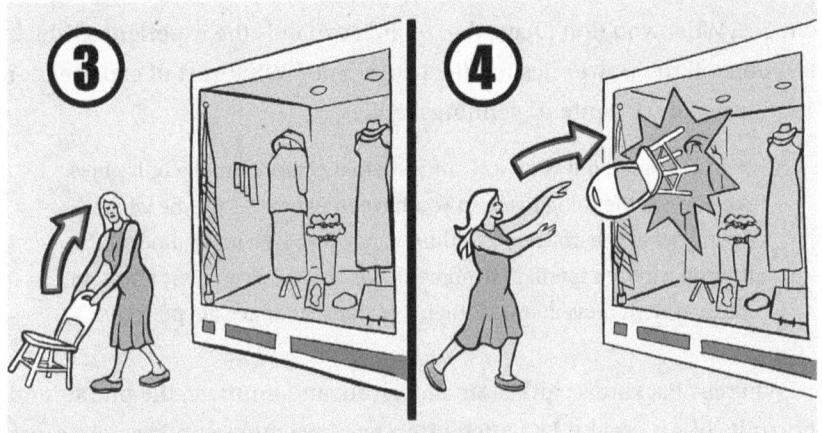

Packard Jennings's Thought Bombs, courtesy of the artist.

commuters on their way to work. It is a simple moment of meaningless surprise.

Charlie Todd, the founder of Improv Everywhere, has deep political convictions and has lent his individual talents to numerous activist projects, so I asked him whether he had ever thought of using Improv Everywhere to advance more "political" causes. In response, he brought up the escalator action. "What would be the effect," he asks, "if right after commuters gave Rob a high-five there was an advertisement for, say, hand sanitizer? They'd feel betrayed, like they were duped. What was a beautiful experience would be ruined, and just another reason to be cynical." Instrumentalizing the performance in service to an advertising campaign would ruin it, as would using the whole performance to forward a specific activist agenda.[33] But for Todd, there *is* a politics in the performance. Encountering a creative intervention whose purpose is not immediately identifiable (and dismissible) as a sales pitch for a product or a political cause creates a "politics of wonder." It disrupts the hegemonologue.[34]

The ability of art to create a sense of wonder, even awe, is one of its super powers. Good art is hard to immediately categorize, sort, and thus classify. It refuses common sense. It upsets expectations and opens up new ways of thinking, feeling, and doing. The element of surprise is also at the heart of good artistic activism. Chris Dwyer, one of the leading evaluators of artistic activism and someone we will spend more time with in the next chapter, sums it up nicely: Art "creates sometimes almost a dissonance. Sometimes just a pause. An arrest of attention whether it's something beautiful or shocking or you've never seen before." Or, as Luis Camnitzer, an esteemed and experienced political artist wrote to me: "art does not simply help make sense of life, but it also helps to challenge that sense. At least for me, art is anarchy at its best."

Artistic Activism Disrupts

"I paint street art with a purpose: to entertain, inform, and sometimes shock," says the street artist FINK from Dublin. Art has long had the capacity to shock. Indeed the *raison d'etre* of modern art has been characterized as "The Shock of the New" (to crib the title from a once-popular art history textbook and British TV series). Bogad underscored the ability of surprise to open up the "hegemonologue" so that "anything can come in," but artistic activists also emphasize the capacity of surprise as a way to shock people in order to push them out of their complacency with the status quo.[35]

Early in his career, while still a student at the School of the Art Institute of Chicago, Dread Scott created a piece that invited the audience to walk over an American Flag. The artwork, *What Is the Proper Way to Display a U.S. Flag?*, received such notoriety that it was denounced on the floor of the U.S. Senate and called "disgraceful" by President George H. W. Bush. When we asked Scott what "work" his piece did when most of the response was negative — more of a closing down than an opening up — he responded:

> I wanted to do artwork people couldn't just dismiss the politics of. Whether they liked it or didn't like it, whether they agreed with me or didn't agree with me, I wanted them to have some engagement with the work....It was debated.

Scott's work was more than merely debated, it was outlawed: a local ordinance was passed banning the desecration of the American flag — and then overturned after a lengthy fight involving the American Civil Liberties Union. By generating shock and provoking a reaction, Scott revealed the reactionary reality hiding behind liberal democracy.

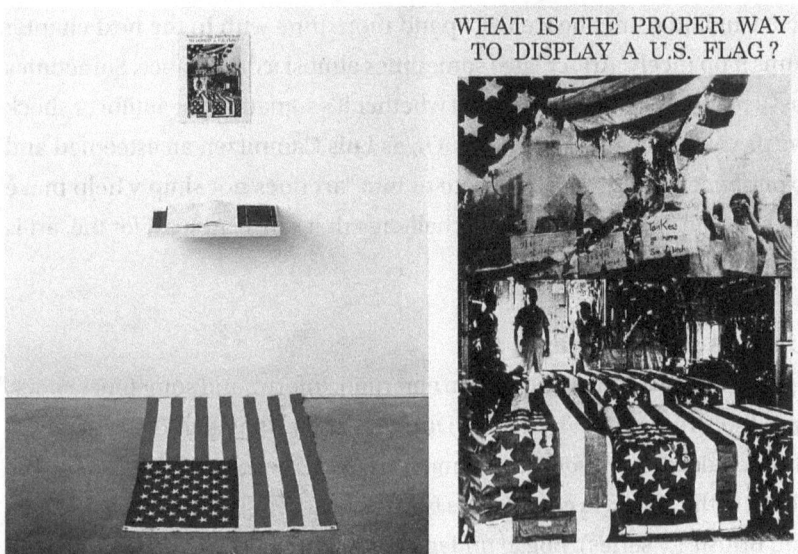

The "Proper Way to Display an American Flag" by Dread Scott, courtesy of the artist.

The Center for Political Beauty, mentioned briefly above, has been criticized across the political spectrum for being insensitive and exploitative and crossing ethical boundaries; they have also been recognized for their æffective use of shock. In one of their interventions, *The Dead Are Coming*, the group exhumed — or claimed to exhume — the body of a Syrian refugee who died in her attempt to travel to Europe. The group then staged a formal burial for her in Germany, the country she was migrating to. In another, *Eating Refugees*, Political Beauty built a model of a colosseum — with four live Libyan tigers — in Berlin and then asked refugees to volunteer to be eaten by the beasts in a modern version of the colosseum games of ancient Rome. When asked why Political Beauty seems to willfully court controversy, "privy councilor" André Leipold explained: "Traditional humanistic work is very polite, usually, and what we are saying is that we need other ways to communicate humanism within Germany and the European society.... Aggressive humanism means throwing out politeness for the sake of the work."

Political Beauty's call for "throwing out politeness for the sake of the work" resonates with the tradition of the avant-garde artists who swear fealty to the truth of their art and are resolute in their determination to shock the bourgeoisie.[36] As artistic activists, however, Political Beauty recognizes another value in shock. "It all serves to build the pressure," explains Leipold, "to empower people to start talking. Rarely does society enjoy confrontation, but the stress from confrontation is what can inspire people to act." *Stress* is a word that pops up often when speaking with Leipold, and it gets at his approach to his practice. Artistic activism works by putting stress on the system, causing it to break down and reveal the horrors that lie beneath.

Wafaa Bilal, the Iraqi-born artist who invited people to shoot at him with remotely operated paintball guns, explains shock value in terms that would be familiar to the The Center for Political Beauty. "Since my work is political," Bilal says, "it alienates more than it engages."[37] He goes on to discuss this "alienation" in terms of "aesthetic pleasure versus aesthetic pain" and "the conflict zone versus the comfort zone." By encouraging his audience to "Shoot an Iraqi," or make a conscious choice to refuse to do so, Bilal hopes to replace the aesthetic pleasure that people often desire when seeking out art with a sort of aesthetic pain, as they are forced to confront their thoughts, feelings, and actions.

Watching a squad of soldiers in combat fatigues confront, handcuff, and throw bags over the heads of civilian protesters on a public street, amid screaming and loud commands is shocking, to say the least. Hughes, who created this performance with the IVAW, explained the shock value of *Operation First Casualty*. It forces "a choice," says Hughes, "whether to be ignorant of their own structures and systems that they're perpetuating, or to be aware of them and acknowledge that there might be a problem with it." For Hughes, the shock of a U.S. population seeing a uniformed occupation force in their own cities held the promise of disrupting the mediated vision the U.S. public had of the war in Iraq. "Rupturing the spectacle, that's where I'm at," he explains. Then, in his next sentence, Hughes makes clear that shock is not an end in itself. The rupture of one reality makes room for another. As he puts it: "Creating a space for people to think about their experiences."

Artistic Activism Makes Space and Place
To state the obvious, artistic activism happens someplace — on the street, at a park, inside a bank or a museum — but there is a branch of artistic activism whose primary aim is to create places for creativity to flourish. The established version of this practice is called "creative placemaking," and the definition of the practice provided by the United States National Endowment for the Arts goes like this:

> In creative placemaking, partners from public, private, non-profit, and community sectors strategically shape the physical and social character of a neighborhood, town, city, or region around arts and cultural activities. Creative placemaking animates public and private spaces, rejuvenates structures and streetscapes, improves local business viability and public safety, and brings diverse people together to celebrate, inspire, and be inspired.[38]

At its worst, creative placemaking is a top-down development-led scheme to revalue real estate and generate profit through the introduction of arts and culture into poor neighborhoods. As the NEA report cited above goes on to trumpet: "These creative locales foster entrepreneurs and cultural industries that generate jobs and income, spin off new products and services, and attract and retain unrelated businesses and skilled workers."[39] At its best, however, creative placemaking recognizes the importance of culture and creativity in the vibrancy of a community, as well as recognizing community spaces as places of creativity. Best practices of this sort of creative placemaking within the United States include Theaster Gates's *Dorchester Projects* in Chicago and Rick Lowe's *Project Row Houses* in Houston.

Artistic activists push placemaking in a more activist direction. Not content with merely providing space for "creativity," they create places to open up space for creative activities they hope will bring about social change. Phoebe Davies is interested in audiences having conversations about feminism and sexuality. She does this by creating what she calls "constructed social spaces," such as

> a feminist nail salon that was developed in conjunction with different women's groups locally to where it was toured. We designed not only the space as a site for conversation around contemporary gender politics and what was relevant to the groups we were working with, but it also hosted a series of workshops and events and talks, *and* it was a functioning nail salon.

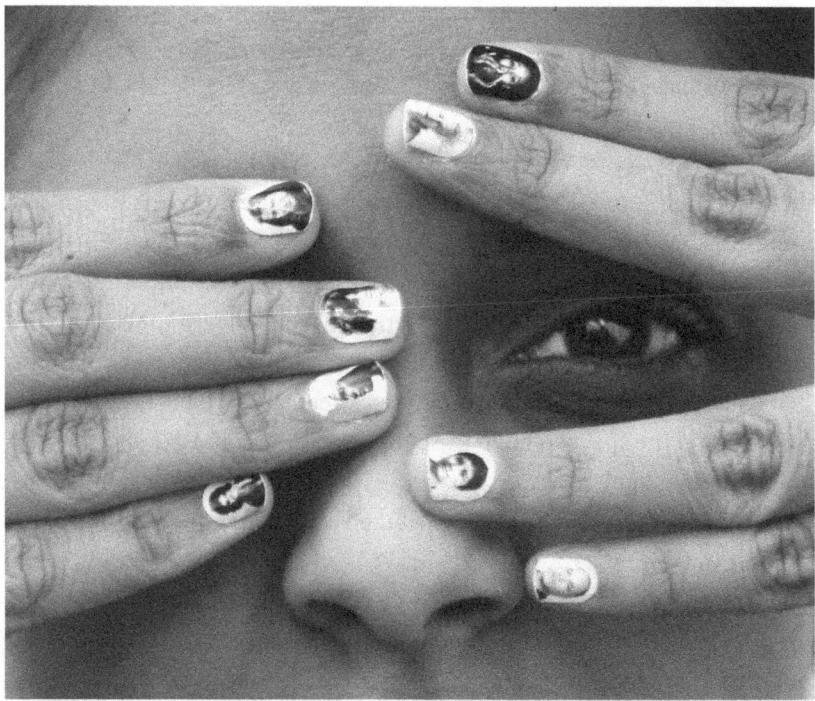

Intimate politics in Phoebe Davies's Nail Salon, photo: Rowena Gordon.

In the salon, women have their nails painted with their choice of feminist icons, designed in conjunction with local activist groups and selected in order to generate discussion around social change themes. Unlike an art gallery, "it's not only a space where you come in and cruise around and look at stuff," Davies explains, "but more that you're sitting in it, you're learning in it, you're hosting conversations in it." The nail salon is a creative place, but it's also a social, educational, and activist space.

Creating activist space through creative place (or vice versa) is central to Fernando García-Dory's artistic activist practice. These places can be shepherds' huts where young people stay and learn history, lore, and practical skills from working shepherds, or an international art conference used as an excuse to bring isolated shepherds from around Europe together. His latest project is "a whole abundant village as an infrastructure for farms, craft, and art production with a community of practice, a collective of people that run it and live in it." For García-Dory, the importance of creating a place is what happens in that space:

> It's more about creating a space for other forms of life — a collective life with a land-based economy, a community of practice that's beyond the discursive aspect of activism. With this, we're challenging ourselves with making and seeing what one makes.

Place as a space for alternative activity — "other forms of life" — is what's important for García-Dory, but the place itself is integral to the transformation. "It's not so much what we talk about or how we talk about it, but where we talk about it, " he says. "The context of the production is important." What García-Dory is drawing attention to here is that creativity happens within a "context of production": a metaphoric space and a concrete place. It is only in a place where one is free from physical need and critical oversight that one can find the space to build the confidence and self-assurance to think and articulate one's own thoughts and express one's own creativity. Space, however, is not always equitably distributed and creative places come easier to some than others.[40]

Inspired by what the scholar José Esteban Muñoz calls "world-making," Marlène Ramírez-Cancio argues for the importance of places for people who feel out of place.[41] "World-making," she says, "is the willful and relentless enactment of the self that creates a world in which they are possible." That's beautiful, but a bit abstract, and so when asked for an example, Ramírez-Cancio recalls how the queer performance artist Holly Hughes described wow Café in New York City in the 1980s, how she "talked about going to that tiny, tiny space for women and for queers as almost like going to church because it was a place where they felt they were creating the possibility for their very existence in a world that wasn't there for them." For Ramírez-Cancio, this "church" is not a retreat from the world as much it is a safe space for those battered and belittled by the dominant society to gather strength before going back out into the world to change it, akin to how Black churches functioned as places of black self-recognition, self-affirmation, and self-power that provided the space for the work of the civil rights movement. For Ramírez-Cancio, a precondition for political action is a sense of personal political agency, and this is something that creating spaces for creativity fosters. As she concludes: "Yes, in here, we are creating this world for ourselves first, and that matters. Because without that, how do you then go out there?"

Artistic Activism Imagines New Realities
Sometimes these openings for new forms of language and living can be created within the real world.[42] At other times, however, they exist only as spaces of imagination. Artistic activism can make this imagination manifest.[43] "I think that art is the language of possibility," Favianna Rodriguez says. "Art is the language of the future, and through art, we can actually create the vision of the world we want to see."

As a trans person, Berlin-based artist Joey Juschka is acutely aware of the limitations of existing spaces. So Juschka writes stories about spaces like bathrooms. Not bathrooms as they are, which force people into a binary choice of sexual identity, but bathrooms as they might be in an imaginary future. "I write about observations of things that I don't like and change it fictionally," she says. We ask, "what good does that do?," and Juschka describes what she noticed in her audience during her readings. "Even though they can't do anything in the end — because it's only a fictional law — for a second their reality was changed. For a second there was an opening into another world of possibility." This sense of fictive possibility can have real world applications. Juschka continues:

I believe once you experience this moment of "Oh! There actually was a solution to a no-solution problem," then the next time there's an apparent no-solution problem, you know that maybe it isn't a no-solution problem after all. You can go back to that experience and hook into it, get reassured that there is a solution — maybe a real wacky one, but way wacky is way better than being stuck in thinking that there's no way one can change anything. You can change everything.

"Way wacky." Like the power-generating windmills atop the Brooklyn Bridge represented in the fanciful artwork of Andrea Polli. "Obviously it hasn't gotten built yet, maybe never, right?" Polli admits, "but I think it inspired people to say: why not come up with some really wild pie-in-the-sky idea? And try to push it through as much as possible. So, I think it was successful in that way, or effective in that way." Like Vladimir Tatlin's plans for the Monument to the Third International, a structure commissioned by the Russian revolutionary government in 1919 but designed so large, complex, and unrealistic that there was no possibility of it ever being built, Polli's proposals fire the imagination.[44]

Aaron Gach designed the *Tactical Ice Cream Unit*, an old ice cream truck tricked out with loudspeakers and surveillance cameras, from which he distributes free ice cream and propaganda at political protests, to be, in his words, "of practical service" to activists. Yet, as Gach describes his project, it becomes clear that he has an expansive definition of practicality. The truck's real function, he explains, is to "manipulate reality." And, as Gach continues, "this is where the magic comes in. It's all about giving people a show that elicits a broader sense of reality, that reality is bigger than what we're told reality is."

As discussed above, the purpose of artistic activism can be to reveal reality and unveil the truth. But for Gach, whose artistic training included studying with a magician and a locksmith, the goal of artistic activism is to open doors (of perception) so that people might imagine reality in entirely new ways. As he describes:

If they can see that there is an alternative to the way that reality is packaged and sold to them, then all of a sudden they can also begin to think on their own about how they might manipulate reality. How they might manifest their desires in reality. And that's a big forward step. If one comes across an ice cream truck handing out free ice cream *and* political propaganda, then what else is possible?

For Oumy Regina Sabou, who describes herself as an "anticonformytsical" journalist and has organized an artistic activist campaign against corruption in Senegal, dreaming and social movements go hand in hand. Listing off the objectives of her campaign, she describes aims that would be at home in any advocacy campaign: "mobilizing and ensuring the ongoing battles against corruption, reinvigorating them, giving them a boost to refresh and really motivate." And then she adds, "on an emotional side, we also wanted to make people dream."[45] Sol Aramendi, an Argentina-born artistic activist living in Queens, New York, works with immigrant communities whose precarious actualities often overwhelm their sense of possibilities. A photographer (as well as architect, educator, and labor organizer) by train-ing, Aramendi asked immigrant women in a workshop she was running to take pictures of themselves as they wished they could be. One woman took a self-portrait of herself as a Zapatista, another as a baker, and a third as a piñata maker. Six years later, Aramendi revisited these women and took formal — and strikingly lush and gorgeous — portraits of the women as they are now. One now runs a baking company, and another makes a

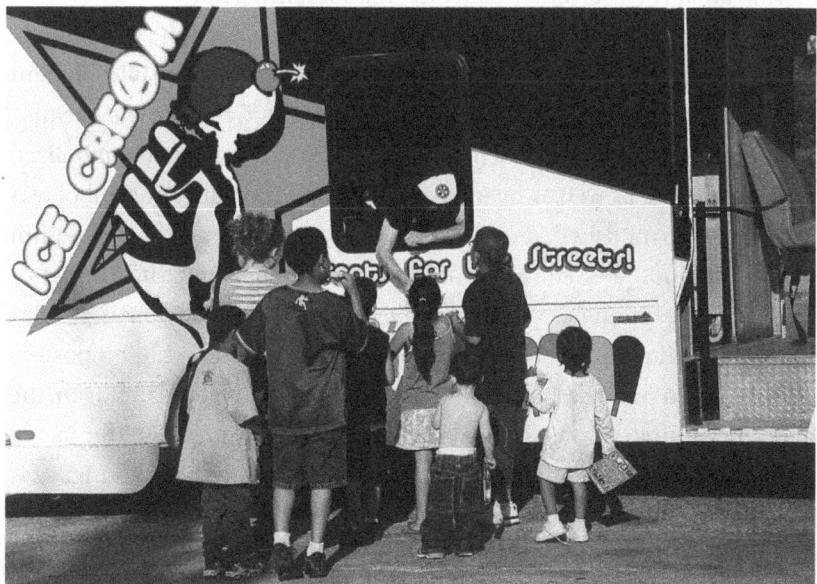

Aaron Gach delivering politics and popsicles in his Tactical Ice Cream Unit, courtesy of the artist.

living making piñatas. And the revolutionary Zapatista? Her daughter is going off to college to become an immigrant-rights lawyer.

Artistic Activism Aids and Amplifies Social Movements

Some artistic activists see themselves as relentless critics, others as bold visionaries, but a number of artistic activists we talked to, including some of the best-known names in the field, speak in the humble language of service. The function of their work, as they articulated it, is to amplify the impact of preexisting social movements and activist organizations. "There are things that already have momentum," explains Jacques Servin of the Yes Men. "These movements already exist; there's already stuff going on and we can just add a little bit." Often this "little bit" added by the artistic activist is furthering the nascent creative tactics already in play in movements and campaigns. "What are the songs, the stories, the memes, the hashtags, the aesthetics, etc., that are being used, and how can we help to make that more legible, and can teach us and signal a counter-power?" These are the questions that Beka Economopoulos, a co-founder of Not an Alternative and The Natural History Museum, asks herself as she enters into a project. "It is very important to us," adds her partner, Jason Jones, to be "building off of what already exists rather than creating something new."

An example of this creative amplification is the work done by Favianna Rodriguez with migration activists that we encountered in the introduction. The symbol of the monarch butterfly was generated by activists because its annual migration takes it across the U.S.-Mexico border and symbolized the naturalness, as well as beauty, of migration. The butterfly symbol was then taken up, polished, and popularized by Rodriguez. "It's a metaphor that's been out there," she explains; "I was able to maximize it." Rodriguez did this by designing a colorful image, devising a catchy slogan, "Migration is Beautiful," and then plastering this image and slogan on posters, T-shirts, and other merchandise. As a value-added image and a slogan, the migratory monarch was then cycled back into the movement for use in their campaigns. What is important to recognize here is that Rodriguez is not claiming the traditional artistic role of original creator. She is an artistic facilitator of ideas and images that come up from the movement and then go back to it, and it's because of this relationship that her creations are æffective.[46] "It's important," Rodriguez says, "that we create objects that people can attach themselves to."

John Leo, who works with a New York City chapter of Augusto Boal's Theatre of the Oppressed, sees his role as bringing creativity into otherwise non-creative social and political spaces. He describes how his group was once asked for help by a city council member: "He was like, 'I want to do this in my district! I want an emergency response team of actors where if a problem happens, you can make a play about that thing and then go and address it with legislators.' TONYC answered the call by staging "performances" in municipal spaces to help citizens understand and enthusiastically participate in mundane governmental procedures like the budgeting process. "I think what [we] are trying to do is changing or shifting the atmosphere in which more tangible political struggles or policies are in or take place," explains Mark Read, a long-time artistic activist and another member of the The Illuminator collective (along with Rachel Brown, mentioned above). The atmosphere to which Mark refers is not a physical space of policy-making that Leo works within, but more the cultural terrain — the sets of meanings and a values — in which policies are made and enacted. As Read elaborates: "We are not directly effecting policy, but we are trying to affect the conditions under which the discussion about policy take place."

Ummi Yakubu uses the word "bridge" when she talks about her role as an artistic activist working with social change organizations in West Africa. These organizations work on worthy causes, they have information and resources that are of vital use to people, and they organize campaigns that have the potential to have a direct impact on people's lives. But none of these good works do any good unless people *feel* the importance of the social concerns at hand and want something to be done. As Yakubu puts it, "The social change organizations are desperate to get people to care about this, or people moved enough to do whatever it is." And this is what Yakubu sees artistic activism can do: "This is the bridge," she says, "if we can get people to feel something about this particular issue, then they can give them the tools to do something about it."

Bridges are sometimes also necessary to navigate between the expressions of artistic activists and the expectations of social-change organizations. Ricardo Dominguez tells the story of working with migrant-rights groups, trying to convince them that poetry was integral to the *Transborder Immi-*

grant Tool, the phone app he and his fellow artists had developed to help migrants cross the U.S.- Mexico border safely. The first meetings were a bit strained:

> First, they didn't think it would work, as a tool. [And then] they had a lot of conflict over why poetry . . . was part of the tool. And so it took about a year of dialogue in terms of thinking about the border as an aesthetic project and the availability of a different formation of language — aesthetics and disturbance.

But perseverance paid off for Dominguez and his comrades, and by working alongside the activist groups, going out on weekends to the desert and putting out water caches for the migrants crossing the border, "we were able to coalesce with these communities and have them begin to think about art in relationship to their work, as a way to amplify their work." Working with organizations and within movements means doing a certain amount of teaching about "how artistic activism works": what it can do, what it can't do, and what it can do in ways that surprise you. And artistic activists often find themselves having to explain the importance of *affect* to those who are used to only thinking about *effect*.

But the learning happens in both directions. The politically minded art critic Ben Davis says that he frequently talks to activists in community organizations who complain about "what a burden artists were" because they need extensive training to understand the basics of effective activism. Artists interested in social change, Davis explains, often "start from the position [where] you're assuming that you're a special visionary person and that you're going to bring your solution to something." Working with social movements and organizations, however, demands a reorientation of the way artists are taught to think about their creative contribution. Sol Aramendi describes this shift that is needed as one from innovating and telling to asking and listening. When she first started out as an artistic activist working with social movements, " it was more, 'Okay, I have an idea. Let's do something, or let's work on something together,'" Aramendi explains. "But now more and more, since I understand my place in a community, it is a lot of listening. And asking: 'What questions do you have? What do you want to do? What is your campaign? What do you want to work on?' That's how a lot of [projects] started." Sometimes an artistic activist needs to turn down the voice of their creative muse and listen up to the words and wisdom of people in the communities they work.

Artistic Activism Keeps You Going

As with the case with their "theory of change," artistic activists rarely gave a concise, definitional answer to the question of how their artistic activism worked. Most provided multiple hunches or hopes, and some offered up vague and almost mystical explanations. (Aaron Gach's invocation of "magic" was not the first or last time that word was used to describe artistic activism's æffect.) This lack of clarity regarding the external outcome of their practice, however, is not just due to oversight or lack of introspection, it points to another way artistic activists think about what artistic activism does. Faced with uncertainty as to how their projects actually impact other people and the wider world, artistic activists find a certain level of surety by turning their attention to the impact their practice has on something smaller and better known: themselves and their creative practice.

"Sometimes we try to accomplish too much," the renowned artist Alfredo Jaar explains with great humility. "So here it's really like the minimal strategy: let's see if we can insert this word, which is a concept, a story, a history, blah, blah, into their conscious or even unconsciousness, and let's see what happens." Referencing Antonio Gramsci's maxim that what a revolutionary needs is "pessimism of the intellect and optimism of the will," Jaar tells us that "deep inside I share ... Gramsci's intellectual pessimism and, of course, I still have this optimistic will — because I have no choice. If not, I would just commit suicide."

Despair or create, that is the choice an artistic activist makes. "I have an idea about radical resistance that is somewhat romantic," admits ACT UP's Avram Finkelstein.

> What was the Marx quote? Something about capitalism is so ingenious because it's the only system that has constructed itself in such a way that it can never be dismantled. And I think I'm over mourning the fact that it can't be dismantled....I feel like you have to fight anyway. Because, what's the alternative?

Lack of clarity regarding how and why artistic activism works and the immensity of the problems it faces off against can lead to a sort of existential theory of practice that goes something like this: I cannot predict exactly what my work will do and what impact it will have but I know change is essential, so *I must do something*.

Or nothing. I remember once being invited to speak at Rensselaer Polytechnic Institute, a renowned science university in upstate New York that is also home to an exciting experimental arts program. I was giving my stump speech on the necessity of evaluating the impact of artistic activism when one student, visibly agitated, raised her hand and blurted out: "But I don't want my art to do anything!" I asked her to tell me more, and she explained that what was wrong with contemporary society was that it was excessively instrumental and that the only way, as an artist, to challenge and change such a society was to produce art that did nothing useful.[47] *L'art pour l'art*.[48] But I then asked her how she would know if her art did nothing? After all, against all her intentions it might turn out to do *something*. Without some sort of evaluation and assessment, how could she ever be sure? We ended up having a fruitful conversation about whether it is necessary to be instrumental in order to ensure anti-instrumentality. I'm not sure I convinced her, but she did convince me. Within the specific context of an overly instrumentalized society, one of the functions of artistic activism could be to do absolutely nothing. Which is, of course, something.

So ... What Does Artistic Activism Do?

As with the philosophers and critics, amongst artistic activists there is no one, universally agreed-upon notion of what artistic activism does. Depending on whom you speak to, artistic activism makes ideas accessible *or* it surprises and confuses, it reveals realities *or* it imagines new ones, it creates conversations *or* facilitates participation, it circumvents barriers to acceptance *or* creates spaces and places for creativity, it generates affect and empathy *or* shocks and disrupts, it is aimed outward toward social movements *or* inward toward oneself. Or it is some of these, or all of these, or some of these all of the time or all of these some of the time.

For those keeping track, I outlined twelve ways that practitioners believe that artistic activism works. And I am not alone in arriving at a multitude of answers. In recent surveys of the field, former Creative Time curator Nato Thompson recognizes six ways that artistic activism might work, while professional evaluator Christine Dwyer provides an alternate half dozen. The team at Animating Democracy outlines an even ten, and arts educator Beverly Naidus offers up another twelve.[49] It is also important to acknowledge that all these categories are, again, "ideal types." Grouped or divided another way I could have arrived at ten or fourteen instead of the twelve above,[50] then maybe synthesized these down to three or four.[51] With enough time and patience, I might even be able to sift all these theories and practices into a grand master theory of what artistic activism can do — complete with a clever diagram with balls and stars and arrows that accounts for everything.

If I could develop a singular, unified theory of what artistic activism does, it would make evaluation easier. If artistic activism causes X to happen, then all that's needed to evaluate whether it works is to look for changes in X. However, I don't think this is the right way to proceed. In the last chapter, I developed a singular, albeit complex, theory of change for artistic activism. Because it is based upon universal human capacities to think, feel, and do, and upon the fact that all societies possess both Culture with a big *C* and culture with a little *c*, I stand by the universality of the model. It does a good job helping us think through how artistic activism works in the abstract. Artistic activism, however, is an applied practice: it never functions only in the abstract; it is created, staged, and made sense of by concrete people, working on concrete issues, operating within concrete historical and cultural contexts. Because of this, there will always be a multitude of applications of artistic activism, all of which are trying to do different things.

The fact that there are so many theories as to what artistic activism can do, and so many different aims in doing it, tells us something far more useful than an authoritative answer to the question "what does artistic activism do?" It tells us there is no singular correct response to the question.[52] Why is this useful? Because it demands an approach to evaluation different from a one-size-fits all model. In order to assess the æffect of artistic activism, we need a methodology that can account for, and even embrace, this diversity.

CHAPTER THREE

Does Artistic Activism Work?

HAVING NOW EXPLORED HOW ARTISTIC activism works, and what it does, we are now ready for the question of "does it work?" In other words, we are ready to address *assessment*. Assessment inspires fear and loathing amongst many artistic activists. Like an evil talisman, the concept conjures up images of actuaries in gray flannel suits sucking the color out of creative projects so they can be safely written up and stored in drab metal filing cabinets. But evaluation, done correctly, needn't be this scary. Evaluation is as common as creation and something we do every day. Learning not to pick up hot objects, much less undertaking more complex tasks like cooking a meal, could not be done without an assessment of what works (or hurts) and what does not. Basic human activity would be impossible without some sort of evaluative feedback loop.

Broadly speaking there are two types of measurements used in evaluation: *quantitative* and *qualitative.* Quantitative assessment, as the name suggests, entails measuring things in terms of quantities that can be counted and, for this reason, is favored in the sciences. Galileo, one of the pioneers of the scientific method, wrote in the 1600s of the necessity of distinguishing objective attributes that "exist in external bodies" and can be measured, like size, shape, quantity, and motion, from more subjective qualities like color, smell, and taste. The former have autonomous and verifiable reality, while the latter, in Galileo's words, "exist only in the sensitive body, for when the living creature is removed all these qualities are carried off and annihilated."[1]

To return to our everyday example of preparing a meal, a *quantitative* assessment might consider things like the cost of ingredients, the weight or volume of each ingredient used, the times and temperatures of cooking, and the number of portions created. This, however, is a woefully incomplete measurement of a meal. While Galileo was correct in relying upon quantitative measurements when it came to things like assessing the velocity of an object reacting to gravitational pull, counting only upon things that can be counted limits the range of things that you might evaluate. Chief among these omissions are things that "exist only in the sensitive body." Knowing the measures of ingredients might tell us something about a meal, but we would never consider such evaluation sufficient if we didn't also assess how the meal *tastes*.

This is where *qualitative* assessment becomes essential. It measures the quality of the object or experience in terms of the impact it has on Galileo's, appropriately named, "sensitive bod[ies]." To measure human senses, of course, is a great deal more difficult than measuring the weight or volume of an ingredient. In order to determine something like the taste of a meal — or the æffect of an artistic activist intervention — we have to resort to more subjective measures. For example, when we follow a recipe that calls for a teaspoon of salt, we are using a quantitative measurement, but when we taste the dish and assess whether it needs more salt we are engaging in a qualitative evaluation. Both are useful. Quantitative measures give us exactitude and allow for easy verification and replication through cookbooks and the like. Qualitative measurement allows for a much more nuanced and rich evaluation of a meal. Yet, such assessment is also subjective to the "sensitive body" doing the tasting. What is perfectly salted for me may be too salty or not salty enough for you. This is why we have quantitative measurements in recipes, and saltshakers on the table.

Models of Evaluation

Evaluation is as essential for æffective social change as it is for a good meal, and within the larger field of social change, artistic activism and its kindred fields employ a dizzying array of assessment measures.[2] Every theory of change generates multiple understandings of what might work to generate that change, and in turn, each change-making activity calls for multiple ways of evaluating whether it worked or not. As such, the possible metrics of impact expand exponentially. It is beyond the purview of this chapter, and my capacity, to account for all the types of metrics employed for assessing the impact of creative interventions. I will, however, try my best to provide a broad-brush picture of the field, and a more finely sketched portrait of what artistic activists themselves think and say about the assessment of their practice.

For this study, I reviewed every white paper, report, article, and essay in the English language I could find on assessing social impact in the arts, including the few that address artistic activism more directly.[3] Despite all their variations regarding theories of evaluation, methods of implementation, what is to be measured, what tools are used, and of course the mandatory number of steps an assessment process demands, most sound methods of evaluation share a few foundational premises in common, three of which I describe here briefly.

Creative impact is hard to measure. In part this is due to the difficulties in assessing social change writ large: there are simply too many variables in play to determine with any exactitude that what you are measuring actually has the effect you think or hope for. This challenge is compounded by the particular type of work art does — that is, its affective power. Claims by neuroscientists aside, feeling, perception, and sense are notoriously resistant to measurement.[4]

Metrics are meaningful only insofar as they are appropriate. Metrics need to match the creative intervention and its desired outcome. It does little good, for instance, to measure the number of international Facebook shares of an artistic activist project if it was designed to foster an intimate conversation within a local community. Who is doing the assessing also matters. A number of reports on assessment called for participatory evaluation, such as including the community æffected in the evaluation process itself. Others called for the participation of the artists themselves.[5]

Evaluation should not be an afterthought. Assessment needs to be built into projects from the beginning and used as part of a reflective process throughout. Measurement will be appropriate only if it flows logically from a plan that includes a clearly defined goal, creative interventions that are directed toward that goal, and appropriate indicators that let you know whether you have moved closer to or away from the goal of your project, or met it exactly. Assessment is also only useful if the knowledge it generates feeds back into the overall plan so you can revise and replan accordingly as you move forward.[6]

Instead of providing a tedious literature review detailing the methodologies espoused in all of the reports read, I want to focus the discussion by highlighting the methods of three of the best "arts for change" evaluators in the United States: Jan Cohen-Cruz, Chris Dwyer, and Pam Korza.

Jan Cohen-Cruz was for many years the director of field research for A Blade of Grass, a New York City–based organization that funds and supports artistic activists.[7] A well-known scholar in the field of performance studies, Cohen-Cruz brings her ethnographic and observational skills into her work as an evaluator — except that she would never call herself an evaluator. "There are so many associations" with the term, she explains.

> [Associations] of somebody from the outside who is applying a set of values to your work that may or may not be relevant, . . . and I've had so many artists, working with them, and at first, I feel there's a resistance: "ugh, I'm going to be evaluated." And I don't want to be that person.

Instead of being "that person," Cohen-Cruz sees her role as "a kind of witnessing, . . . an active witnessing where someone is giving you feedback. It's dialogic as you go, and that to me is a lot of the value."

Witnessing, in Cohen-Cruz's case, is not passive spectatorship. Her ideal is more in line with religious witnessing, a form of active discipleship. Here, however, the job of the witness isn't to spread the words and deeds of a divine savior, but help the profane creator realize their own vision. By talking the artist through their project and using her experience to notice things they may not, Cohen-Cruz reflects back upon the artist a picture of their own work so it might be altered, improved, and redrawn.

The data Cohen-Cruz collects and analyzes for her research rarely takes the form of a formal observation of audience participation or community responses to a survey. Her "data" is generated out of an ongoing process of conversation and reflection between her and the artist, one on one. This process-oriented approach to evaluation reflects Cohen-Cruz's ideas about how artistic activism works. She believes that the greatest impact of an overall project or particular intervention may not be the end result; instead "indicators of change" are often embedded within the creative process itself. "It is always a process over time," she explains.

> The evidence that [change] is happening is never just at the end. It's not like a play where at the end you can say, "Oh, the process was hell, but what a great play." That wouldn't hold up here because the process is as important as the product.

This unfolding process, of which she is both witness and coach, is then communicated in "field research reports" shared with the wider artistic activist community through the website, a magazine, and books produced by A Blade of Grass. Cohen-Cruz, however, sees her ultimate responsibility as not to the organization or the funder, or even to a wider audience who might read her reports, but to the artist, helping them to be more æffective. As she poses the question: "How can I, as a witness, contribute to them doing their job better?"

If for Cohen-Cruz evaluation is a process of dialogue and discovery, for Chris Dwyer it is an opportunity to clarify, define, and set clear goalposts. Dwyer is a senior vice president of RMC Research, a national research and consultation firm that specializes in evaluating healthcare, education, media, and the arts. She began her career as an evaluator by researching children's television, assessing the impact of popular public shows like "Reading Rainbow" and "Behind the Scenes," a program that featured famous artists and unpacked the "magic" of art-making. It was this latter experience that led Dwyer into arts evaluation. Early on she realized how evaluating arts was different from assessing education: "In education we have . . . the standard outcomes that people want you to look for. . . . Those outcomes are all pretty well known and there are measures for them." Whereas: "In the arts, you often need to do a lot more upfront work with a client because the measures, the indicators, are not as well understood or known."

Part of the reason these measures are not well understood has to do with the complexity of what is being measured. Dwyer explains that, "because of both the process and product nature and the instrumental nature of the arts, especially with arts for change, there are multiple outcomes that you're always going for at different dimensions." In addition, evaluation and measurement are not "known" in the arts. As she elaborates, "I think a lot of folks in arts are not used to thinking about outcomes. So they don't come to you with, you know, 'here's what we think our impact is and here's what we'd like to measure.'" Because of this, there's no one universally accepted metrics for artistic activism. Dwyer explains: "It's much more challenging because you've got to find, and sort of peel back to figure out, what the outcomes are that are meaningful to people."

Responding to these challenges, Dwyer takes what she calls a "case-making" approach. She works with the client to clarify the audience for the evaluation and what the arguments are that will be most compelling for that specific audience. She then determines the best measures for "making the case" for the impact of an artistic activist project. A good example is an evaluation Dwyer did for the Art at Work project in Portland, Maine. Art at Work was spearheaded by feminist artist Marty Pottenger in order to "improve municipal government through strategic art projects," through workshops led by local artists inside city agencies.[8] The Police Poetry Project, for instance, paired poets and photographers with local police, writing poetry and taking photos together to address low department morale and strained relationships between police and the public. For Dwyer, the first and most important step in evaluating this project was "identifying the various audiences for evaluation results and their top issues and interests ... [and] what would be convincing to them."[9] With the idea of what sort of proof each of the stakeholders in the project — artists, police, community, and government — needed in order to be convinced that the project was a success, Dwyer developed an elaborate evaluation plan.[10]

Dwyer's plan is impressive and formidable. If properly implemented it would take years and a staff devoted solely to evaluation to pull off — all for a relatively small project in a small city. In our conversation, however, she revealed that the plan serves another important function: "What I try to do through the case-making approach is to get people to think systematically about: What story do you want to tell? What story would you like to be able to tell? [And] Who do you want to tell it to?"

It was then that I realized Dwyer's brilliance in developing such a detailed evaluation plan. Regardless of whether it is ever implemented, merely creating a plan forces artistic activists, and their supporters, to think systematically about what they want their project to do and who they want it to reach. Forget outcome (for the moment); what evaluation is really about is clarity of *intent*. "[With] a really good planning of evaluation," Dwyer says, "people think the evaluation is done because they've gotten so much clarity out of the planning of it that they think, "Oh, I've got it now." In other words: the value of evaluation is not just on the back end in determining what happened, but on the front end in helping people think through what they want to have happen. Sometimes, this is as far as Dwyer's evaluation goes. "I've done a ton of work," she says, "where basically I'm just doing the front-end piece for those people, . . . just training them on how to do a plan or helping them refine a plan they may or may not carry out."

None of this is to say that the final results of evaluations are not important for Dwyer. The results make the case for the social impact of the artistic activist project, and social impact is, ostensibly, the reason for doing the project in the first place. It's just that Dwyer, like all evaluators I've talked to, understand that a critical function of an evaluation is to get the artists, and the supporters and facilitators of these artists, "into that habit" of "do[ing] something systematically," thinking carefully and critically about what they want their project to do.

There are few people in the United States, if not the world, who have provided more resources for artists, cultural organizations, and funders to help them think, systematically, about the impact of socially engaged art than Pam Korza. Along with Barbara Schaffer Bacon, Korza was, until recently, the co-director of Animating Democracy, a program of Americans for the Arts, a large arts advocacy organization located in Washington, DC. Animating Democracy turns out a steady stream of studies, reports, and tool kits designed to help connect arts and culture to community-building and social change, and within the field it is nearly impossible to miss their work. While many of the materials produced by Korza and her colleagues have an evaluative thrust, this interest was evolutionary. "The investigation in the early years of Animating Democracy was: What does this intersection of arts and civic dialog look like?" Soon, however, this concern with *what it is* grew into an interest in *what it can do*, and then *whether it is doing it*. "We chose to take up the question 'How do we know what difference we're making? How do we evaluate this work?' . . . really trying to get at some practical ways that artists and cultural-organization folks and their partners could kind of do a little more DIY work."

The do-it-yourself approach underlies many of the resources that Animating Democracy produces. Their *Continuum of Impact* guide, for example, takes the artist or organization through a process of articulating their creative strategy, desired outcomes, indicators of change, and potential data sources in order to "create your own evaluation plan."[11] Their *Aesthetic Perspectives* model provides different arts-appropriate assessment buckets — disruption, emotional experience, openness, sensory experience — with which to evaluate artistic activism.[12] Both resources are meant to be used as tools, and are loaded with things for the artistic activist to do: questions to be asking, like "How does the work highlight or challenge sensory expectations?"; and schematic worksheets to be filled out, with prompts like "Your Outcome (What are your intended outcomes?)" and "Your Indicators (What specifically will you track or measure?)." This prompted participation is buttressed by easy-to-understand definitions of wonky research terms and case studies that illustrate a particular concept or process. Understanding that artists, activists, and organizations often do not have the resources to hire an outside evaluator or the time to devote to a multimonth study (because, as Korza says, "just getting the work done is about all everybody can manage"), Animating Democracy works hard to make it as easy as possible for artistic activists and their supporters to do their own evaluations.

I find Korza's, Dwyer's, and Cohen-Cruz's approaches so useful because they suggest three different approaches to evaluating artistic activism. For Cohen-Cruz, evaluation is primarily an ongoing dialogue between the evaluator and the artistic activist. Dwyer concentrates on the power of the plan to focus and clarify the intentions and desired outcomes of the people she's working with. And through her guides and other resources, Korza puts an emphasis on providing artistic activists with the tools to do their own self-evaluation.[13] Standing on the shoulders of these giants, I draw upon their approaches to guide the model of evaluation presented in the next chapter. But before we can go there, there's another group of people we need to be listening to: artistic activists themselves. Artistic activism is a deeply subjective, profoundly creative human process. And any system of metrics that hopes to be *useful to* and (equally important) *used by* artistic activists needs to take into account their practices and their concerns.

Evaluation in Practice

Artistic activists have seemingly paradoxical positions on evaluation. All those we interviewed wanted their work to have social impact yet, almost as universally, assessment of the social impact of their work was an afterthought if thought of at all. Some of the reason for this has to do with the fact that many artistic activists, befitting the activist moniker, identify with Napoleon's famous dictum: *on attaque, et puis verra* — "we attack, and then we see." Artistic activists put their time and effort into the creative intervention itself and then look around to see what impact it may have had. (There is even an evaluation methodology popularized by the Ford Foundation called "outcome harvesting" that endorses this approach.)[14] However, this seeming contradiction between interest in impact yet lack of interest in assessing that impact has deeper roots. Many artistic activists we talked to are skeptical of the ability of artistic activism to be evaluated correctly, or even evaluated at all. However, by listening closely to what artistic activists have to say, we can begin to recognize the points of resistance to formal assessment, as well as observe the types of, often informal and ad-hoc, evaluation that they are already doing. To create a model of evaluation that works for, and with, artistic artists we need to know both.

Pulling It Off

Perhaps the easiest impact measured, yet also the most critical, is the creative intervention itself. Last chapter, I discussed what I called an "existential theory of practice." Faced with doubt as to how their creative contributions bring about change, some artistic activists conclude that one thing they can know, and control, is their act of creation. Consequently, when it comes to evaluation, one of the measures used by artistic activists is whether or not their intervention actually happens. Dara Greenwald, who once fabricated an inflatable recreation of a historic, forgotten African American church in upstate New York where the abolitionist Henry Highland Garnet once preached, explains her evaluation criteria: "Why it was successful to me is: (A) it worked (B) no one got killed." Laughing, she elaborates: "It's just that we made this huge inflatable church and then people went inside it. It stayed inflated, it didn't collapse, so...there's structural success in that what you make actually functions as you intend it to."[15]

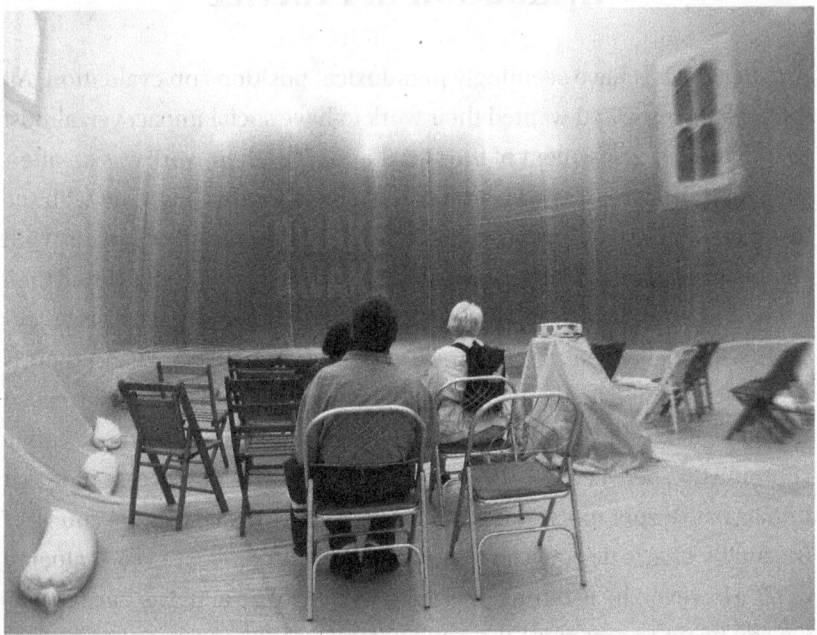

Worshiping history in Dara Greenwald, Josh MacPhee, and Olivia Robinson's Inflatable Church, courtesy of the artists.

Public Interest

It doesn't take a close reading of the response above to realize that there is another variable in play here in addition to the success of the structure: the public, who in Dara's case are the people who came, went inside her installation, and didn't get killed. This concern with the public contrasts with the romantic ideal of the artist isolated in their garret, painting paintings only they will see. As Hank Willis Thomas, co-founder of the U.S. artistic activist organization For Freedoms, points out, this idea of the artist was probably only a myth to begin with: "A lot of people will say: 'I don't make work for an audience, I make work for myself.' I would say every person, and every artist, wants to be validated by someone." "So to me," Thomas continues, "that's what success can be."

The artistic activist concern with a public audience goes beyond self-validation. All the artistic activists we interviewed recognized that, in order for their work to effect change, it needed to affect people. Like the proverbial tree falling in the woods when no one is there, artistic activism without an audience of some kind guarantees that it will not have a social impact. Discovering who that audience is and what impact your work has on them is where some sort of evaluative criteria sneaks into even the most assessment-averse artistic activist.

The definition of what constitutes "publics," of course, varies widely. It can be a mass and anonymous public of passersby on a street, or as we've seen in previous chapters, it can be an individual in one-on-one engagement. "Public attention" is such a broad term as to be almost meaningless until you realize what it *does not* include: money, sponsorship, exhibition space — the traditional evaluative markers of artistic success. "For me publics are very, very important," says Elena García Olivares, a feminist artistic activist from Spain. "For other artists perhaps the price of the piece could be an aspect of success, or perhaps the money they could earn, or the sponsorships. Well, that's not my case, " she explains; "the number of people and the engagement of the people is a key aspect." Since social change is the goal of artistic activism, what constitutes success is primarily its æffect on those who make up the "social" — that is, the public. But as García Olivares stresses, assessing the audience is not only a matter of "the number of people" who show up; a "key aspect" is "the engagement of the people."

"I can show a piece and that's great," says Sheba Remy Kharbanda, a New York–based British video artist whose nonlinear storytelling explores subjects of migration and displacement in the Indian diaspora, "but [if] I don't have feedback from people who might not otherwise go and see something like that, then I'm not really convinced that it's been successful." Reaching those "who might not otherwise go and see it" is particularly important for Kharbanda, as she defines what success means for her, both artistically and politically: "I feel like a piece has been successful when it can reach people who are not otherwise reached by this medium. I can open people's eyes to what the possibilities are, the potential for these kinds of nonlinear narratives." Part of the power of artistic activism, as you'll recall, is its power to surprise and shock, to step out of the ordinary, and ordinarily dismissed, modes of art and activism. Kharbanda's nonlinear narratives do this. Yet, she is acutely aware that, in order for her work to be successful, she has to make these available, and at least partially understandable, to a wider public than those who might frequent an experimental video screening.

Expanding your public by maximizing exposure has its own challenges. The "publics" for artistic activists intervening on the street are usually whoever happens to walk by — and this makes assessing impact difficult. Looking for a way to account for public interest, street artist Posterchild likes to hang around his pieces to see if people stop and take pictures. When asked why he does this, he replies: "That means someone noticed it. The first big step when you're working on the street, in the gallery, anywhere, is to get noticed, to rise above the visual cacophony on the streets. People don't notice ads, people don't notice tagging, but people notice my shit." Posterchild's mention of picture-taking is telling, as it hints at what constitutes public attention in a mass-mediated age. When asked how he knows one of his street theatre performances has worked, political puppet maker Elliot Crown says, "if I'm looking out and there's ten photographers all shooting, it's working."

Media Attention

To be seen is one thing, but to be seen, recorded, and then distributed via the media amplifies the public attention that a project — and the issue it speaks to — might receive. It's no real surprise, then, that mentions in the media, or "hits" as they are sometimes called, are the single largest verifiable, quantitative measurement used by artistic activists to determine success. FINK, a street artist from Ireland, told us that he is "extremely proud of creating my artwork and promoting/influencing social change through my artwork." How does he know that his artwork is "promoting/influencing social change"? Because, as he explains in his next sentence: "Not only was my marriage-equality artwork featured on the front page of the *Irish Times* here in Ireland, but [it] also had internet features across the globe in Los Angeles, India, Australia, and more."

FINK isn't the only artistic activist making this sort of assumption. Jacques Servin talked to us about what is probably the Yes Men's best-known intervention: impersonating a Dow Chemical spokesperson on the British

Broadcasting Corporation. On December 3, 2004, the twentieth anniversary of the infamous Bhopal chemical leak, Servin appeared on BBC's *World News* as "Jude Finisterra," representing the Dow corporation. In front of an international audience of millions, he proceeded to pledge to use Dow's profits to properly compensate its victims and take full corporate responsibility for the disaster. When asked if the intervention was a success, and how he could tell, Servin explains:

> There are a couple of different measurements. One is simply the number of articles or amount of media attention and the quality of media attention. So, because of the BBC thing, there were six hundred articles in the U.S. press that wouldn't have been there otherwise. They are writing about [the intervention] but had to communicate all the information about Dow and so on. So that was very successful. Even though nothing happened, even though it didn't force Dow to change, it was successful because it actually got that attention and successfully got people talking about Dow.

Servin is careful to point out that media attention in artistic activism is merely a means to an end: drawing attention to social issues, in this case, creating an opening to talk about corporate responsibility. Still, the impact equation is much like FINK's: media = attention; attention = people talking; people talking = impact.[16]

Part of the appeal of media attention is that it's easy to measure. By monitoring the number of media hits, artistic activists can easily assess whether their action has had some sort of result. While many artistic activists we talked to shied away from quantifying the impact of their work, veteran artistic activists Beka Economopoulos and Jason Jones are proud of their numbers. Referring to the media coverage of one intervention in their campaign to get climate-change-denying corporations and individuals removed from boards of museums, they boast: "It was something like 150 news hits around the world in the biggest outlets, and covered by news, science, climate, higher education, philanthropy, and arts and culture reporters. That's impact!" But successful as they are at garnering media hits, Economopoulos and Jones also see the problems of what they call the "by-the-numbers stuff." After listing their litany of successes, they then ask: "Is just getting news coverage enough to change the game?"

Media Impact

Numbers of media hits are really valuable only as *proxy indicators* of public awareness and attention. They are easy to measure, but they reveal little about whether the people watching, listening, or reading are actually paying attention, changing their hearts and minds, or altering their actions — that is, whether the intervention is having a social impact. Recognizing this, some artistic activists look deeper into what their media hits mean. As Economopoulos and Jones continue:

> You can suggest that [media attention] is changing the conversation, but then we look for some qualitative assessment of that news coverage. Is it good? Is it on message? Is it communicating something different? [Has it] actually impacted the conversation in the sector we're trying to transform?

This sort of qualitative assessment of quantitative metrics was repeatedly brought up by the artistic activists. Marisa Morán Jahn, for instance, tells the story of working on her *NannyVan*, a project that aims to educate workers and the wider public on the rights of domestic labor. She was in a workshop with other artists ostensibly interested in social change where "people were identifying what they wanted in terms of media coverage and what that meant for their project." But, Jahn noticed, "they were really concerned about the messaging around the poetics of their project." In other words, what her fellow artists were interested in was the media coverage of their art project, not necessarily coverage of the social cause their art was serving. It was then that Jahn had an "aha" moment. "I don't care if the project is even mentioned," she realized. Maybe, "the reporter came to the event because they were like, 'What's that quirky *NannyVan*? What the heck is that thing?' Or even like, 'I love cars.' But they're really writing about domestic workers. It's like a hook."

Having worked with the Yes Men for years, I have watched countless media interviews in which the reporter wanted to talk to them about how the Yes Men pulled off a daring, creative prank, only to have them deftly redirect the topic back to corporate responsibility, global warming, the war in Iraq, or whatever cause they were currently working on. For artistic activists like Jahn and the Yes Men, art is a hook on which to hang their activist concerns in order tempt the media to bite.

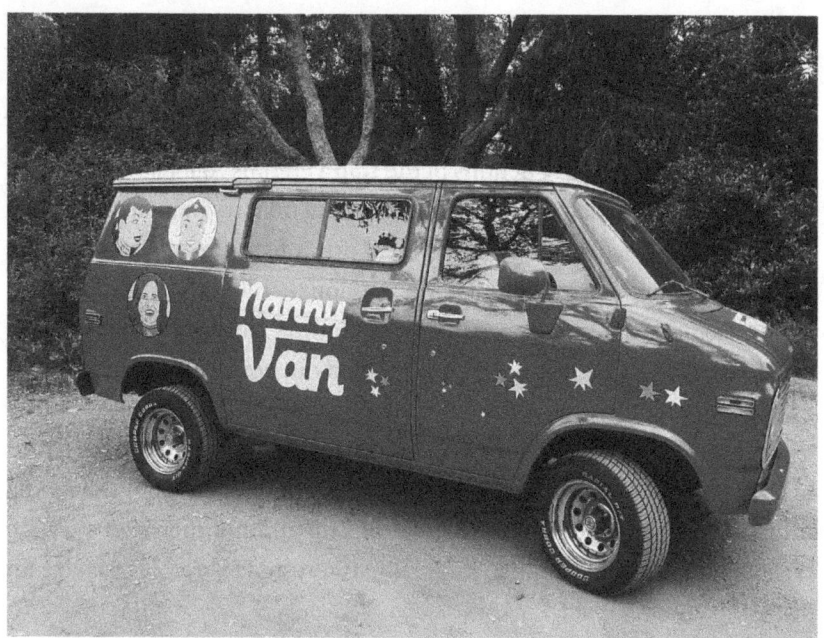

Marisa Jahn mobilizing domestic workers with the NannyVan, courtesy of the artist.

If mentions in the media constitute a measure of success, then it's no surprise that artistic activists will be tempted to stage interventions tailored to what the media wants. As a political puppeteer, Elliot Crown recognizes that, in order to get his message out to a wide audience, he needs to provide the media with an attractive image. "Most of my stuff," Crown explains, "is geared toward finding a simple, direct image with as few words as possible, or none, that visually encapsulates a critique, a message, so that someone will go, 'Oooo, my editor is going to want to publish that!'" As much as artistic activists may turn to attention, mass-mediated and otherwise, as a metric of success, there is also an underlying unease: a fear that what is used as a measure will end up becoming a guide, and that attention itself will become more important — and better recognized — than the social issues that motivated the work in the first place. Hans Haacke, whose artwork generates no shortage of media, reflects that:

> Success would mean, in today's arts, media attention. I'm a bit uncomfortable with that because it means that, ... if it doesn't get picked up, then therefore it was a bad work, and something that, for sensational reasons, is being bandied about therefore is a good one, a successful one.

The fear is, in Haacke's words, that artistic activism "becomes too much of a prisoner of media attention."

"The media is still the spectacle," argues Aaron Hughes, who helped plan many of the media-savvy actions of the Iraq Veterans Against War (IVAW). Using the performance of veterans carrying out military maneuvers on U.S. city streets, to use an example mentioned previously, the IVAW was aiming to get people to question popular assumptions — often aided and abetted by the media — about heroism and war. "So we can rupture that shit. We can do that," says Hughes, but "we didn't find out how to fill the hole. We're not going to fill that hole through media hits, because that's just another spectacle. That's more telling people what to think." Hughes wants to use his interventions to shock, surprise, and disrupt, yes; but after the media rupture, then what? In response, he holds up another metric of success: creating *less* mediated relationships: "I'm interested in creating a space for people to choose, react, have a voice."

Audience Engagement

Asked to explain the "success" of one of her public readings, Joey Jushka mentions news coverage — "The newspaper published the story afterward" — but with the familiar lament that "there wasn't much discussion of the content." Media quantity or quality, however, is not how she evaluates her work. Instead, Jushka explained, "one reaction that I remember was a fifty-five or sixty-year-old woman coming up to me after another reading of the story that I did, and she said, 'This is literature that I've been waiting for.'" For Juschka, that "one reaction" is a success. More intimate than public attention or media mentions, what matters is this sort of personal connection with her audience.

Looking for connections with their audience was what was behind *Stripperoke*, an intervention staged by artists and sex workers in South Africa where audience members were encouraged to take pole dancing lessons in public. One of the organizers, Mia Arderne, described how they evaluated the success of their project. "There were some positive," responses, Arderne relayed,

> like a student walking by saying "this is amazing." And some negative,
> like an older man with teenage children who we approached and said

"Just move on, I don't want my kids seeing this bullshit." The audience was mixed in their reaction but took on the issue themselves.

When asked what she meant that people took on the issue themselves, Arderne elaborated, describing how, "when some people heckled, others in the crowd would say, 'that's fucked up,' back to them.... They stuck up for us." Arderne went on to tell the story of how "a stereotypical, conservative old man came up and learned a few moves and danced and the crowd went wild." Why was this a success? Besides the obvious stereotype-defying, crowd-pleasing element of surprise, it signaled a success because, as Arderne discovered, "once someone tried it, and saw that they could do it, they would defend it." Audience response can become audience participation, which leads to audience investment, and this is a mark of success.

While participation can mean an audience member swinging on a stripper pole for a few minutes, it also can entail people participating in the act of creation itself, crossing the line from spectator to creator. Gustavo García Solares, one of the founders of Central de Artivismo e Innovación, an artistic activist collective in Guatemala City, was drawn to art, and artistic activism precisely for its ability to lower the barriers to participation. He describes his experience of the local activist culture in Guatemala as "closed," limited to the usual hardcore activists and left intellectuals, whereas he "feel[s] like art, everyone can be part of it, right?" One might well argue that the art world is just as elitist than intellectual and activist circles, if not more, but what defines artistic activism for García Solares is its DIY, amateur ethos, which he compares to punk rock, another of his creative passions: "You know three chords? There's a song!" Because there's such a low bar for participation, the best artistic activism, in his opinion, is that which draws people in, not just as audience members but as co-participants in creation. "I have seen a whole community doing a mural," he says. "People that don't get along, but everybody working together to see a mural. It's just a beautiful thing that happens. And I want to be able to find a way to make that happen in more places."

Emulation

When asked about how he measures the "success" of his very successful web-based rap news show *Journal Rappé*, Cheikh "Keyti" Sène immediately mentions media analytics, where "you can see the data in terms of traffic, gender, geography." "But still," Ketyi says, in a now familiar refrain, "those are just numbers." So he looks to other metrics of success. One of those measures is feedback from his audience, which he tallies, "when people meet you in the street, when people send emails or send text messages or call you." But as we talk some more, it becomes clear that there's another marker of the success of his project: the global spread of the *Journal Rappé* model. Beginning with a chance meeting in Germany with a reggae band from Jamaica whose members watched *Journal Rappé* and wanted to emulate it, *Journal Rappé* quickly spread across West Africa, then East Africa, then Central Africa, then to other islands in the Caribbean, and on to Vietnam and beyond. While it began accidentally, emulation is now part of the project's design as Ketyi and his partner, Makhtar "Xuman" Fall, offer encouragement, feedback, training, and technical, financial, and political advice to help others copy what they are doing. "You know what they say," says Ketyi, "plagiarism is actually recognition for a good work you are doing."

Freely admitting that his Billionaires for Bush project failed in defeating the presidential election of George W. Bush, Andrew Boyd points to a measure by which it succeeded beyond his expectations: the replication of his project and inclusion of hundreds to thousands of participants through "copycat chapters.... We started with a chapter in New York and another chapter in LA, ... and it grew to up to one hundred chapters." Similarly, when asked what he wanted the audiences for his artistic activism to do, Amin Husain answered simply "replicate it" and then went on to list actions similar to the ones he had helped plan that took place at other sites, even in other countries, and staged by other people. "Contagiousness," is what Jason Jones calls this, explaining that "the measure of success is that [the signs and symbols and stories created] become something that other people pick up and use."

Contagion is consciously factored into Ketyi and Boyd's plans, but sometimes it's unplanned emulation that demonstrates a project's success: "When something got proceduralized in an unauthorized fashion," as Marisa Jahn puts it. She reflects on one instance:

> One of the domestic worker groups was having a celebration for themselves, internally, and they made a piñata in the shape of the *NannyVan*. They didn't tell me about it and they didn't ask me. They didn't need to ask me. It was such a joyous thing for them that they did it for themselves. It was like, "Oh, they feel like it's theirs.[17]

Empowerment

Eve Mosher and her team designed and built one hundred simple "green roofs" on New York City tenement rooftops. "The effectiveness" of which, she explained, "is measured by how many green roof plots actually get out there, *and* how much beyond those initial one hundred the project extends," inspiring others to build their own green roofs. In other words: emulation. But Mosher also has another, less quantifiable, variable in mind when she evaluates her work on that project. She describes it as "giving that knowledge and confidence. Empowerment, whatever. I hate that word, [but] sometimes it's the only term." I must admit to hating the word "empowerment" too. It's a mushy term used to describe everything from people shifting power relationships to new-age self-actualization. Yet, over and again, artistic activists whose creative work I admire and whose commitment to social change is unimpeachable would raise, if not the word, then the idea of empowerment as something they used as a measurement of success.

"Evaluating an art project along the same terms that you might evaluate an engineering project or something like that can be problematic because it can limit the project," says Andrea Polli. The comparison between art and engineering is not a hypothetical one for Polli. In addition to her masters in fine arts, she holds a doctorate in computing, communications, and electronics and has worked with NASA and the National Science Foundation. Speaking of her artistic activist project that envisions power-generating wind turbines on NYC landmarks, she elaborates: "It's tangibly important to produce energy, and that's great, but if you're changing the way people are thinking, then you've got more people starting to do projects like that." Pressed on what she means by "changing the way people are thinking," Polli explains:

> It has to do with agency. It's having the attitude that you can come up with new ideas and they can be implemented. Or they can at least be tried out. Changing people from taking a passive point of view to an active point of view.

Numbers of wind turbines created and the energy generated are easily measured, just as you can count the numbers of newspaper articles or people attending an event. It is even possible to account for changes in the way people think through opinion polls and the like. But when it comes to things like assessing the transformation in a person from "a passive point of view to an active point of view," precise metrics become elusive.

There are a handful of projects referenced over and over, in articles and lectures and reports, to demonstrate that artistic activism works. Sol Aremendi's *Wage Theft App* is one of these oft-cited examples. Aremendi was working with fellow artist Tania Bruguera on the Immigrant Movement International, an immigrant-rights organization cum art project in Queens, New York, when she noticed a dire need amongst immigrant day laborers. Painters, carpenters, and other construction-trade workers would work an entire day and then not be paid, or paid less than agreed upon, by unscrupulous employers exploiting the workers' precarious legal and economic positions. In collaboration with the day laborers, workers' centers, unions, and a computer programmer, Aremendi created an app that made it easy for workers to snap photos of employers and their vehicles, report their experiences, and share these reports. The result is a user-generated database of useful knowledge that "empowers" the workers to improve their working conditions. This is artistic activism's success story, proof of concept for what Bruguera calls *Arte Útil*, or "useful art."

Except that Aremendi tells another story of the app's success … and failure. Judging by the utility of the app to help day laborers be better informed about employers, she is frank: "They're not using the app. So it's not successful in that way." *But*, she continues, "if I understand what happened as a process I can continue." Aremendi explains:

> It was a three-year project, and all the relationships that have happened around that [are the real successes]. … For example, at the workers' center they told me, "We didn't have a project together." This was a project that brought them together. It was crafting these relationships, and then it was like fifteen meetings in different workers' centers in the U.S. So it started getting bigger for the workers. They also started going on TV, doing things with the publication [we put out]. We did photography. We did a photo exhibit at the Queens Museum. All this stuff, … all these empowerment activities where art could be the skills.

Success for Aremendi was not the product, but the process of building it. Through that process, relationships were formed and a sense of *creative empowerment* was forged. The app was merely the catalyst.

The Spanish artistic activist Jordi Claremonte once talked to us about "increasing the repertoire" of a community. "What is a 'repertoire'?," we ask, thinking we had misunderstood a Spanish term. "For a musician," he explained,

> a repertoire is a collection of songs or music you have and which you can play confidently because you are able to work with all of them. So, you are as good a musician as you have a good repertoire, right? So, to me one of these campaigns or actions would be working when we increased the repertoire of the community.

Seeing the blank look in our eyes, Claremonte continues, explaining what this had to do with social change. Because of the artistic activist projects his group did with communities, he continues,

> they could do more things, and they could understand more things, and that's a very important philosophical issue for me in this approach, which is increasing your ability to do and your ability to understand. So, when you are able to do more things, and when you are able to understand more things, you are wiser and you are happier, and you are stronger.

"And that," Claremonte concludes, "is a very effective thing."

(Self)Empowerment

The evaluative question implicitly asked by the artistic activists above is whether those people who are impacted by their projects have more confidence, better skills, enhanced knowledge, stronger social relations, and a greater desire to act — to use Claremonte's phrase, "an increased repertoire" for social change. Empowerment, in these cases, is something to actualize in, and with, *others*. Some artistic activists, however, look for empowerment a bit closer to home.

Adelaide Damoah, for instance, is careful to point out that she measures success as "that response that you get from the public," and by whether "people understood what I was trying to say." But she then goes on to admit that another one of the metrics she uses in her assessment has to do with an internal state. "It's the feeling that I get when I finish making the work," she says. "It feels like I'm being my most authentic self, and so I'm the most comfortable with it. When we do a performance I'm not nervous, I'm not scared; I'm content, I'm happy." This experience that Damoah is sharing is not, I believe, an instance of the stereotypical artist that Hank Willis Thomas critiqued: someone interested only in themselves as the audience. Instead, Damoah is demonstrating an awareness that personal and creative empowerment may be necessary to produce work that can empower others and transform society.

"If you're talking about delivering fifty thousand gallons of milk to the community, that's a different goal," says Marlène Ramírez-Cancio. "But," she goes on to say,

> when you're talking about the arts [you need to] understand well-being as a holistic thing that [has] to do with how you feel when you wake up in the morning and how you're making people around you feel and how you're making a community feel.

For Ramírez-Cancio, other-directed work, affecting the feelings of those around you (and perhaps even the effective delivery of milk), is wrapped up in personal well-being; without this as a base of operations nothing else can happen.

Thokonzani Ndaba, Refilwe Nkomo, and Mark Rautenbach make up the Izindlovu Collective in South Africa. Following a creative workshop they organized to destigmatize and decriminalize sex work, they discussed with us how they evaluated its success. They shared an imposing-looking evaluation form with qualitative survey questions and quantifiable checkboxes that had been filled out by all their participants. They showed us the empirical data the form generated and described how it was useful in assessing the impact of their project and giving direction for future work. As we continued to speak, however, it was clear that there was also another set of metrics that were important to their project. Nkomo then explained there were really two measures: "There's what the participants got, and what we got. That connection. We were all hugging at the end of the workshop, and to *feel* that a difference was being made. It's difficult to translate that. It's even hard to express with you."

Material Outcomes

"My first demonstrations resulted in people in power resigning," reflects Ron Goldberg, the "chant queen" responsible for crafting the many memorable chants used by ACT UP. "You would actually see movement; not as fast as we wanted, but you don't usually get to see it in front of your eyes." Demonstrable social change, like the resignation of people from government agencies, is an elusive marker of success in artistic activism, but it does happen every once in a while, and for most artistic activists, it is the ultimate goal. Popular interest, media attention, and audience engagement are all important indicators of success for artistic activists, but in the end they are a means to a greater end: social change. As we explored in previous chapters, social change can be ideological and/or emotional, but for Goldberg, what matters most is the change in structures of power: "people in power resigning."

For Vivien Peng, who for many years worked with the advocacy organization Doctors Without Borders on their access-to-medicines campaign as a communications specialist and artistic activist in residence, describes one of her interventions against the pharmaceutical giant Pfizer:

> The day before Pfizer's shareholder meeting, we organized a live stunt where seventy-plus people slowly and deliberately placed a total of twenty-five hundred flowers into a crib to illustrate the number of kids who die from pneumonia each day. On the crib, we wrote the names of all the people who signed our petition asking Pfizer to lower the price of the pneumonia vaccine. Pfizer accepted our crib, and it sparked a lot of internal dialogue from their employees when they came across this work of performance art.

This discussion amongst Pfizer employees was certainly a success at the level of ideas, but Peng had other objectives as well:

> The next day, we attended their shareholder meeting and asked the CEO what he would do to reduce the price of the vaccine. In his response, he mentioned our stunt and casually said that he would be glad to meet with our director. Because he said this in an open forum, we were able to publicly hold him accountable to the meeting. This opened up a direct door to dialogue.

Another marker of success. Yet, the shifting of power that enabled the CEO of Pfizer to meet with the director of Doctors Without Borders resulted in demonstrable material change only *after* this meeting. It was then that the real success of the action was realized, when, "after seven years of campaigning, Pfizer finally agreed to lower the price of the pneumonia vaccine to nine dollars per child for all humanitarian organizations." For Peng, "success" looks like a long line of successes, each building upon the last.

Material outcomes are most often the result of longer campaigns waged by social movements or social-change organizations. It's worth noting that Goldberg's success as a "chant queen" was within the broader social movement of ACT UP to which he lent his creative talents, and Peng's success came as part of a large campaign by a multinational advocacy organization. To develop a working relationship with a social movement or organization, then, is also a mark of success. "When a social movement is able to use your productions, we can talk about success," explains Democracia's "Pablo." More often than not, however, there are no clear markers of demonstrable change that can be directly traced back to an artistic activist intervention or engagement with a social movement, and even those artistic activists most committed to material change recognize that there is no simple causality between their creations and social change.

"My goal is rooted in material reality: making revolution in an imperialist country," Dread Scott boldly states, before more humbly reflecting, "how do I measure my art against that?" As a committed revolutionary as well as a prolific artist, Scott has probably given more thought than most to what his art does and how its impact might be evaluated. He's worth listening to at length:

> Art is contributing to that [revolutionary] process. And again, not in instrumental or reductive ways, but is it contributing to people further wanting to get rid of a society that's based on exploitation and oppression and seeing the means to do that? And since the work isn't always, or even usually, tied to "come to this demonstration!" or "write this letter to the editor!" or something like that, it's not so simple.... From my perspective, the yardstick is whether it's contributing in as strong a way as possible to revolution and communism. Again, that's not like asking, "is it making people want to go out and take up arms right now?"

But is it contributing to a process where they find this system that we now live under worthless and that another system radically better?

The yardstick with which Scott measures success is daunting: "contributing in as strong a way as possible to revolution and communism." He's careful, however, not to define impact solely in terms of immediate material outcomes; there's an intermediary between the act of artistic activism and people going out and taking up arms. Before people violently overthrow capitalism, they have to think the current social system is worthless and another could be radically better. They need to desire change and feel they have the means to make it happen. In other words, people need to think and feel before they do. Dread may begin his jeremiad with "material reality," but he ends up with the acknowledgment that, to get there, you need to change hearts and minds. It's not only the effect of artistic activism that must be accounted for, but also its affect. In sum, its æffect.

Missing a Universal Measure

Unsurprisingly, there is no universal set of metrics that artistic activists agree upon to gauge success. There is, however, some common ground. Most artistic activists interviewed mentioned the importance of public attention, be that in a direct form through audience interest or indirectly through media coverage. This makes sense: without publicity and some sort of public, the driver of change — the social — is absent. It also makes sense because these metrics, like simply "pulling it off," are low-hanging fruit effects that are relatively easy to attain and even easier to measure and report. Although these are the measures most often employed, they are also widely understood to be insufficient. Artistic activists understood that the potential power of their practice was more than merely attracting attention. Audience engagement, project emulation, and personal and social empowerment are essential for interventions to transcend their impact in the moment and have any lasting outcomes. But it is exactly because these *aeffects* are long-term that they are harder to capture, and thus, while acknowledged as important, are less often accounted for. Finally, the effect of the affective practice of artistic activism — its material impact — is recognized as important, but here too evaluation happens less readily. In part, this neglect occurs because it is so exceedingly difficult to account for the impact of the project amongst the myriad of variables that go into transforming systems and structures of power, but also because the social and material effect of artistic activism is all wound up with its personal and emotional affect and it is impossible to pry the two apart. While universal agreement amongst artistic activists regarding what sort of measures are appropriate for assessing the success of artistic activism remains elusive, there is remarkable consensus on one thing: *metrics are problematic.*

Suspicious Minds

Again and again, prompted only by "positive" questions regarding how they evaluated their own work, the artistic activists interviewed launched into passionate and thoughtful critiques of evaluation. While the comments vary by individual, practice, and context, taken together they sort out into several general categories of critique.

Who Measures?
Favianna Rodriguez is in the minority of artistic activists in having a fully thought-out, and seemingly uncritical, approach to assessment. "I deal with funders all the time and they always ask me [how I measure success], and I look at it in a few different ways," she explains:

> First, I look at what the impact on the people who experienced the art was. Did they have fun? Did they learn a new skill? Did they see something they hadn't seen before? Were they moved by the art, did they get excited by it? What was the quality of the interaction with the work or the experience? ...
>
> The second thing is, Do movement people now have another tool in their tool box that they can leverage? Are they able to tell stories differently? What changes for them? What do they notice that is different for them?
>
> And the third thing I look at is, artistically, what was the experience for the artist?"

In a few deft sentences, Rodriguez sums up several of the ways in which artistic activists determine success: audience, engagement, and empowerment. But I want to return to the words with which Rodriguez began: "I deal with funders all the time and they always ask me ... " In that line lurks a recurring criticism of assessment: Who is the evaluation for, and what are their interests?

"Who are we trying to convince, and of what?," Gan Golan asks: "Are we trying to convince funders? Are we trying to convince economists? Are we trying to convince advocacy organizations? And to do what?" Eric Gottesman of For Freedoms has a ready answer for Golan's questions: "Social practice," he says, "was invented as a term and then employed as a tool for art institutions, art funders, to say 'Look, we're having an impact!'" Jacques Servin of the Yes Men piles on: "I think it's the whole NGO system, the NGOs who want funding are like, 'We'll guarantee your investment by measurements. We can measure our impact.' I think it's as simple as that. I think it doesn't do any good for activists." "Bullshit" is how one prominent artistic activist, preferring to stay off the record for this comment, described the usefulness of a professional evaluation of one of their group's nation-wide projects. "When somebody brought the idea of impact assessment to [us] we were like, 'nah, it's stupid.' But as we recognized what it could do, we decided to go along with it." And what did they recognize the assessment could do? "Generate data, some data that we can send to our funders." The skepticism toward evaluation shared by these and other artistic activists runs deep, and its roots are in the economics of the practice. Since artistic activism does not produce objects to be sold in an art market, artistic activists are often supported in their work by philanthropic funders and nongovernmental organizations and, particularly outside of the United States, governmental organizations, all of whom, understandably, desire "accountability" for their investment. What measures these bureaucratic organizations demand, when they ask for them, and how they want them accounted for, however, is often at odds with the priorities and capabilities of the artistic activists.

Jon Rubin has had many successful projects. Conflict Kitchen is one of them. Created with Dawn Weleski, it's a take-out restaurant in Pittsburgh that serves food from nations with which the United States is in conflict. Aiming to build empathy, each serving of food is packaged in a wrapper printed with the thoughts and stories of everyday citizens from that country. To fund large projects like this, Rubin and Weleski write grants, to granters who want measures:

> I remember us spending an enormous amount of time writing grant reports to validate the money we had received. Often in these kind of like spreadsheet ways which were antithetical, to be honest, to the nature of the conversation and the activity we were doing and concerned about on a daily basis.

Rubin continues, pointing out how this mismatch between what the artistic activist wants to do and what the funder wants is endemic to the practice: "Where art meets activism, you see a kind of problematic space occur. You create rhetoric around the work that's not really based on the values that you're wrestling with on a daily basis, just in order to validate it to granting organizations."

The "rhetoric around the work" is seen as part of the problem with assessment. "If you use 'measurement' and 'evaluation' with my local [artistic] activist group," says Beautiful Trouble's Nadine Bloch, "they're going to be like, 'yeah, whatever,' and give you the glazed-over look." Evaluation, like any specialized practice, has developed its own language and terms, like "qualitative measures," "quantitative data," "metrics," "variables," "log frames," and "theory of change," and this language can be alienating and intimidating for those without the professional training or advanced education. And rewarding for those with it. During a recent forum on impact and evaluation organized by a group of New York–based philanthropies (as well as your author), Risë Wilson, a founder of the artistic activist organization the Laundromat Project, made the point that, although artistic activism has long been a practice of people marginalized by race, class, sexuality, and legal status, "the folks who have the clearest fluency in the majority language are able to gather the resources because they can describe the impact, [while] the people who have been doing this for their survival don't speak that language."

Another cause for distrust has to do with who is doing the evaluating. In the same forum at which Wilson spoke, Cohen-Cruz stressed that "it becomes important to ask *who* is the field researcher or the evaluator." This is critical, she argues, because, "based on who your writer is, what will be evaluated, what will be lifted up, will be different." As Cohen-Cruz went on to explain, the problem with evaluation often has to do with using evaluators and methods of evaluation that are foreign, and sometimes even inimical, to the artistic activist and the intentions of their project.[18]

The solution to the problem of outside evaluators who don't understand the projects they are evaluating would seem to be simple: the artistic activists set the criteria for success and then goes about measuring it themselves. "You need to have your own tools of measuring success," Prince Afful says, discussing an empathy-building intervention he staged in a shopping mall in Accra, Ghana. In his piece, Afful held up a sign admitting he had mental health issues and asked people to simply embrace him. He then talked to those who chose to embrace him about mental illness (still a taboo subject in much of Ghana), how to understand and accept it, and offered information about professional help people could receive for themselves or their loved ones who might be suffering. Asked about its impact, Afful says

> I felt like the social experiment was a success because I followed up with a psychologist and found out that people were actually going to therapy sessions just from that. Okay, so it's a success for me. Some other people out there would have just counted the number of people who hugged them. That's success for them.

Afful identified an objective and a means to measure it: how many people followed up on the healthcare information he handed out by making appointments and getting help. But there's also a recognition within Afful's statement that it's not only the artistic activists' objectives that matter. There are multiple audiences — "some other people out there" — who may have their own, different, ideas of what is to be valued and how it might be measured.

In conversation, several artistic activists underscored how measures meaningful to the communities within which they work matter as much as their own. Owen Griffiths, for example, spoke of a collaborative garden project he did within a youth prison and how, "you'd have to ask them what made it a success, because my criteria would be different to theirs." Griffiths goes on to explain: "My criteria are from the perspective of someone who leaves at the end of the day, and their criteria are that they managed to stay out there [in the garden] without misbehaving or being sent back in or being restrained." "So," he concludes, "I think the markers of success are always kind of moving." In Griffiths's case, the concern is not some powerful outsider forcing their ideas about what should be measured on the vulnerable artistic activist. It's an acknowledgment that a certain humility is needed on the part of artistic activists themselves to recognize that their measures may not always be the most relevant markers of the success of their own work either.

Lastly, there is the problem of evaluation within a context hostile to activism, artistic or otherwise. "I think this whole thing about measuring social impact is kind of a very American thing," says Sim Chi Yin, the photo and video artist who grew up in Singapore and lives in China, and whose creative work has taken her to North Korea. "Increasingly I've had a problem with grants that require me to quantify my social impact," Sim says. Her problem? "Neither China nor Singapore are open and tolerant places. So I think it's extremely difficult to measure." This difficulty does not mean that Sim absolves herself from considering, and even measuring, the impact of her work. A project she did on unsafe conditions in Chinese gold mines and the effects it had on the health of the miners was censored in China, so there was no way to measure her audience and no "media hits" to count. "You cannot measure things that were not allowed to be published." Yet, as Sim recalls, there were more informal and roundabout measures of success. "Random Chinese people came up to me and said, 'Hey, I saw that on social media.'" Even though officially censored, the project circulated privately, and it raised a hundred thousand Chinese *renminbi* for a family featured in the project in two days. "I can measure the money," Sim says — "I think that says something."

Evaluation Takes Time, Money, and Skill

Measurement and evaluation take time, money, and technical skills that are often in short supply amongst artistic activists. When we asked Diana Arce whether she evaluates the impact of her *Politioke* project, she replied: "I mean, I try, but it's an issue of time." Arce is genuinely interested in the social impact of her shows, and even has ideas about how to measure that impact: audience interviews at the end of her shows and newsletter surveys are two tools she mentions. But she asks herself, "Do I invest energy in researching the effectiveness of the shows or do I continue doing shows? And I always happen to choose to continue to do shows or work on new projects."

Regardless of whether one has the time to do evaluation, "it's something that requires different skill sets than what we have," Igor Vamos (a.k.a. Mike Bonanno) of the Yes Men explains. And if you don't have the skills, it means paying for someone who does. "We were looking into prices of doing research through a focus group company," Vamos continues, "and the prices were so exorbitant that there was no way we could afford to do it anyway." Given the creative skill set of artistic activists, as well as limited resources of time and money, doing evaluation can seem like an unnecessary indulgence. Even Paolo Pedercini, whose artistic activism takes the form of subversive video games where audience and interaction are easy to track and who possesses the technical skills to do the data collection and analysis himself, reasons, "I could probably create a system and do some kind of data analysis, but," he concludes, "I don't have the time." And then adds: "I don't really care."

The Long Arc

When pressed on the issue of the problems in evaluating artistic activism, a number of artistic activists interviewed raised the problem of time. Not the time that it takes to do evaluation, as mentioned above, but the duration of social change itself. Evaluation and measurement are usually carried out at the time of, or soon after, the intervention takes place, yet the effect of that intervention, particularly its affective impact, may occur over long periods of time. "It took three hundred years to get rid of slavery and segregation in this country," Coco Fusco reminds us, before asking:

> So do you think that means that the people in the nineteenth century who were abolitionists or who were anti-lynching activists were losers and that they failed? How long did it take the nonviolence, through nonviolent means, to decolonize India? Decades of struggle. So does that mean that each individual instance is a failure?

Fusco sees a lesson in this for artistic activists who are quick to evaluate their actions as a success or failure. "If you can't measure the effect of individual art practices directly on social formations in this immediate sense," she asks, "then do you want to consider them all failures? Or shouldn't we start looking at the big picture?" To recast a phrase made famous by Martin Luther King Jr.: The arc of the moral universe bends toward justice, but it is *long*.

"It's a long wave," muses Beatrice Glow, whose multisensory work often grapples with our understandings of history. She then elaborates:

> I think of everything as being interdependent or part of an ecosystem, philosophically and biologically. There are urgent moments of crisis where the waves are crashing on the land, which are the moments that activists quickly rise to. But then there's the long waves, behind them, that are holding a space. They're affecting generational change, through educational, cultural methodologies. I see myself as being part of that [long] wave.

"But how do you measure that?" Glow asks herself, acknowledging, "That's going to be difficult;... people used to say that it takes about sixty years to see a change. So, I hope that by the time I'm an old woman I might be able to see a little bit of change, if I get to be lucky and see that." As Antanas Mockus, former Mayor of Bogotá, Colombia, recalls, "[Argentine author Jorge Luis] Borges once said something: 'Where are the heroes? We don't see them, but perhaps they will be seen as heroes ten or twenty years later.'" The long-term impact of artistic activism, like the long arc of social justice, may be missed by short-term measurement and evaluation.

There's another problem with time. How evaluation is carried out frequently privileges things or events, which can be stopped in time, over processes, which take place *through* time. "You cannot understand anything about activism at the moment, everything is a long process," says Gloria Duran, from the Spanish artistic activist group Intermedia. "And when you go to a demonstration, and there is some beautiful poster, or a nice performance, or whatever, it has nothing to do with the moment, [it] is the long process of political articulation." It is this long arc that matters, Hank Willis Thomas explains: "Regardless of [whether] this project was the one that turned the corner. Great! It turned a corner! But what was that thing that actually started the engine? So we have to see ourselves as part of a much longer discourse, and chain reaction."

For artistic activists like these, artistic activism is most æffective when imagined as a string of actions unfolding over time and not measured as moments of discrete interventions. To use language an activist might understand: metrics, as they are frequently employed, emphasize the impact of *tactics*. In order for tactics to be effective, however, they have to be a part of a longer *campaign*. In language more familiar to the arts, the question is one of *product* or *process*. The former is relatively easy to evaluate, but the latter may be what's more important for success. "It gets back to this idea, like, what system of measurement are you looking at?" Sam Gould asks, before elaborating:

> Each project can't get you to your goal. It's just one more step toward reaching that goal, which is always on the horizon. But, you need this belief that, like, walking there is totally good enough, you know? Even though, in your mind you know you can never actually reach the horizon. It's so trite, but it's the journey, man! It's the journey.

Judging each of these small steps on a long journey as a success or a failure obscures the fact that it is an accumulation of steps, right- and wrong-footed, that gets you closer to your destination.

Evaluation Hinders Creativity

Most of the arguments above are based on understanding evaluation as something that measures (or fails at measuring) the *results* of artistic activism, but when speaking to artistic activists about evaluation, another criticism comes up, one that locates the problem at the very beginning of the process: the initial act of *creation*. Evaluation, it is feared, hinders the artistic activist's creativity. Some of this critique takes the more traditional form of the ideal of artistic autonomy: to be true to your vision, you must turn inward and not listen to outside voices.

Adelaide Damoah articulates this sentiment well: "The minute you start thinking about the audience, you get confused [and] you start creating things that are not authentic; ... it's not coming from me, it's coming from somewhere outside." Damoah is deeply committed to her work having an impact on her audiences in challenging the ways that Black and female bodies are observed and imagined. So why the evocation of artistic autonomy? What Damoah is getting at is the problem of the critic-in-the-head: the voice of judgment "coming from somewhere outside." The worry with assessment is that it gives this critic a loud megaphone and that their voice will drown out the creator's.

Evaluation is a rational endeavor, and the concern with assessment hindering authentic expression and free creativity is also rooted in the belief that art's power — and by extension, the power of artistic activism — resides in its ability to transcend rationality. Part of the promise of artistic activism is to generate the unexpected: to create novel perspectives on the past or new visions for the future. To accomplish this, it is believed, artistic activists need to be able to trust their own creative senses; taking their own path even if what they do doesn't measure up.

Failure Is Part of the Practice

Alfredo Jaar speaks eloquently about the "failure" of his attempt to capture and convey the horror of the massacres in Rwanda in an activist art piece:

> I created different works. All failures. I did twenty-five works in six years....And each one had a different program; it failed and I moved on to the next one; it failed and I moved onto the next one. Of course, at the end, I learned a few things and I affected a few people.

It should be noted that Jaar's *Rwanda Project* is widely recognized as one of the most impactful pieces of political art in contemporary times. Nonetheless, if it is a success, Jaar got to it through failure.

Failure is a recognized part of the creative process of artistic activism, yet verifiable success is also the understandable goal of social movements, as well as funders, artistic institutions, and NGOs. By emphasizing markers of "success," artistic activists worry that measurement and evaluation will punish "failure" and thus discourage innovation and experimentation... or even creation of a project in the first place. "We're often asked what are the metrics, how do you measure it, how do you calculate impact?" Hank Willis Thomas explains, but, he continues, "if you are 'making art,' would you ever want to measure the impact? How defeated would you feel, oh, if I'd just done one more thing it could have reached another million more people." As an evaluator, Korza sees the resistance to evaluation from artistic activists, in part, as a way of avoiding the possibility of failure. Or, as she puts it, "a nagging fear that we'll find out that we aren't making a difference, or to the degree that we hope we are." Not only can evaluation raise the stakes on failure, and thus potentially undermine creativity, but it makes the artist acutely aware they may have "failed" in the first place. In other words, not knowing you've "failed" may be exactly what keeps you going. Evaluative ignorance is creative bliss.

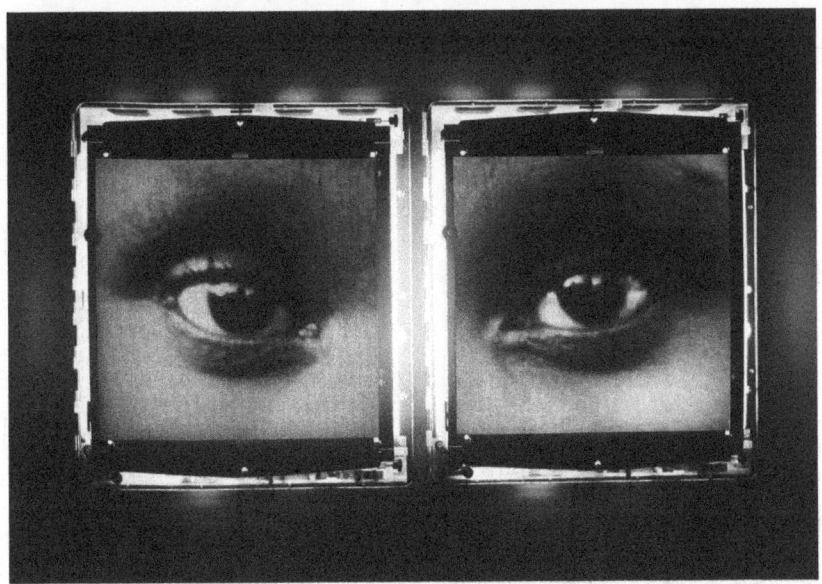

Inappropriate Tools

The reservations artistic activists have about evaluation and measurement go beyond the issue of who measures and why, whether it's politically or logistically possible, time frames, and creativity and failure. There is serious skepticism about how artistic activism can be measured and the tools that might do that measurement.

"Was Rosa Park sitting on the bus effective?," Vamos asks rhetorically about the performative action that signaled the start of the Montgomery bus boycott in 1955. "Was that effective? . . . I think if you asked most people, they would say, 'yes, it was.' But I don't know how you would actually measure it." What Vamos is pointing at is the difficulty of measuring the effect of affect. How can you measure the impact of Parks's performance that day? Yes, you might count the news stories, or how many African Americans boycotted the bus system, or measure the eventual effect of ending the segregation of the Montgomery bus system, but would that account for the *feeling* of rage and pride and possibility that Parks's act generated that was an essential component in broadening and deepening support for the civil rights movement?

Asked to discuss what is arguably his most "successful" artistic activist project, Billionaires for Bush, Boyd tells us:

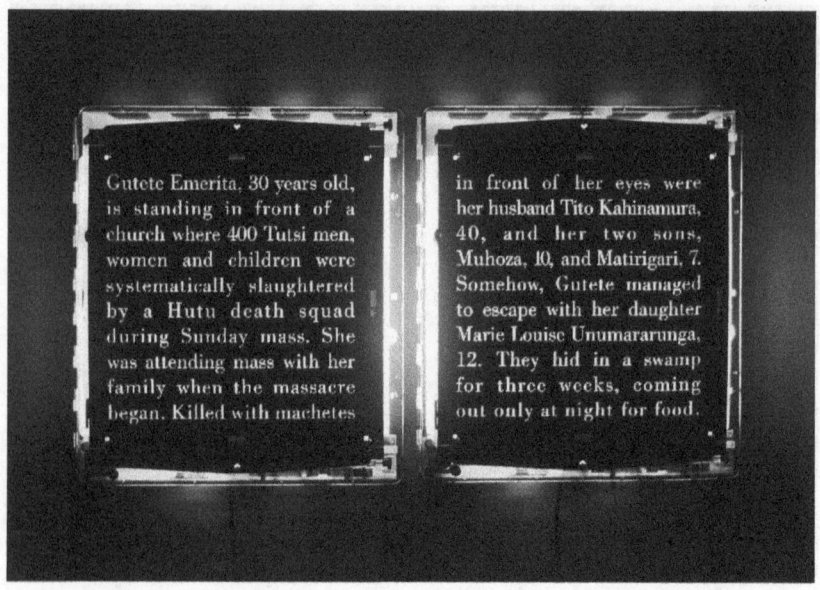

Representing the unrepresentable, Alfredo Jaar's *Rwanda Project*, courtesy of the artist.

> There were a lot of measurable metrics that we knocked out of the park. Like if you were going to measure by column inches you know, newspaper real estate that we captured, it would — well, I don't have an actual final number but it was like, you know, three hundred articles.

"But," he qualifies:

> Politically, we have absolutely no metrics. We have a few anecdotes about sort of little moments when we would have interactions with people and they would have these "aha" moments, but we really don't know what was going on inside their heads even. We have no metrics for persuasion. We have no idea if we were successful. We have no idea if we persuaded a single voter.

Part of Boyd's frustration, and Vamos's skepticism, has to do with the scale of measurement and the resources available for evaluation. It is easy to hit the "News" toggle of a Google search engine to see whether anyone has written about your campaign; it's much harder to account for its long-term impact on voting patterns, or how a creative action served as a catalyst for social change. But underlying Boyd's and Vamos's laments is something else: a recognition that the type of work that artistic activism does is difficult to measure with traditional metrics.

Gan Golan points out how metrics — like column inches or numbers of social media hits — don't really capture what is important, and worse, fool artistic activists and their supporters into thinking they have. "We're tricking ourselves in the lab, so to speak," he says, "I don't think we have yet found metrics that really show meaning. Meaning is what motivates people to do work." A sense of "meaning," or Boyd's elusive "what was going on inside their heads," is not something that can be easily measured by social media use, or attendance numbers, or media coverage, or many of the other ways that artistic activists are asked to account for success. And this is a problem because, again, it is these largely affective impacts that distinguish artistic activism from other forms of activism. Golan concludes: "I think a lot of the conversation on metrics has been actually damaging, because the things that are the most measurable are sometimes the least important. And I think that the most important are the least measurable."

Outside Measurement

Aware of the shortcomings of the standard tools of measurement for capturing the æffect of artistic activism, some practitioners come to the conclusion that *no* method of evaluation or tools of measurement can ever work. That is to say, metrics don't work because what artistic activism does best is immeasurable. "What may be the most effective element isn't necessarily measurable in any sort of empirical way, and that's a real challenge," admits Aaron Gach, who then provides an illustrative scenario:

> So, if you set up a blockade and it actually prevents the police from getting in, that's sort of a concrete effect. But a psychic effect is difficult to measure. So if you curse the police, and they go home and they have nightmares at night, chances are you're not going to know about that.

Gach is only half-serious (he does believe in magic, after all), but he articulates a widely shared belief that is taken seriously: the "magic" of artistic activism is outside of rational calculation. When asked about metrics, Leónidas Martin responds: "That's a very tricky question, because it's not easy at all. Since we [are] working with little parts of rationality, you know, we cannot measure it in a very rational way."

Part of the problem of measuring the impact of artistic activism, as Keyti pointed out in the previous chapter, has to do with the unpredictability of its æffects on the audience. "I hate it," Marlène Ramírez-Cancio says:

> When it's like "I'm going to do this performance and you're going to think this and I'm going to pass this information to you," ... you might think that you're doing one thing and it might be received in a completely different way.... You have no freaking idea.

Having "no freaking idea" what's happening seems like an odd stance for someone so experienced and committed to the practice as Ramírez-Cancio, but her nonchalance is based upon her theory of change. "It doesn't bother me, I guess, to not know," she says, "because at a base level, ... there's already probably some 'work' being done, some transformational things happening." Similarly, Packard Jennings, who aims to facilitate "the idea of dissent" through his how-to insurrection pamphlet, "thought bombs" sent out to audiences he will never see or meet, understands his artistic activism as "just planting that seed into someone, and who knows how it will germinate." Transformation this opaque, inchoate, and potentially multidirectional is, needless to say, resistant to evaluation.

The problem of measurability, however, goes even deeper than not being able to always observe and account for audience response. What is at stake is a problem of epistemology: how can we know what we know? Even those artistic activists who eschew magic for science, and are interested in pragmatic changes here and now, acknowledge that there is something about the magic of artistic activism that makes it hard to measure. Antanas Mockus, famous as mayor of Bogotá for such creative interventions as replacing the entire city's traffic-police force by mimes (and lowering traffic fatality rates by fifty percent), is a firm believer in measurement. A mathematician and philosopher by training, his creative interventions are based on survey data he collects about the problems he faces and the people he hopes to æffect. When possible, he also assesses the impact of his interventions after the fact through more attitudinal surveys and hard data on traffic deaths, violence, and so on. Yet, in a long conversation we had about the value of empirical data in planning and evaluating artistic forms of activism, even Mockus got to a point where he acknowledged the magic that results from using artistic means for activist ends. "There are some epiphanies," he explains, "moments of light when you see your Utopia, realize it partially, for an instant. *Avistamiento!* [you see the Virgin Mary!]" It goes without saying that divine sightings are notoriously hard to verify.

All the artistic activists we talked to, regardless of their particular philosophies or methods, are committed to social change, often radical social change. But, if change is truly radical, it will by necessity appear foreign to our current ways of making sense of the world. Martin raises this problem while discussing the 2011 occupations of public squares in Spain. Despite being a veteran artistic activist, what he saw and heard in those squares did not always make sense to him: the ideologies, their expressions, the occupation itself — none of it fit into the standard protest handbook he was used to. But instead of rejecting these new forms of protest because he didn't understand them — as a number of more traditional leftists did — he pushed himself to be attentive to what he describes as, "something happening just right before it gets organized, [when it is] undefined, because these kinds of things contain more than the things that are already organized." It is in these moments, in forms of thinking and feeling and doing in a stage of becoming, before they get organized and codified and contained, that we get a glimpse of radical social change, or what Martin describes as "new forms of politics that actually are almost un-politics."

But this radical transformation, if it were ever to occur, poses real problems for evaluation. What would be evaluated? What would be measured as an indicator of success? What would success even mean? To adapt a famous saying of Audre Lorde: you can't use the master's ruler to measure a liberated world.[19] Truly radical change requires radically new forms of evaluation, as it renders all forms of measurement that came before — and that we might currently understand — useless. "So the world of metrics lives down here," explains Beka Economopoulos, alluding to her project's success with mailing list numbers, petition signatures, and media hits, and ultimately getting eight major cultural institutions to divest from their connections with the fossil-fuel industry, but "above that there's [another] level, and above that there's universal egalitarian emancipation, you know? I don't know how you fucking measure that!"

Underlying many artistic activists' criticisms of evaluation is also a question of means and ends. They worry that, by emphasizing what can be measured, the affective qualities that are the unique contribution of artistic activism will be disregarded. By measuring in the moment, the long-term effects of artistic activism to create new perspectives and sensibilities will be overlooked. By stressing what "works," experimentation and "failure" will be punished. By giving time, money, and emphasis to evaluation, it takes away from scarce resources available to the artistic activist's creation. And by using the metrics urged upon them by funders, their work will bend toward pleasing those criteria and away from the affects and effects that matter to them, and the communities in which they work. In sum, the fear is that evaluation and measurement, instead of being a means with which to create more æffective projects, will become the goal, an end in itself.

Moving Toward a Method

Anyone wanting to create a model of evaluation of artistic activism that is useful to, *and actually used by*, artistic activists has to reckon with the reality of this field. This is what I have tried to do above and in previous chapters. To review: (1) There is no consensus on how artistic activism works, nor a clearly articulated theory of change that all artistic activists ascribe to. While I have tried my best to create such a model, I am not naive enough to think that the next generation of artistic activists will carry my diagrammatic wheel of change in a laminated card in their back pocket as they plan their creative interventions. (2) There is no common agreement on what artistic activism does, or even aims to do. Not only do the individual artistic activists hold different beliefs and engage in different practices, but how artistic activism works across the board is deeply dependent on the context in which it is created and enacted: its audiences, their cultures, the historical moment, and so on. (3) There is also no consensus on how to measure artistic activism. Indeed, amongst practitioners, there is skepticism on whether one can or should measure it at all. While most practitioners generally agree that it would be nice to know the impact of their creative interventions, they are wary of, and even hostile to, a specific evaluative approach — particularly when it is imposed from on high by funders, support organizations, or dare I say, an "expert" like myself.[20] These challenges can be cause for despair. Why create yet a model of assessment that will be at best ignored or at worst met with hostility?

But simply put, knowing whether artistic activism works *is* important. To repeat what I've said in the opening pages of this book, assessment is absolutely essential to creating more affective and effective artistic activism. Without a way to account for its æffect, artistic activism's claims for social engagement, social impact, or social change ring increasingly hollow. Furthermore, assessment of artistic activism is already happening, and will keep happening. Funders, NGOs, arts organizations, critics, the art market — all employ implicit and explicit mechanisms for determining whether a work is a success or not. The question is not to evaluate or not to evaluate; it's whose evaluation and for what purpose.

Honestly assessing the field can lead to despair, and inaction, but this reckoning can also prompt a new perspective on assessment. This new approach entails rejecting the sort of top-down, one-size-fits-all model of assessment that artistic activists themselves rightfully reject. It means honoring and accounting for the plurality of ways in which artistic activism is imagined to work. And it necessitates looking at the challenges that face assessment from another vantage point.

The vantage point I am proposing is erected upon the pioneering work of the Brazilian educator and theorist Paulo Freire. I have neither time nor space to do justice to the full range of Freire's thought, but I want to highlight several key aspects of his approach that may be useful here. In the course of attempting to teach poor campesinos to read in Latin America, Freire developed both a critique of traditional teaching and a model of liberatory learning. Traditional education, Freire argued, is based on a "banking" model, with the teacher as the determiner and holder of knowledge that is then taught to the students to regurgitate in the form of tests, exercises, and essays. In Freire's own words:

> Education thus becomes an act of depositing, in which the students are the depositories and the teacher is the depositor. Instead of communicating, the teacher issues communiques and makes deposits which the students patiently receive, memorize and repeat.[21]

Not only does this model of education recreate a hierarchical social relationship of powerful and powerless, it also fails a more basic test: it doesn't work to teach peasants to read. Presented with abstract words and ideas divorced from their own lives and experiences, such as *communiques*, they understandably don't see the relevance of education.

Freire proposes another model of learning; a "dialogic and problem-posing" approach.[22] This model begins with the assumption that education is a two-way street, a dialogue between teacher and learner. Instead of the linear and hierarchical model in which the teacher teaches the student, who then dutifully spits out the answer, education is understood as a reflective and reflexive communication process between teacher and student. In another reversal of the traditional model of education, the pedagogical content is not set by the teacher, but by the student. The subject matter of any lesson, as Freire explains, is "constituted and organized by the students' view of the world, where their own generative themes are found." [23] In other words, learning happens in dialogue, reflecting upon and puzzling through those things that are immediately relevant to people' lives and practices.

Freire, however, is not suggesting some free-flowing rap session on everyday experiences that merely reinforces what is already known (or not). Instead the point is to begin with what is most relevant in people's lives and use this as a starting place — what Freire refers to as a "cognizable object" — to generate critical thinking.[24] In this pedagogical process, the teacher still has an important role. "The task of the dialogical teacher," writes Freire, "is to 're-present' that universe to the people from whom he first received it — and 're-present' it not as a lecture, but as a problem."[25] In short, the teacher is no longer an answer-giver, they are a problem-poser, and by asking questions of what is familiar, students and teachers figure out together new ways of understanding and acting upon that reality.

How does an approach to pedagogy developed to educate and liberate Latin American peasants apply to a model of evaluation of artistic activism? While the contexts are wildly different, I think that the challenges faced are the same: the tendency, on the one hand, for evaluation to be a top-down, expert-driven process that disregards the knowledge and interests of artistic activists and the varying contexts in which they work; and the tendency, on the other hand, for artistic activists to distrust and distance themselves from practices of evaluation that seem abstract from and foreign to their own practices.

The solution inspired by Freire is a method of evaluation that starts from the bottom up. In this model, the evaluator is not the person with all the knowledge bestowing it upon (or using it to monitor) the artistic activist. Instead, we begin with the artistic activists themselves: with their own artistic aims and political objectives, and those developed in concert with the communities in which they are working — that is, their *intentions*. The evaluator then enters the picture as a problem-poser: asking critical questions in order to "re-present" the artistic activist's project back to them in such a way that they can clarify and strengthen what it is they want to do — that is, their intent, and how to know whether they have done it — as their own methods of measurement. In this model, the artistic activist and the evaluator are in conversation with one another: discussing, reflecting, analyzing, revising, and recreating in a dynamic process of learning. Indeed, with this method of evaluation, the goal is for artistic activists to become their own interlocutor, developing a continual practice of self-reflection in order to become their own best evaluator. At its worst, evaluation is a form of external monitoring determining the success or failure of a project at its completion. At its best, assessment can be a continual process of learning led by artistic activists themselves.

For this method to be useful, it needs to be both universal and contextual: *universal* in that any artistic activist can use it; *contextual* in that it accounts for the artistic aims, goals for social change, creative practices, and cultures of a specific artistic activist and their project. The trick here is to balance the two. Again, it is Freire who suggests a solution. Instead of a model of assessment, I want to propose a model of problem-posing...that leads to assessment. The foundation of this model is not built upon answers, but upon questions: a set of common questions that will necessarily result in uncommon answers. These prompts, posed to artistic activists throughout the process of their projects — no matter what they want to do, with whom they want to do it, where they are doing it, and what impact they want to have — will lead them to critically reflect upon their practice so they can assess what is working, what is not, and what might work better. Because the *raison d'etre* of artistic activism is social change, part of this reflection, by necessity, will be to assess what sort of change has happened. However, what is measured, how it will be measured, and what instruments will be used to measure will all be discovered through a process of questioning and conversation.

My proposal here is for a query-based, artistic activist-centered method-ology to assess the æffect of artistic activism. This methodology is not wholly original. In addition to the ideas of Freire, it draws upon the dialogic method of Jan Cohen-Cruz, it incorporates the extensive foreplanning of Dwyer, and like the evaluation tools created by Korza, it is designed so that it can be implemented by artistic activists and their supporters themselves. Other researchers have also stressed the importance of contextuality,[26] focusing on intent,[27] and an evaluation process that begins with conceptualization.[28] Originality is not my aim here; utility is. The methodology is created from what I've learned from others, not least of all what I've heard from artistic activists. It is an open, creative approach in tune with the culture of artis-tic activism, a method that does what artistic activism does best: engage participants, ask questions, challenge perspectives, provide alternatives, and move people toward action.

CHAPTER FOUR

Assessing Æffect

IN THE END, ANSWERING THE question "does artistic activism work?" requires a method of assessing its æffect. In this chapter I will be presenting just such a method, which I'll call the *Æffect Assessment Method*, not by providing prescriptions, but through posing questions — questions designed to put the artistic activist at the center of the process and take into account the particular variables and specific contexts of their artistic activist project. I'll demonstrate this æffect assessment method through a short script of queries (a full script can be found in the appendix) and a hypothetical case study that extends these questions and applies them to planning and evaluating a project. I'll then conclude with four real-life examples of the method in practice around the world. This method is composed of many questions, followed by sub-questions that generate even more questions, but its structural integrity relies upon only a handful of prompts, seven in all. The first is the all-important question of intention:

What do I want my project to do?

For artistic activists, intention is a matter of both aesthetics and politics, affect and effect. Reflection on this question gets us thinking broadly about the "look and feel" of what we want to create, as well as what sort of social impact we want our project to have. It gets us thinking about grand, utopian goals, as well as specific attainable objectives. "What do I want my project to do?" is a question that also entails thinking deeply about what artistic activism *can* do, as well as a theory of change that explains how it does it.

Who do I want to engage?

This question prompts the artistic activist to reflect upon public reception, the powers and potentialities of different audiences, and the forms of expression that resonate — or don't — with different publics, depending upon the geographic, cultural, demographic, and political contexts in which they live. Considering the audience is critical because the social impact of artistic activism is contingent upon the impact it has on the public, for it is only through the persuasion and mobilization of others that social change happens. This avenue of questioning helps us think through what audiences we hope to engage and why, and explore what we want these audiences to *think*, *feel*, and *do* in response to our project.

How do I want to act?

Because artistic activism is necessarily a public intervention, the *ethics* of the practice need to be considered. This is why it is important for artistic activists to develop an ethical code that guides our work. This set of ethics can begin with the values we currently hold and those that guide the world of the future we want to help build. These ethics also need to take into account the concerns and conditions of the communities within which the project is situated and the audiences being addressed. The ethics of intervention, creative or otherwise, are often fraught with moral uncertainty, and this can lead to paralysis as the artistic activist is concerned that, even with the best intentions, their project will cause harm. This is a valid concern, yet it is also important to remember that there's a moral cost of nonintervention, of sitting by and doing nothing.

By interrogating goals, audiences, and ethics, we artistic activists will arrive at a place where we know what we want to do, whom we want to do it with, and how we will do it. In brief: we will be clear in our *intent*. With this we are ready to plan the look and feel of our intervention.

What do I want to create?

Often artistic activists start with an aesthetic inspiration triggered by social concern, and this is the beginning and end of the planning processes. The æffect assessment method upsets this ordering by posing the question "What do I want to create?" only *after* we have given thought to what effect and affect we want our project to have, who we want to engage, and the ethics of our practice. This reordering asks artistic activists to express our creativity within a larger context. It transforms what is often a self-centered response — *I* want to create — into a far more complex inquiry into what I want to create *in order to* impact an audience *in order to* generate social change. This concern with change raises the next question.

How will I know if it works?

The aim here is to move from intent to outcome, proposing what success would look like and designing research practices and evaluation instruments that might measure this. This question transforms diffuse goals into *concrete objectives* and asks us to think about how we would know whether the audiences are impacted in the way we want them to be. Such a question nudges the artistic activist into the role of evaluator, as we explore and develop ways to measure impact and gauge our project's success — as well as account for unexpected and surprising æffects. It's only after we've figured out what "working" will look like, and how we might observe and account for this, that we enter the area that is too often thought of as the entirety of assessment: evaluating the impact of the artistic activist's project.

Did it work?

Once the evaluation data is gathered, analysis begins. This analysis is not aimed toward a final judgment of success or failure. Rather, the objective is a rich understanding of the project and its impact. The first step in the process of analysis is to generate a thick description of our project, a non-evaluative picture of what happened ... and what did not. From here we move into analysis, and using the data generated through measurements we ask ourselves: What worked as intended? And what didn't? How did the different audiences respond? What did they *think, feel,* and *do*? What sort of political, social, or cultural impact did the project have? The magic of creativity means not always knowing what will happen, so we also ask: What happened that surprised us?

What do I do next?

The ultimate goal of the æffect assessment method is to produce better, more engaging, and more impactful work, and the last framing question of the æffect assessment method prompts the artistic activist to learn from experience and analysis and move forward. Knowing what we now know, this question asks us to think about what could be done differently next time. It leads us to think about how æffect might be cumulative, each intervention building on the other, as part of an overall campaign instead of a one-off expressive gesture. In short, it prompts the artistic activist to think strategically about our practice and encourages us to be thinking about our long-term trajectory as artistic activists.

This small cluster of framing questions concerning goals, audience, ethics, intervention, measurement, and iteration provides the structural foundation of the æffect assessment method. In practice, each of these questions is built out and expanded to create a more comprehensive evaluation edifice that prompts the artistic activist to think even more deeply about what it is we really want to do and how to know whether we've done it. Artistic activism, like all forms of creativity, is as much about the process as it is about the end-product. As we develop our project, the answers to the questions posed above will change, as they should; and as these answers change; the shape of the project — including even our intentions — may change as well. Assessment is not something to be done only at the end, or even just at the beginning of a project, but constitutes an ongoing reflective process that encourages artistic activists to shape and reshape their efforts in response to fresh ideas, practical challenges, new knowledge, and changed conditions. The mission of this method is not to train artistic activists to become professional evaluators. Rather, the aim is to provide an easy-to-use process of rigorous self-reflection — from planning through project execution to final evaluation — in order to make more æffective artistic activism.

The æffect assessment method can take many forms. It can be a script of questions, either brief and broad like the ones above or dense and detailed like those I sketch out below through my hypothetical example (and provide in full in the first appendix: "Æffect Assessment Script"). These questions can be self-administered by artistic activists or be posed to them by evaluators. This questioning can take the form of a pen-and-paper worksheet or a digital form to be filled out. One can also engage with the æffect assessment method though an online, interactive app. All these mediums exist, are freely available and free to use, and are licensed under Creative Commons. (You'll find URLs and QR codes for both the Æffect Toolset and Æffect App at the back of the book.) The æffect assessment method has taken on other forms as well, as artistic activists around the world have used the basic ideas and prompts and adapted and altered them to their specific contexts and particular needs.[1] Regardless of its medium, this method is meant to be a dialogic process: a conversation between the artistic activist and the evaluator, even when they are one and the same person. Here, however, I am constrained by book and page. And although it lacks the dynamism of human interaction, and the sorts of explanations and follow-up questions that are a natural part of such a dialogue, the examples that follow, one hypothetical and four actual, will hopefully provide a basic understanding of the process.

The Æffect Assessment Method at Work

As I've argued above, assessment works best not as an abstract set of prescriptions applied, but as a set of prompts worked through over the course of an entire project. To demonstrate this, I want to start with an example of the æffect assessment method at work. It's a hypothetical case study with a hypothetical artistic activist, but it is based on real people, real places, and real issues we've worked with at the Center for Artistic Activism.[2]

Fatoumata, or Fatou she's usually called, is a sculptor and installation artist from the Republic of Guinea, or Guinea-Conakry as it is commonly known, on the coast of West Africa. She lives in the capital city of Conakry, which, like many places, has a garbage problem. Garbage is piled on the side of streets, lies strewn across what would be beautiful beaches, and clogs the waterways that wind through the capital. In addition to being smelly and ugly, the garbage creates unsanitary and unsafe conditions for the people of the city, particularly those who are poorest and spend most of their life out of doors. Garbage collection is run by the city government who, in turn, contract out to small private enterprises, but governmental and business corruption means services are insufficient, inefficient, and underfunded. Politicians don't seem to care, and everyday people dump their trash where they can. Fatou loves her city, but the garbage drives her mad. It is a daily, visible reminder of the rampant corruption that plagues her society and the thwarted beauty of her country. She wants to do something that will address the problem. As an artist, Fatou is often inspired by an idea of what she wants to create: what it will look like, and she begins her projects with this aesthetic vision. But as an artistic activist Fatou also wants her project to have a demonstrable social impact. So before thinking about the form of her work, or even its content, she asks herself:

What do I want my project to do?
Fatou thinks about all she'd like to change about the horrible current garbage situation in her city, but also what she'd like her city to change into. With this vision of the world she'd like to help create, she asks herself further:

What is my activist goal?
Thinking big, she decides her goal is to make Conakry beautiful.

Now that she has a handle on the *effect* she wants to have, she turns to what she knows to be art's special power: its ability to generate *affect*. Thinking about how she wants to move people emotionally with her project she asks herself:

What is my artistic aim?
Fatou decides that her *artistic aim* is to create a project that helps people to feel as if they can do something about large social problems like garbage and corruption.

Make Conakry Beautiful! Help People Feel Empowered!! After a moment of elation, reality sets in. These are inspiring aspirations, but how and where does she start? Fatou realizes that, if she's going to ever get anything done, she'll need to scale down her ambitions to something she can work on. She needs an objective. Whereas goals are big and bold and sometimes unrealistic, objectives are demonstrable, measurable milestones that will let her know whether she is making progress and moving in the right direction. So Fatou asks herself:

What is the objective of my project?

Recognizing she needs to begin somewhere and reflecting upon how garbage made her think about how badly she wants her city to be beautiful, she decides she'll start with the problem of garbage. "Raising awareness" or "starting a conversation" about the issue of garbage is not going to be enough. Everyone in Conakry knows that garbage is a problem and they talk about it all the time. The problem is that nothing is being done. After thinking about it for a while, she comes up with the *concrete objective* of mobilizing people to clean up a local beach.

Fatou knows it's a good objective, but she wants to make it even tighter so she can know where and how to focus her efforts. Thinking back to a business class she took at university, she recalls the concept of S.M.A.R.T. objectives: that a good objective should be Specific, Measurable, Achievable, Relevant, and Timed. The business class only confirmed her desire to be an artist, but she figures that it's worth seeing whether this wonky concept can help her clarify her objective. Since Fatou is interested in social justice, not maximizing profit, she also adds two more criteria: an *I*, for Inclusive, and an *E* for Equitable. She asks herself,

How is my objective S.M.A.R.T.(I.E.)?

Fatou determines that her objective is *specific* because it's focused on a specific action, cleaning up trash, in a specific place, a local beach. It's *measurable* because she can compare the cleanliness of the beach at the end of her project to what it looked like before, and she can also "measure" how many people take part in her intervention. Her objective is *achievable* because a project to mobilize people to pick up garbage from a public beach was carried out with great success in nearby Ghana, and one of her artistic activist heroes, Modou Fall, a.k.a "Plastic Man," has been organizing volunteers in Dakar in Senegal to do grassroots clean-up projects for years by dressing up as a traditional kankurang with a shroud of plastic bags. Even though the contexts are different and the Ghanaian project wasn't very artistic, these successes in other West African countries convince Fatou that hers can work here in Guinea-Conakry.

Her objective is also *relevant* because, even though getting rid of garbage on one day on one beach isn't "making Conakry beautiful" by itself, mobilizing citizens to do something about the garbage problem and rediscover the natural beauty of their city is moving toward that goal. When she gets to the *timed* question, Fatou realizes that she had not thought about a time frame. She thinks about the other responsibilities in her life (her job at the pharmacy, helping her sister out with childcare, and other projects she's already committed to), stresses a bit about all she has to do, and then decides to give herself three months to accomplish it. Having made her objective S.M.A.R.T., Fatou continues on with the social justice *I.* and *E.*, reasoning that her objective is *inclusive* because she will be including everyday people of Conakry in the execution of the project, and *equitable* because public sanitation is a problem that impacts the poorest people the most, while mobilizing people to take power into their own hands addresses inequities of power. Fatou now has an *activist goal*, an *artistic aim*, and a thoughtful *concrete objective* for her artistic activist project. But who is her project for? In other words, she asks herself:

Whom do I want to engage?

To answer this question she asks herself another:

Who has the power to realize my objective?

Because Fatou has translated her big goal into a do-able objective, the answer in this case is pretty clear: the people with the power to clean up the beach are the everyday people of Conakry she wants to mobilize. This, she decides, is her "primary" audience, answering the question of:

Who is the audience I want to engage?

To make sure this is really the most important audience to engage, she asks herself:

Why do I want to engage this audience?

Thinking about this, Fatou concludes that, since politicians and officials are often corrupt and rarely do anything for the people, the problem of garbage in Conakry is best addressed through the efforts of everyday people. Fatou knows she could further refine this audience too. She could target school children, or street kids, or people who live within walking distance of the beach, or those already involved in civil society. Distinct sets of signs, symbols, and stories will resonate with each of these audiences, and knowing who her audience is and what they respond to will make her work more affective, and therefore effective. But for now, Fatou is okay with identifying the broad audience of "everyday people of Conakry."

With her main audience in mind, Fatou goes deeper into the reactions she would ideally like these people to have. She asks herself: if everything goes perfect with my project:

What do I want this audience to think, feel, and do?

Since her overall goal is creating a beautiful Conakry, and the people who live there already know that garbage is a problem and talk about it a lot, Fatou decides she wants to push her audience further than just knowing and talking about the problem. She wants people to feel that they are the solution... and then do something about it. Fatou decides that:

> I want my audience to *think* that social problems like garbage collection are fixable.

> I want my audience to *feel* empowered that they can fix these problems.

> I want my audience to *do* something to beautify Conakry by picking up trash and staying civically active.

Thinking deeper about audience, Fatou realizes there are some other audiences she wants to engage, and asks herself similar questions to those above:

Who is my "secondary" audience? Why do I want to engage this audience? What do I want this audience to think, feel, and do?

Fatou decides that there are two additional audiences she wants to engage, or at least not upset and alienate: *politicians* who determine and enforce policies about garbage collection, and the *news media* who can publicize her project to the public and create more pressure on the politicians.

Fatou considers how her project might speak to these *secondary audiences* as well as her *primary audience*. For example, she — and many of her fellow Guineans — think most politicians are corrupt, but since she is counting on politicians to be a possible sympathetic audience, she doesn't want their corruption to be a central message of her piece. And knowing a bit about what the news media need to create a story, she considers creating a compelling visual element as part of her project that will make for good photos and video, and hosting a press conference to provide information about the event and the issue to reporters.

Fatou also thinks of a possible "unintended" audience: people who she's not targeting but who will likely encounter her intervention. Because artistic activism projects like her own are often carried out in public, Fatou knows she can't always control who comes into contact with her work, and people can have all sorts of reactions — both positive and negative — that are unexpected. This is a hard audience to plan for because it is, well, unintended, but she knows it's important to think deeply about *all* the possible audiences for her work, so she asks herself:

Who might be a possible unintended audience? Why do I need to consider this audience? What do I want then to think, feel, and do?
Fatou thinks of the workers at the local sanitation companies. She worries they might misunderstand her project as an attack on their livelihood and disrupt it. She decides that, whatever she plans to do, she'll try her best to make sure her project is not perceived as a threat to them.

Having spent time thinking through her audiences and how to prepare for them, she turns to the ethics of her intervention, considering:

How do I want to act?
Fatou begins by exploring her own values, asking herself:

What are the core values that make up my ethical code?
Fatou reflects upon values she admires, those she doesn't, the values of her community, and those of the "beautiful Conakry" she wants to create, and comes up with a list:

Honesty
Autonomy
Community
Collaboration
Caring for my city, my country, and my continent
Honoring nature
Helping others to create
Learning from others
Valuing tradition
Celebrating innovation.

She jots these onto a piece of paper that she hangs on the wall of her workspace so she can consult them regularly throughout her project, using the list as a guide in making the myriad decisions that need to be made when working on a public project over a series of months. But right now, Fatou considers:

How will I apply my ethical code to my project?
She thinks about this, and then writes down:

> I will apply my ethical code by creating a collaborative project that facilitates the creativity of all the participants. My project will do good for Conakry, Guinea, Africa, and the natural world. At all stages in my project, I will solicit input from the communities in which I work. My project will work with local symbols and artistic traditions, but also push new boundaries with aesthetic forms and uses. I will be transparent in how decisions are made and how resources are allocated, and I will not take any money or assistance from politicians or officials who want to shape my project.

With all the thinking through of the intentions of her project done, it's *finally* time for Fatou to think about:

What do I want to create?
Keeping her goals, objectives, audiences, and ethics in the back of her mind, she begins imagining, asking herself:

What is my idea for an intervention?

Fatou thinks of herself primarily as an installation artist. She loves to create built environments that people can interact with and, through that process, transform their understandings and perspectives. Ever since first conceiving of the idea of creating a project around garbage, she knew she wanted to make some physical object that everyday people could help create. After brainstorming on her own and with her friends, and then some more on her own, Fatou comes up with an idea and writes it down in the notebook she's devoted to this project:

> I will create a massive collaborative sculpture out of all the garbage picked up from the beach. This sculpture of found objects will stand at the head of the beach and will be in the shape of an elephant. Why an elephant? Because an elephant is a symbol of Guinea and the name of the beloved national soccer team. It is a powerful symbol that all local people know. I also like that it reminds people that there is an "elephant in the room" — the corruption and apathy that keeps Guinea from being the country it can and should be. The elephant can also be a motif in the flyers, posters and a social media campaign publicizing my project.

It's only just a rough sketch right now, but it gives Fatou something to work with. In revising and expanding this idea, the first thing she does is reflect back upon her original intentions and see if her current project does what she set out to do. If not, she knows she can revise her project so that it does, or even go back and revise her original intentions. To begin this stage of reflection and revision, she asks:

How will my intervention get me closer to my goals, aims, and objectives?

Fatou thinks back to her *activist goal* to make Conakry beautiful, her *artistic aim* to help people feel as if they can do something, and her *concrete objective* of mobilizing people to clean up a local beach within three months. Because her intervention entails (1) creating a collaborative participatory artwork that (2) prompts people to clean up a beach and (3) produces something of beauty while doing it, Fatou decides it checks all the boxes and doesn't need to be revised just yet.

The next question she asks herself has to do with her intended audiences:

How will my intervention address my audiences?

Fatou has a number of audiences she wants to engage: Her *primary audience* is the everyday people of Conakry she wants to attract to participate in her project. She also has two *secondary audiences*: the news media who can cover her event and spread her message, and politicians who have the power to pass laws and enforce policies. She also worries about an *unintended audience* of sanitation workers whom she does not want to upset.

By making something beautiful and symbolic out of garbage, Fatou hopes to demonstrate to the people of Conakry that they can have a demonstrable impact on their city by using their creativity. She'll use social media, flyers at schools, and her connections in artist circles in Conakry to recruit participants. Fatou also plans on inviting local civic groups who can work with the participants and channel their enthusiasm and commitment into longer-lasting campaigns.

Her intervention will also address the needs of one of her *secondary audiences* — the news media — by staging a story and photo-worthy spectacle of a large sculpture built out of garbage in a public space. She plans to hold a press conference at the end of the event, and she'll reach out to this audience directly by writing up a press release and sending it out to TV and radio stations, news websites, and bloggers. Creating a public and publicized intervention that draws attention to the problem of garbage in a spectacular way will also invite politicians, her *other secondary audience*, to become part of the solution... or stay away and be recognized as part of the problem. Fatou decides she'll appeal to this audience by sending ornate "special invitations" for the unveiling of a new public sculpture erected by the citizens of Conakry, and then follow up with phone calls asking the politicians if they want to be involved in this important civic event.

Finally, Fatou thinks about how her project might play with her possible *unintended audience*, sanitation workers. She decides that it's best to engage this audience directly by visiting the local companies that are contracted to pick up garbage and talking to the workers, reassuring them that her intervention is not targeting them, but the larger system, and persuading them that better sanitation policies would mean more jobs.

The final check-in Fatou does is with her ethical code. She plans on reflecting back upon her ethics often as she moves from the planning to the execution and evaluation of her project, but now that she has a basic idea of what her intervention will be, it's time for her first check-in:

How will my intervention meet my ethical code?

Looking back at her ethical code, Fatou thinks about several ways her project matches her ethics. It is an intervention that invites people to participate in a creative collaboration that will benefit the community. The cleaning of the beach will make her city, country, and the continent more beautiful, and the natural beauty of the beach will be in full view. As important, everyday people will be empowered to take control of and transform their material environment. And while she will invite the politicians to come, they will not have any influence over her project.

This process of reflection doesn't demand a lot of revision of her original plan at this stage, but it does push Fatou to think in more detail about how to appeal to the audiences she wants to engage, and how she wants to handle the two potentially tricky audiences: politicians who might compromise her project and sanitation workers who might disrupt it.

Fatou is halfway through the evaluation process, and nothing yet has been evaluated. Instead, she's spent all her time on clarifying intent, audience, and ethics and using these to hone her project idea. Why? In part because, until she defines these variables, she won't know what to assess in terms of outcomes later. But also because a great deal of assessment isn't about outcomes at all: it's about strengthening the creative process through clarification and reflection.

But now that she's done this clarification and reflection, Fatou directly addresses the question of:

How will I know if it works?

Fatou begins this evaluative state of the process by coming up with ways she can assess whether her project does what she set out to do, asking:

How will I know if my project is a success?

Her first step is to think back to her *activist goal* to create a beautiful Conakry, her *artistic aim* to create a project that makes people feel they can do something about social problems, and her *concrete objective* of mobilizing people to clean up a local beach within three months. She asks herself: "If everything goes amazingly well with my project, if it is a grand success, how will I know?" She'll know if it's succeeded, she decides, because, quite simply, the beach will be clean. Not only will this make Conakry more beautiful, but people will get a sense of civic and creative empowerment because they cleaned it themselves and erected a public sculpture together.

Fatou is excited by her vision of success, but quickly wonders how she'll know whether any of what she wants to happen will actually happen. Moving from wishful thinking to empirical evidence means measuring impact, and she knows that, in order to do this, she'll need some tools. As a guide, Fatou asks herself two questions:

What evaluation tools will I use to know if my project is a success? What can I learn from each of these tools?
Fatou knows from her university classes that social scientists have devised ways to measure impact — documentation, observation, interviews, surveys, focus groups, publicity analysis — but Fatou doesn't want to limit herself to only these traditional tools. She knows of artistic activists who have created "comment walls" so their audiences can write out their thoughts and feelings. Others have concluded their interventions with speak-out sessions to solicit feedback, facilitated a call and response to voice division or unity, and built interactive props into their intervention that measure public opinion. She considers all the traditional and creative ways of accounting for impact that she's learned and does some further research. She asks for advice from friends and teachers, brainstorms a bit, and comes up with a set of tools she thinks can help measure the success of her project. She jots these down, and what she hopes to learn from each, in her notebook:

> *Documentation:* taking before and after pictures of the beach, to provide visual evidence of everyday people making a more beautiful city.

> *Observation:* watching people participate and interact with my intervention, to discover how people interact and participate.

> *Spot Interviews:* talking to people who are helping with my intervention, to tell me how people are feeling about what they are doing.

Fatou knows that these tools will help her know — in general — whether her project is doing what she hopes it will do. But she also wants to go deeper, to discover whether her intervention is engaging her particular audiences in the ways that she wants. For this, she needs to ask the question for each of her audiences:

How will I know if I've engaged my audience?

From these answers, she will come up with ways to measure whether she's done this. Fatou begins with her *primary audience* of everyday people of Conakry. She thinks a bit, and concludes that she'll know if she's successfully engaged this audience if enough people of Conakry, from all walks of life, show up and participate in her intervention. Fatou considers tools that might help her know whether this happens and writes down the following:

> *Documentation*: photos and videos of building the statue, to have a visual record of the process of people's participation.

> *Observation*: counting the number of people who come to work on my intervention, to determine how many people participated.

> *Interviews*: asking people why they are participating, to know what people are thinking and feeling.

> *A Visual Comment Wall*: providing a space for free expression, to capture and display how people imagine a beautiful Conakry themselves.

Fatou turns to her other audiences and asks herself the same series of questions: *How will I know if I've engaged my audience? What evaluation tools will I use? What can I learn from these?* Starting with her *secondary audiences* of politicians and the news media, she figures that she'll know whether she's engaged them because politicians will attend the opening of the project and the news media will show up and report on the event. With this in mind, she comes up with some tools that might provide some evidence:

> *Observation*: of politicians and the news media, to know who and how many news outlets and politicians showed up.

> *Documentation*: of media hits, to show how many times the event was mentioned in the news.

> *Publicity Analysis*: of the news coverage, to determine the quality and tone of the news coverage. Was it positive, negative, sensational, or

dismissive? Did they mention the larger issues of social services and corruption?

When it comes time to think about how she'll know if she's engaged her *unintended audience* of sanitation workers in the way that she hopes, Fatou concludes that the best indication will be the lack of one: sanitation workers will not disrupt her project. To know whether this has (not) happened, she decides to use:

> *Interviews*: of sanitation workers before the event, to learn something about how sanitation workers feel about the garbage problem, their jobs, and my project so I might better understand their concerns and assuage some of their fears.

> *Observation*: of the crowd during the event, to note and record any disruptive elements that might have a negative impact on my project.

By this time, Fatou has a good idea of what evaluation tools she'll use to evaluate the impact of her project, but now she has to put it all together. After a coffee and croissant break she asks herself:

What is my evaluation plan?

Fatou thinks about what she has the time and talents to do, and quickly realizes that she'll need help. She wants to concentrate on the creative side of things on the day of her action, so she'll need others to help her with the actual measures. First, she'll need someone to take pictures and videos for documentation. She has a good friend, a film-maker named Bilal, who has helped her in the past with this, so she decides to ask him to come. Then she realizes that she needs people to observe the action: recording who shows up and what they do. The professor who taught her research methods at the university might be able to convince some of her students to help, so she decides to ask her. Fatou thinks she can also ask these students to do some spot interviews. She figures she'll need to work with them beforehand to let them know what she is looking for, and maybe even design a simple observation form with her professor friend so they can easily record their observations. She'll also need to come up with a short interview script — only three or four questions — for the spot interviews.

The comment wall Fatou is planning is based upon some of the works of the U.S. artistic activist Candy Chang. She's impressed by the simplicity of them and plans on using a similar form: just a black wall, with a white question above, and a box of chalk for people to write or draw in their responses. She did a little scouting of the area and noticed the breakwater walls will work nicely for this.

Interviewing the sanitation workers before the action is definitely something she can do herself, Fatou decides, as well as recording and assessing the news coverage after the action. But she'll also ask Bilal to help her with the analyses of the TV news because he has a good eye for visual communications.

With all her advance planning done, Fatou gets busy with the on-the-ground work of her project. Periodically, she checks back in with her goals and objectives, and her audiences and ethics. As things change, she adapts. It turns out that the public beach where she was planning her action had been sold to private developers — another instance of corruption — and she has to find a new location. But finally, all the pieces come together, and on a beautiful, sunny day in late February, people show up, a public beach is cleared, a trash elephant is built, and Conakry is just a little bit more beautiful.

After taking a week off to rest and recover, Fatou is ready to address the *big* question:

Did it work?
To begin to answer this daunting question, she asks herself a simpler one:

What happened?
Fatou thinks back to the day on the beach, looks over the documentation, and writes up a description of what took place in her project notebook:

> The day began at 10:00 with me and my team of friends at the beach waiting for people to show up. For the first half-hour, no one did. Then a bunch of artists from La Muse, a local art space, turned up, bringing with them a locally famous comedian. Soon after, a group of school kids in uniforms arrived, led by their teacher. Some activists I met while doing a project with OSIWA (Open Society Initiative for West Africa) walked up, members of an environmental club came together, and a handful of individuals wandered in — including the foreman of one of the sanitation crews with his teenage daughter!

We all sat in a big circle and I explained the project and its goals. I unrolled a large picture of an elephant as a guide and hung up blank sheets of paper on the breakwater walls. For the next hour we brainstormed how best to build the elephant with the artists from La Muse and the sanitation worker offering their technical skills. The kids volunteered to start collecting trash, directed by the environmental club who brought with them huge bags to hold the garbage. And I recruited an artist I know to paint one of the breakwater walls black, and then paint in white letters across the top: "What Would a Beautiful Conakry Look Like To You?"

Over the next couple hours, people set to work cleaning the beach and making a big garbage pile. Working with the artists from La Muse we started assembling the garbage in the form of an elephant. My experience as a sculptor taught me about the importance of a strong armature, so I had brought materials to build this. We were struggling with attaching the garbage to the armature until the daughter of the guy from the sanitation company suggested we fashion ropes from the ubiquitous discarded plastic bags to tie things in place. It worked brilliantly.

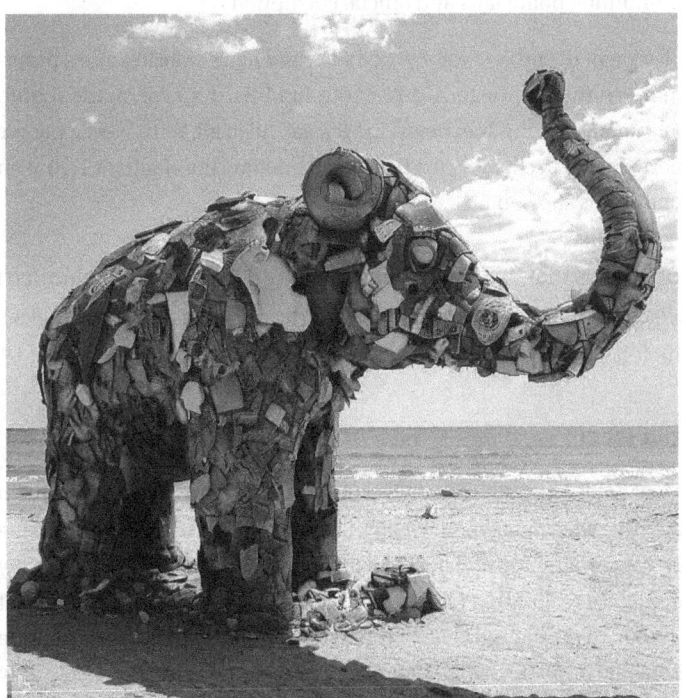

Building an elephant from beach garbage, courtesy of AI assisted imagination.

Around noon, we stopped for lunch of konkoé turé gbéli (smoked catfish stew) and cassava fufu donated by one of the restaurants that overlook the beach, and a few musician friends came by to play drums. Then back to work. As the garbage pile grew, so did the elephant, and the beach got cleaner. Even some street kids got into picking up garbage and putting it on the sculpture. Every once in a while someone would wander over to the comment wall and draw or write something about their vision for a beautiful Conakry.

A reporter for the local paper stopped by and interviewed me. I told him to interview some of the other folks helping out and he did. By 15:00 the beach was almost clear, and by 17:00 the elephant was done. It was a bit scraggly looking but at four meters tall, bigger than a real elephant. A TV crew showed up and a few reporters from local radio and news websites too. Photographers shot pictures of people picking up garbage and of the comment wall. We staged a press conference in front of the elephant where I explained the purpose behind the project, what the intervention signified, and a chorus of kids talked about creating a new, cleaner Conakry. The comedian did a funny bit on camera about do-nothing politicians and official corruption.

That night the project was on TV, radio, and news websites and a prominent Guinean blogger wrote about it. I heard it even made it onto *Journal Rappé*, the "rap news" in Senegal. All in all, thirty-seven people participated in cleaning the beach and building the elephant, . . . but no politicians showed up.

Fatou knows that, by recalling our feelings, we sometimes notice things otherwise left out of more matter-of-fact descriptions, so she checks in with how she felt during and after the event, asking herself:

What did I feel?

Most of all I feel exhausted! But also really happy. It's hard for me to describe what made me so happy, but when I think of those kids picking up the garbage and making something beautiful, it brings a smile to my lips. I also realize that I feel proud. When I looked back at the beach at the end of the day, all clean, I was overwhelmed with a feeling of pride in what Guineans were able to accomplish together. I'm also pretty proud of myself for pulling this whole thing off.

Most things went — more or less — according to plan. But, of course, not everything. Fatou knows from her experience as an artistic activist to expect the unexpected, and how to learn from it, letting surprises — whether happy wonders or unpleasant blows — teach her new ways to approach her projects and her practice. So she he asks herself:

What surprised me?

> I was surprised by a few things. First, who showed up. I cast my net wide with my main audience being "everyday people," but who ended up coming, for the most part, were people already organized in groups: a school class, an environmental group, activists from an NGO, and the artists from La Muse. Second, I was surprised by how amazing the kids were. Not only as participants in picking up the garbage and making the elephant, but how eloquent they were at the press conference. My *unintended audience* of angry sanitation workers turned out not to be a problem at all — in fact, one even showed up with his daughter to help out, and now she wants to train with me to become an artist! Finally, I was surprised (actually, more confirmed in my disappointment) that no politicians or government officials showed up, even after I spent so much time inviting them and following up with their staff. Several promised, but none came.

With her broad descriptions done, Fatou digs into the evaluation, starting with her audiences, since the impact upon them will largely determine the social impact of her project. She asks herself:

How do I know if I've engaged my primary audience?

Reviewing all the information she gathered from counting participants, doing spot interviews and documentation, talking to friends who were there as informal participant-observers, and looking over her initial description, she concludes that she engaged her *primary audience* because thirty-seven people showed up and that was enough to clean the beach and build the elephant. However, Fatou also realized that "everyday people" was way too vague. Who really showed up were folks who were part of organizations: schools, clubs, NGOs, and cultural centers.

A quick count lets Fatou know how many people were "engaged" well enough to show up. But she is well aware that counting participants is low-hanging-fruit; equally or more important is what they were thinking, feeling, and doing. This is why Fatou asks herself the questions:

What was my audience thinking? feeling? doing?
and
How do I know this?

Fatou talked to people the day of the action and later listened to the interviews that were recorded by the students. Participants said things like, "It is great to see what the power of people can do" and "Conakry doesn't need these corrupt politicians; they just need more people doing things like this," so Fatou has a general idea that this audience was *thinking* they were doing something really empowering. Reviewing the video and photographic documentation of the intervention gives Fatou a sense of what people might have been *feeling*. Several people who were interviewed by the reporters said how proud they were to do something to make the city better, and Fatou observed another feeling: Fun! She knew people were having fun because they had big smiles on their faces. As for what her audience was *doing*, her documentation of the event demonstrated that, most obviously, they were cleaning up the beach, but also that they were creating collaboratively. The comment wall also expressed people's creativity in how they imagined and envisioned a beautiful Conakry.

What Fatou doesn't know, she realizes, is whether there will be any follow-up action on the part of the people involved and whether they will stay involved in the issue. She heard through the grapevine that a few folks from the intervention joined the environmental club whose members showed up. But because she never took down a list of the names and contact information of all the people who participated, she has no easy way of tracking them down and asking what they are up to now. Next time, she promises herself, she'll do this.

Fatou had two *secondary audiences* in mind: the news media and politicians. She considers the students' observation notes and the documentation of the event, as well as the media coverage and reports, and concludes she successfully engaged her news audience because she spotted a TV crew, as well as two reporters from news websites and another from a local news radio. A political blogger she talked to when was planning the event must have been there too, because she later saw her post about the event. The TV and radio news coverage were positive, with the kids doing a great job being spokespeople. Of the two news website reports that made it online, one was very positive, and the other was good but a bit snarky — making reference to the fact that Fatou once received funding from George Soros's Open Society Foundations before launching into a full-blown conspiracy theory. The blog report was terrific, however, and really explained her project and its goals.

That her audience of politicians didn't show up was no real surprise to Fatou, but what was surprising was what happened with her *unintended audience* of sanitation workers. Not only didn't any sanitation workers show up to disrupt anything, but the opposite happened. The foreman she talked to earlier to explain her project came with his daughter to help out with the intervention, and now Fatou's mentoring her to be an artist. Furthermore, Fatou knows from her interviews with sanitation workers before the intervention that not only did they not perceive her project as a threat, but they actually thought that the intervention was a good idea to draw attention to the problem of garbage collection in the city.

Done with the evaluation of her audiences Fatou turns to ethics, assessing how the project conformed to her ethical code by asking:

Did my creative process and product follow my ethical code?
Thinking back upon her project and all the work that led up to it, Fatou concludes that, for the most part, she followed the values she inscribed in her ethical code: honesty; autonomy; community; collaboration; caring for city, country, and continent; honoring nature; helping others to create and learning from others; and valuing tradition while celebrating innovation. She did this by creating a collaborative project that addressed the real problems of Conakry and the region, like garbage, civic empowerment, and the natural environment. She used a symbol — the elephant — that has meaning in the country and to the local community, and she didn't bend her project to the interests of the powers that be. Finally, Fatou concludes, she created an intervention that tried to take into account the skills and creativity of all the participants.

But Fatou also knows that, no matter how hard we try or what good people we are, we inevitably fall short when it comes to applying our moral code. We are human, after all, so she also asks herself:

How did my creative process and product fall short of my ethical code?

Thinking back, she realizes that there were places where she fell short, or was simply blind to some ethical considerations. For example, her project fell short of her ethical code by not reaching out earlier to the many interested communities already in existence — in schools, in artist centers, in civic and ecology clubs — for their input and wisdom in advance. Because of this oversight, it was pretty much *her* project and *her* intervention. As much as she tried to create opportunities for people to participate, she has to acknowledge that her project was not as truly collaborative as it could have been. After beating herself up a bit for not being the beacon of moral virtue she aspires to be, she admits to herself that she succeeded in following her code more often than not.

Fatou has been able to assess a lot of the immediate impact of her project: the public participation, a cleaner beach, publicity about her issue, and even things she did not expect: like finding a mentee in the sanitation worker's daughter. But her goal is so much bigger: creating a beautiful Conakry, and this is something that can't be accomplished in just one day. She wonders:

What might be the long-term æffects of my project?
and
How might I evaluate these?

Fatou knows she is a long, long way off before Conakry is the image of beauty she has in her mind, but she also truly believes that her project might have nudged things in the right direction. She hopes that the people in Conakry who worked on her project, or were even inspired by seeing or hearing about it secondhand, will realize they can do something on their own to make the city more beautiful. Fatou figures she might assess whether this actually happens by noticing whether other citizen-led initiatives happen in the future to better the city and its natural environment. By interviewing leaders of those projects, Fatou could find out whether any of them took part in or were inspired by her project, and this might demonstrate at least one of its long-term æffects.

To conclude the assessment of her project Fatou considers her original intent, the *artistic aims*, *activist goals*, and *concrete* objectives she began with, asking herself:

Given my original objective, aims and goals, how does the outcome compare to my intent?

Fatou looks over her notes, thinks a bit about her original objective — mobilizing people to clean up a local beach within three months — and concludes that, compared to her intentions, the project's outcome was mostly on target. She succeeded in getting people from Conakry to clean the beach, and her project from start to finish took only ten weeks. She realizes now, however, that she left out a really important aspect in her original objective: having people create something beautiful with the garbage they picked up. This creative empowerment turned out to be as important as picking up the beach.

Fatou widens her scope to reflect upon her *artistic aims* and *activist goals*. Her *artistic aim* was to create a project that "helps people to feel as if they can do something about large social problems like garbage and corruption," and her outcome was pretty close to her intention. She succeeded in mobilizing people to create a sculpture built of trash they picked up from the beach. In this, she was able to use her art to draw attention to the garbage problem and get people to feel they could do something about social issues by actually doing something — if only a little something — to better their environment on their own.

Fatou's *activist goal* was "to create a beautiful Conakry." It was ambitious, a bit utopian, and unsurprisingly, not realized...yet. Compared to her intention, the outcome of her project was definitely in the right direction, but Fatou is honest enough with herself to recognize that she still has a long way to go. She created a community art project that succeeded in mobilizing thirty-seven residents of the city to clean up a beach. She organized their creativity to turn all that garbage into something really beautiful: a garbage elephant. And she got pretty good publicity about the intervention and about the problems of garbage collection in the city too. All of this is great. But walking by the beach just yesterday, Fatou noticed there are already plastic bags and bottles and other garbage washed up on shore. On her walk there, she passed open sewers running at the side of the street and piles of garbage that looked like they hadn't been picked up in weeks. The sight of kids out in the street with no jobs and no schooling depressed her too. And she just heard the head of public works for Conakry went to Paris for a shopping trip. All this makes Fatou realize there are lots of other kinds of ugliness in Conakry that need to be cleaned up for her city to become truly beautiful.

This honest assessment of her accomplishments and the realization of all that remains to do are a bit depressing. But, looking back at her project, Fatou recognizes all the ways in which her project did have an impact. So, instead of getting depressed and giving up, her mind turns toward:

What do I do next?

Through experience, Fatou knows that one of the frustrations of the creative process is that it's often not until the end of your project that you realize what you might have done better. But one of the joys of the creative process is that there's always a chance to do it over, and do it differently. Creativity, she knows, is all about *iteration,* so she asks herself:

Knowing what I know now, how might I change my project?

Fatou takes out her notebook again, gives it some thought, and then lists what she might do differently next time. If she were to do her project again, she would:

> Target sympathetic groups of people to help, not just put out a general call to "everyday people."
>
> Integrate participants into the creative process much earlier so the project is truly a collaboration and participants have more creative ownership.
>
> Find more people who could interview more participants on the day of the action.
>
> Do more prep work for the press. The press conference at the end worked, but it was mainly the kids who saved me. There should have been press releases, press packets, quotes, and so on all ready to go.
>
> Figure out a better way to approach or confront politicians and officials who are responsible for sanitation policy and garbage collection.
>
> Plan a follow-up fun event with everyone who participated to help create a lasting community.

Fatou knows her goal of a beautiful Conakry is far out on the horizon, but it's a goal she holds dear and wants to devote her skills and passions as an artistic activist to make happen. Her experience with her past project taught her that she'll need to come up with other projects, over a longer period of time, in order to help her reach her utopia. So she turns to the future with a question of:

What comes next?
Fatou answers with:

> I realize, that in order to create a "beautiful Conakry," I'll need to develop other projects that look wider and take on the rampant corruption that siphons money out of the country so there are no resources for public works and social services. It's exciting to think of all the projects I can do to address these issues, but also daunting to take it on by myself, so I think it's time to start collaborating with others — the artists from La Muse, the school kids, civic advocacy groups, the NGO activists — in order to do all I want to do. My goal still seems far, far away, but thinking about it step by step makes it easier to reach.

Hopefully, this hypothetical example provides a picture of how a typical planning and evaluation process using the æffect assessment method might work. But reality is rarely typical. The method is contingent upon the context of its application and meant as a model for thinking, rather than a pattern to be followed exactly. In this hypothetical case, the artistic activist posed an extended script of questions to herself, essentially being her own conversation partner. In other cases, an outside evaluator, sympathetic program officer, or dedicated friend could act the part of the interlocutor. In this case, the artistic activist went through *all* the questions of the script you'll find in the appendix, but she could just as easily have skipped some, and expanded upon others. This method is meant to be malleable. Alterations are encouraged, and as you will see in the case studies that follow, they are essential.

The Æffect Assessment Method in Practice

What follows are four examples of the real-world application of this methodology. One is with an accomplished artist, another with an advocacy organization, a third with a group of young artistic activists, and a fourth with an experienced group who are mentoring the artistic activism of others. Their social concerns range from human rights, to criminal justice, to economic development for youth, to potholes. Two examples are from the United States, one is from West Africa, and one is from the Western Balkans. In some instances the æffect assessment method is being applied at the beginning of a project, in others it's being used to tweak ones that are more fully developed. The point of sharing these stories is to demonstrate the different ways that this methodology can be adapted and adopted for different needs, in different places, and for different situations. None are ideal; all are real.

Accra, Ghana

It's the end of a five-day Center for Artistic Activism "art action academy" working with young artists from across West Africa: Ghana, Senegal, Burkina Faso, Sierra Leone, and the Congo. The group was brought together by an international NGO interested in developing a cadre of artistic activists to work on youth political engagement. As is our custom, the training workshop ends with a real-world intervention in order to put the ideas we have learned into action. In preparation for the intervention, we lead the group — in English and French — through the series of assessment questions.

The overall goal of youth political engagement has been set by the organization, but our discussion of objectives gives it a focus: developing "a program where young people learn / take action / volunteer / lead artistic activism." Our group is deeply concerned by the lack of economic development in the region that leads to a deficit of jobs for young people, which then results in "brain drain" as people leave West Africa to look for work elsewhere. As we discuss the issue, another even more specific objective is offered up: pressuring "government to implement and fund a youth employment program in one year."

With the *effect* we want identified, we turn to *affect*. What sort of feelings do we want our project to generate? A long list is generated, but responses seem to fall into two camps: hope and curiosity. Hope that something can be done about the problems of lack of jobs for youth. But also curiosity: a sense of wonder that will lead to asking questions and interest in our intervention and the larger social issues it addresses.

But who is our audience? We brainstorm possibilities. These range from the specific, such as "the Ministry of Youth," to the general, like "the Patriarchy." In order to narrow the field, we discuss who has the power to make change. We decide that this power ultimately lies with the youth themselves. If the youth are mobilized, they can then direct their power at the government officials who can make policies and programs. In the discussion, someone points out that access to those politicians is often through the media. With this, we have identified our primary (youth) and secondary (politicians, media) audiences. Raising the prospect of our *unintended audience* triggers a lively discussion with an equally wide range of possibilities, but for the purposes of this test action, we decide upon two: the police, who might disrupt the action, and "the grouchy market lady" who thinks we are wasting her time and intimidating her customers.

Recalling our activist goal, artistic aims, and concrete objectives, we run through what we want our Primary Audience of youth to *think, feel,* and *do*:

> *Think*: Link their unemployment to governmental corruption and inaction.

> *Feel*: Hopeful that they can do something.

> *Do:* Speak out on the issue, engage in conversations with others in their community, and ultimately be moved to become involved in a network of artistic activists.

Finally, we talk about ethics, both in the abstract (What are the group's ethical values?) and the concrete (How will they apply them in their intervention?). High on the list of values is respecting the local cultures in which we work and including the community in the project in all possible ways. There is also a commitment to nonviolence and inclusion — particularly gender inclusion. When prompted to reflect upon how they might apply this ethical code to whatever artistic action they might create, they propose choosing languages (including cultural codes) that local people understand, ensuring that women have leading roles in the planning of the intervention, and being conscious of who is selected to be at the front of the action. The group also suggests we have observers specifically assigned to watch and notice these things.

It's been more than an hour of just talking, and we need a creative break. So the group is broken up into two teams based on common language, and each is given a brief amount of time to create a rough sketch of an artistic activist intervention, while keeping in mind all we have just discussed. After forty-five minutes, the groups come back together and perform for one another. While one group performs, the other forms "the audience" — all of which have been given a certain role based upon the audiences we selected earlier, and from whose vantage point they are asked to view the action. Some are youth, others are media and politicians, and still others are given the roles of police or grouchy market women.

The English Team, as they call themselves, develop an "artful" performance in which one of the team members falls to the ground and, like a human snake, slithers their way below and through the legs of an assembled row of chairs upon which the audience is seated. The audience is then "forced" to make a decision. They can aid or impede the person's journey by moving their chair, ... or they can do nothing. The French-speaking team, self-named Équipe Français, on the other hand, act out a silent but realistic scene that dramatizes the application process for a travel visa, illustrating all of the complications that official corruption brings into the process. In this performance, the protagonist rallies the other people waiting with their luggage to protest in an impromptu sit-down strike until their demands are met.

After each action, the "audiences" are asked to react. Most agree that the first performance was beautiful, interactive, and affective, but also a bit hard to understand when it came to its social message. This is seen as a detriment to most of the audience members — though a possible advantage in confusing the police. The second intervention is easier to understand in terms of its activist message, but maybe too much so: it doesn't inspire curiosity, and it also doesn't ask for any audience engagement. (The grouchy market women despise both.) With this information in hand, the assembled group decides to merge the two actions and come up with a hybrid that will keep the mystery of the human snake, yet have a more didactic political message that's easier to understand. A mix of affect and effect.

Once we decide upon the action, we do a quick check against what we had originally decided upon as our activist goals and our artistic aims, our audiences, and our ethics, and with a few tweaks, decide that the new hybrid intervention conforms to our intentions — at least enough for a test action. Then it's time to discuss metrics. How will we know whether we have succeeded in doing any of these things we set out to do? We are limited by the time we have to work within (less than twenty-four hours), but quickly assign two members of the group to be observers, writing notes on who stopped and watched, who participated and in what ways, as well as the gender dynamics and inclusion of the group and the intervention. These observers will also double as interviewers, conducting spot interviews with passersby they notice who engage with, or ignore, the performance.

These observations and interviews will provide solid data we might analyze later. But far more interesting than these standard measurement "tools" are the creative ideas devised for how measurements might be built into the action. These include:

- A call and response, where the audience will be asked to respond according to where they stand on the issue, both before and after the action.
- A canvas where people can place their handprint if they agree/disagree with the issue.
- A comment wall for participants to share what they *think* and *feel*.
- Using Post-its or sheets of paper for people to write what they are thinking or feeling about the issue.
- A speak-out session at the end of the action, where the audience can take the stage and voice their opinions.

The next morning, we all venture out to Jamestown, a historic working-class neighborhood on the shores of the Atlantic Ocean. In the shadow of a landmark lighthouse and near a youth center, the group performs their intervention. It begins with a game of copycat rhythmic clapping to gather people in the surrounding area and get them curious and engaged in our performance. Once this happens, the group forms a tunnel with legs spread apart and the "human snake" struggles through this tunnel. People in the audience are encouraged to spread their legs and join the line to help or hinder the snake's progress. A pantomime then follows in which artistic activists play the role of unemployed young people who are planning to leave the country. As they march toward an (imaginary) authorities' office they are led in a song — "Fight Against Corruption" — by a member of our group who is an accomplished reggae singer in her home country of Sierra Leone. The marchers, followed by their youthful audience, confront the corrupt official until he backs down and acquiesces to their demands. After the performance and the song, members of the group launch a public discussion with the audience. They announce who they are, what the performance is about, and talk about the politics of unemployment and corruption. Audience members are then invited up to the front to share their response to the intervention and issue. After about an hour, we pack up and sit in a big ring in front of the youth center and reflect upon what just happened.

We go around the circle sharing what we noticed and felt, including what surprised us. The biggest surprise was the most noticeable. We prepared the intervention to engage teenagers and most of our audience turned out to be young children between the ages of six to ten. Because of this, some of the complicated political messaging was dropped or radically simplified on the fly, and it's unclear how much was actually understood by the children who assembled. Since the audience was so young and lacked proficiency with writing, the sheets of paper that had been prepared for people to write out their thoughts and feelings were also useless. And because of the preponderance of young people, the few teenagers in the vicinity tended to keep their distance, not wanting to be part of something identified as meant for children. As such, one of our objectives — recruiting audience members into a larger group of artistic activists — was patently not met.

On a more technical level, the group reflects how the introductory exercise was very good at attracting and engaging young people, but that the main performances were less successful in communicating their social message. Still, participants notice that, during the speak-out session at the end, several of the youngsters — one young boy in particular — had a pretty good grasp on what was going on in the performance and how it represented the struggles of youth in West Africa. The group also recognizes that what had seemed well coordinated in the rehearsals was, understandably, harder to pull off on site. The official observers then share their observations and what they learned from interviewing passersby, essentially mirroring the observations of the participants but also noticing things like the wide smiles and joyful expressions of children as they participated, the mystification of a (not so grouchy) woman on her way to the market who did not understand what the action was about, and another pair of adults who mistook the theatrical miming and clapping for a performance by deaf and mute people.

Finally, we go around the circle again to ask what we had learned that we might apply to other interventions, or future iterations of this one. People respond that:

- We have to choose the right place, and need better scouting to do this. This type of performance should have been done at the market square or around a high school.
- We should have different versions of our action that will suit the audience as back-up plans.
- Most of our physical gestures were small and limited and we should make our actions bigger and exaggerated so they can be seen from afar.
- Since a lot of time was spent on the introductory game, and not as much on the performances that carried the political messages, time management of the intervention should be improved.
- The rest of the performance should be as captivating as the introductory game.

This was a test intervention. Its intent was less to have an impact on the external audiences and political objectives identified, and more to practice putting ideas into action, building reflection and evaluation and bringing the group together. In this, the intervention was a "success." The participants probably learned the most important lesson of all in planning artistic activist interventions: expect the unexpected. You plan to engage teenagers in a serious discussion about their immediate futures, and you get a bunch of small kids who want to play games. Then you learn from it all, and go out and do it again.

As of this writing, members of this group have carried out five more artistic actions across West Africa, using the æffect assessment method both to plan and to evaluate the impact of their interventions. They also integrated the method into a curriculum they developed to train others to become artistic activists. In the process they tweaked its content and changed its form, adapting the æffect assessment method to fit their experiences, needs, and contexts.

New York City, USA

A founder and director of a global nonprofit advocacy organization comes to my university office to discuss a creative project she is planning on launching in New York City. Her organization is committed to sharing the stories of people who speak out and act up for the rights and lives of others different from themselves. These stories of "protectors," as the organization calls them, include a London-based Jewish patrol formed to combat anti-Semitism that also guards Muslim mosques against attacks, two undocumented immigrants from Mexico who volunteered to save flood victims in Texas and perished in the effort, and Syrian refugees who became unpaid search-and-rescue workers within weeks of arriving in their host country of Australia. The advocacy organization hopes stories like these will break down the walls people construct against the so-called Other, as well as inspire people to act in similar selfless ways. In the past two years, they have organized over one hundred events in twenty-five cities, in schools, on the streets, and even at the United Nations. Their new project in New York involves setting up five temporary monuments recognizing five "protectors." They want to use the public spectacle to attract people, and then further engage these spectators through various activities like story-telling, gift-giving, and signing a pledge to become protectors themselves.

As we begin talking, it becomes very clear that this project has been well thought out through by a seasoned professional. She moves rapidly through my questions on *activist goals, artistic aims,* and *concrete objectives,* answering them in quick, fully articulated sentences. She already has her main audiences: "haters," whom she hopes to change, and "nice people who don't know what to do," whom she hopes to give direction. She rattles off what she wants these audiences to *think, feel,* and *do.* When we get to measurements, she is way ahead of me: listing demonstrable, and for the most part quantifiable actions: number of people who share stories, take pictures, send tweets, visit the website, or pledge to be a protector. At this point in this process, I am wondering what I might possibly offer. But then, as we are checking the planned action back against the intentions she has laid out for her audiences, we notice a crack in her otherwise seamless plan.

The main action is a series of public monuments across the city. These will make a striking visual spectacle for passersby and the news media (a *secondary audience* she mentions). But upon reflection, we realize that the very thing that makes this intervention affective as a spectacle may also limit its capacity to move her audiences to the sorts of "doing" she desires. Simply put: her artistic activism asks people to watch, but has no mechanism to move people to actually *do* anything. We imagine a large crowd assembling, feeling some sort of admiration for these heroes and nodding their heads in agreement as they confirm their "nice" thoughts or challenge their "hater" attitudes. We also imagine this same crowd then walking away from the intervention feeling they had done their part as spectators, never engaging in the activities the organizers had planned. It's the old Aristotelian problem of catharsis.

We use this "problem" to brainstorm. I share the ideas of Augusto Boal, and how he demanded that his audiences become "spect-actors" who take an active part in what is happening on stage. This reminds her that role-playing was an integral part of their previous workshops and that they already have a downloadable "tool kit" with instructions for how to actively engage a public audience. We then launch into a conversation about how to transform the monument from being just a sight to see into an opportunity for the audience to role-play what it is like to be someone who acts or is acted upon — making the intervention, as Boal might put it: "a rehearsal for the revolution."

Moving forward again, we notice something else: all the measurements they had planned are both immediate, such as something recorded the day of the action or soon after, and refer back to the intervention itself — documenting it, spreading the message, and so on. What was missing was a way to measure the most important impact of the entire project: whether it moved people to stand up for others unlike themselves. Gauging long-term impact is very hard to do, but this project — with a little tweaking — already had a way to accomplish this built into it: the pledge to be a protector. When people sign the pledge, they could also be asked for a way to be contacted. Then, at regular intervals — after the first week, then maybe once a month or so following — they might be sent a simple message asking: What had they done as a protector? And how might we help you to become a protector? This message would serve multiple functions: (1) as a (slightly guilt-inducing) reminder that they had pledged to do something; (2) a way to offer support and resources; and (3) a source of new protector stories to be shared on the organization's website; finally, (4) provide useful data in accounting for the success of the original intervention.

Although the æffect assessment method is meant to begin before even conceptualizing a project, and designed primarily as an aid for artistic activists who may have never considered things like "concrete objectives" and "secondary audiences," it was still useful in this case. With a project that had been thought through exceedingly well by a person with a great deal of experience and expertise in planning such creative interventions, the method worked as a sort of final check-in. The assessment forced attention on areas that had been previously overlooked, asked questions that had not been initially asked, and exposed potential weaknesses in the project. Most importantly, it created an opportunity to imagine solutions to the problems identified, resulting in a stronger project.

Tetovo, North Macedonia
We are sitting in a circle, sipping strong coffee at a slightly dilapidated outdoor cafe by a beautiful stream on a cool spring day after having just pulled off an artistic activist intervention nearby. It was the first action of a collaboration between the Skopje-based Macedonian Creative Action Team (MCAT) and local artists and activists in Tetovo, a city near the Albanian border. To draw attention to the lack of public services provided by the municipal government, the artistic activists erected a life-sized metal outline of the popular cartoon character from *La Linea* overlooking a washed-out section of a road that, despite repeated accidents, had not been fixed for years. (*La Linea* was an animated Italian cartoon popular throughout Europe in the 1970s and 1980s. The cartoon character travels along an extended line, encounters obstacles, and frequently yells at the cartoonist to fix the line so it can travel on.) Since the problem being highlighted is a journey jeopardized by a washout, and the population in the area is old enough to recall *La Linea*, it is a contextually clever intervention. In theory, at least.

We are gathered to reflect upon how the intervention worked in practice. In attendance are a half dozen members of the MCAT team, another half dozen of the Tetovo "trainees," two members of the funding organization, and two of us from the Center for Artistic Activism. We had not been able to meet with the artistic activists before the action, so we have to move backward before going forward, and ask — after the fact — what *had been* their *activist goals, artistic aims, concrete objectives, intended audiences,* and *ethical principles*. In the conversation that ensues, it becomes clear that the MCAT team and their local partners have an intuitive and astute understanding of what they wanted to do and who they wanted to impact. They wanted to create a public intervention that would be attractive and provocative enough to get media attention so as to embarrass the mayor and other local officials in order to pressure them to fix the road. In this way, their efforts seem to be working. One of the local Tetovo team, staring down at his smartphone, keeps a running commentary on the shares and retweets his social media posts are receiving and the number of media outlets picking up on the story of *La Linea* overlooking a washout.

It also becomes clear, however, that an open and extended discussion of the goals of the project had never been had in advance. The team was operating on instinct, and as experienced artistic activists who knew the political and cultural landscape, their instinct was good, but the process, or lack thereof, left a number of aspects of the intervention unexamined — and a number of the less experienced members of the Tetovo group felt left out. So, we start back at the beginning. In moving through basic questions already decided and acted upon, but never asked in the first place, we discover, together, some interesting things.

The first realization is that there are actually two goals of the project. The first is to call attention to corruption and bad public services in the region. We are on our way to achieving this one. But the second goal is to create an empowering and educational experience for the local team, most of whom had little history with artistic activism. By emphasizing the first goal but not thinking about the second, the MCAT group created a professionally crafted piece of artwork that looked great when picked up by the media. It worked, but it also sidelined the local group's input. Essentially, the MCATS created a project *for* the locals but not *with* them, relegating the local team to spectators of the action instead of participants.

The second discovery is about the audience. The *intended audiences* are politicians, who can solve the immediate objective of road repair, and the media — both mass and social — who can embarrass and pressure the politicians to act. When *La Linea* was being set up, however, a number of local residents came out to ask what was going on. This was an *unintended audience* that had not been given any thought to, and one that could have upended the project. If these neighbors objected to what we were doing, they could easily have prevented the group from erecting the piece or tore it down as soon as we left. Luckily, quick interviews done with residents revealed that they, too, were angry about the lack of road repair, appreciated the intervention, and recognized the character from *La Linea*.

Finally, in the course of discussion, one member of the local Tetovo group, a deeply religious Muslim woman (Tetovo, near the Albanian border, has a significant Muslim population), keeps returning to the theme of the relationship of the group and their mission to the local people, particularly those who are disenfranchised and feel themselves as outside of politics. Her language is not one of politics, but morality. As I confirm later in a conversation with her, she is concerned about the ethical code of the group and the application of their ethics to their actions. Or more to the point: she is concerned that the group has never discussed ethics or how to apply their ethics to their actions.

The reflection on goals, audiences, and ethics, even after the fact, prompts the group to think of what they will do differently in the future. They decide to plan more inclusive "learning" actions instead of "demonstration" ones. One of the MCAT team acknowledges during the conversation, "we should have included them [the Tetovo team] more." Next time, they also plan to canvas locals in order to get a read on their opinions, as well as create a simple flier that explains the intervention to passersby. In addition, the group thinks of ways to further engage their social-media audience by including simple suggested actions in their messaging. By asking people to call the mayor or call mayors in surrounding cities, they hope to move this mediated audience's "activity" from merely spreading the message to becoming activists themselves. Lastly, the young woman who spoke so passionately about morality takes it upon herself to introduce a discussion of ethics into every action planning.

As an evaluation, this was far from ideal: the action was already done and the questioning that could have made it a more æffective intervention happened after the fact. There was no discussion of what was to be measured and how best to measure it. Nor was any data gathered regarding impact other than counting news mentions and social-media shares and conducting a few impromptu interviews and informal observations. But we adapted the æffect assessment method to the setting: spending a great deal of time on clarifying goals and audiences, hinting at an ethical discussion the group might have in the future, and prompting the group to move past the "easy measures" of media mentions. The process wasn't perfect, and it wasn't always pretty — but it worked to push the group into thinking about what they might do differently next time.

Six months later the washout was finally fixed, but the local group had fallen apart. The MCAT team, however, applied the lessons they learned in Tetovo to their work on another project in the North Macedonian city of Štip. Here they settled on a much simpler intervention that did not rely upon their expertise and could be done quickly by the local group. To draw attention to a two-year-old, water-filled pothole in front of a school, they decided — through a collective brainstorming session — to create a duck pond. Bright yellow plastic yellow ducks were purchased and by day's end were floating in the pothole. Pictures of the duck pond make it onto social media and were picked up by the local news, and three days later embarrassed officials repaired the pothole. The Štip group, their morale boosted, stayed together and began planning future interventions.

New York City, USA

I am sitting at a table in the conference room of one of the leading funding and support organizations for artistic activists in the United States. Across the table from me is a well-known artist whose last intervention was staged in the lobby of the Guggenheim Museum. He has been selected as one of the organization's fellows and will receive money and support to restage and expand the project he did at the Guggenheim. The conditions of the fellowship stipulate that there be an evaluator attached to the project. That's me. The artist knows this evaluation is stipulated and seemed amenable to the idea in the email exchanges that led up to this meeting, but *I* can't help wondering whether *he* is wondering about the utility of evaluating a project that has already proven successful in its debut at, of all places, the world-famous Guggenheim.

Putting my doubts aside, I begin. I ask him to describe his project as he would to an old friend whom he has just run into while waiting in line to order at a food truck — in other words, keep it short and nontechnical. He describes a performance project meant to facilitate communication and connection between people from ostensibly warring camps. The project is modeled on a Roman Empire-era sporting event from Florence, Italy, wherein men from the four corners of the city meet and battle one another. In his version, however, it is four "teams" of ideological opponents who meet on the field of battle. The artist explains his artistic activist goal to me. Words too often get in the way of communication, he contends. Hunkered down in our arguments, we ignore who it is we are speaking with, or more accurately, speaking at. By staging a mock battle where opponents cannot speak, but only observe and mirror the bodily gestures of their "opponents," the artist believes that the participants will recognize and respect the basic humanity of those "opponents" and, through this experience, forge a radical empathy.

The Guggenheim event brought together four groups with four different positions on guns. For this staging, the artist, who has worked for years as an arts educator within the criminal justice system, wants to bring together four groups of people enmeshed within this system who almost never communicate with one another: victims of crime, correctional officers, legal activists, and the formerly incarcerated. Over the course of several months, he will train each group through workshops, teaching them to use their bodies as a means of expression and reception. After this training they will "battle." As this is the second run of the performance, most of the more artistic details of the look and feel of the performance have already been sorted. The overall goal of creating the conditions for radical empathy also remains the same. So we concentrate on objectives: the concrete results he wants.

His first objective is to improve communications between these four groups of "stakeholders" in the criminal justice system. This is not a big departure from the Guggenheim project: just a different cast of characters. Through conversation, however, it becomes clear that, this time around, there's an additional objective. The artist wants to demonstrate to local governmental officials — particularly those in the New York City Mayor's Office of Criminal Justice — that these four groups *can* communicate with one another, and therefore *should* be included in all planning discussions on criminal justice policy. In short, his objective is to convince criminal justice system officials of a new way of thinking, not only about who to include in planning and policy discussions, but about how to build æffective communications through nonverbal empathy.

As we turn the discussion toward audiences, we discover his thinking has shifted slightly from the first staging. The *primary audience* remains the same — the participants themselves — but the *secondary audience* is new. At the Guggenheim, the *secondary audiences* were the art-going public and press, but this time, given his new objectives, he needs to address public officials. With this realization, questions start bubbling up: Where should the performance be staged? Is an art space appropriate, or would a space associated with the criminal justice system be better? How can he make a conceptual art piece legible to bureaucrats? What was a taken-for-granted audience the first time around, at the Guggenheim, all of a sudden becomes a lot more complicated when it is public officials and not art lovers watching. When the question of what the artist wants this new audience to *do* arises, we realize that just as important as addressing the problem of how to get public officials to attend is figuring out the best way to follow up with them to make sure that they "get" the implications of the performance and its wider policy applications so they can eventually act upon them.

I also raise the issue of *unintended audiences*. The artist worries about audiences who don't actually experience his performances, but instead hear about them second hand or read snippets in the news. His previous experience taught him that this audience is most likely to misunderstand, misinterpret, and even be hostile to his project: "You did what? Staged a game? Social problems are *not* a game!" Taking on criminal justice, he expects more of the same, if not worse, from victims' rights groups on one side and criminal justice activists on the other. In identifying this audience and thinking through what he hopes this audience might (or might not) *think*, *feel*, and *do*, we start strategizing how to engage them in such a way that they have a fuller experience of his project. Ideas include soliciting testimonials from participants across the ideological spectrum, inviting journalists into the whole creative process, and providing videos of the workshops as well as the final performance. Haters are going to hate, but with some advance planning, he could mitigate some of the misunderstandings.

After discussing his ethical code, and checking back on how the project met this, it was time to talk about measurement tools. Previously, the Guggenheim had hired an evaluator who attended every workshop, interviewed selected participants throughout the project, and administered a survey of all participants at the end. The artist found all these metrics useful, but all of them cost too much money and demanded too much labor time for this nonprofit organization. So we explore the resources he has and how we might replicate some of the evaluation methods he found useful before. His videographer, it turns out, has a background in ethnographic film and can do the interviews on tape. The artist is also teaching a class at an art and design college over the course of the project and can recruit students to do some of the other work. We are off to a good start.

Upon further discussion, however, we recognize that the more traditional interview/survey model used by the Guggenheim left a serious gap in what it measured. It accounted for what people *think*, and maybe even what they think about what they *feel*, but overlooked what participants *do* with their bodies. This emphasis on physical activity is particularly important for the artist because his whole theory rests upon the belief that bodily communication is paramount, and a change here is a precursor to a change in how we speak to one another. With this in mind, we arrive at the idea of filming and recording changes in how people use their bodies over the course of the workshops and into the performance itself. It will mean hours of visual evidence to analyze later, but that's where the students will come in. With the Guggenheim evaluation, there was also no way of knowing what the participants *thought, felt,* or *did* after the performance was over. Since the lasting significance of the experience is key to the project's success, we discuss the desirability for longer-term follow-up interviews of individual participants. Immediately, however, we make plans for two social events after the performance. Both will be opportunities for participants to return and discuss their experience and its lasting significance, but the second event will include an informal debate where we can observe how people approach their positions to the issue and react to their "opposition."

The new audience of criminal justice system officials demands a new approach as well. How will we know whether they are affected by the performance and the effect this has on their actions? The first thing we need to know is whether they attended, so we develop a simple system to record who is in the audience. Second, we need to know whether they gave the performance a second thought afterward. We come up with the idea of sending the officials who attend a video of the performance and a short brief outlining its policy implications, and then follow up with their staff later to see whether they watched it. Most important, however, is whether these officials *understand* the performance and plan on *applying* its lessons. To determine this, the artist will set up meetings with all public officials who attended the performance and received the video and record the quantity of these encounters and the quality of the interactions.

The artist's dream is for the Mayor's Office of Criminal Justice to recognize that these four stakeholders can communicate with one another and, with this realization, begin to include them in policy discussions and decisions. Success at the city level in hand, he envisions a time when his model of playful conflict and empathetic communication is embraced at the state and even national level. At the present, these are long-term impacts outside the scope of this study, but we fantasize about a time in the future when we'll need to come up with an assessment plan for his nationwide project.

A Work in Progress

The æffect assessment method is a work in progress. I find myself altering and adapting each and every time it is applied. This, I believe, is not a sign of its weakness, but rather its strength. While it is a universal methodology, its application accounts for — indeed, depends upon — the specificity of each project: the intent of the artistic activist, the audiences they hope to engage, and the ethical principles that guide their project. As you've seen above, the method can also be adapted to different stages in a project's progression and the different contexts in which it is operating. Yes, the ideal trajectory is a full run, from intention to iteration, but even a little clarity in intent and self-reflection in terms of outcome is better than none.

Experience and skill levels amongst artistic activists vary, time is a scarce resource, and ideas for artistic activism projects don't always flow in such a logical linear order. This is the reality of the practice. One of the advantages of the æffect assessment method is that it is modular and flexible, and questions and prompts can be dug into or skipped over. An artist without much activism experience, for example, might spend a great deal of time thinking about audience and who has the power to effect the change they want, where someone with a great deal of activist experience might skip over those steps. Conversely, an activist new to a more artistic approach might need to spend more time than an experienced artist thinking about the affect they want their project to generate.

The point of this query-based methodology is, again, not to impart a definitive prescription of what will work and how to measure it. The æffect assessment method is meant as an unfolding process whereby the artistic activist (along with their supporters, funders, et al.) discover for themselves what they want their project to do, who they want it to engage, how best to create a project that does these things, and then how to know whether it has worked. The method presented above provides a customized, user-generated plan that the artistic activist can check in with and measure their progress against. This encourages self-reflection and allows for course adjustment as new circumstances arise and unintended consequences occur. Not only does such an approach toward assessment make for a more thoughtful and self-aware creative process, but it also improves the quality and impact of the artistic activist intervention.

The æffect assessment method is not perfect. Perfection connotes completion, and this method is by design incomplete. It is a methodology of evaluation and a tool for doing it, but more importantly, it is a way of thinking about and doing assessment that asks rather than tells and opens up spaces rather than closing them down, providing a platform for ongoing discovery and exploration. It is a method appropriate to the practice.

Formulas and Rainbows

DOES ARTISTIC ACTIVISM WORK? THE simple answer is yes. It has always worked, from the spectacles of Moses to the prefigurative performances of Jesus to the poetry of Muhammad. From the Boston Tea Party through the staged protests of the civil rights movement. From contemporary Chinese environmentalists masquerading an unlawful protest as a dystopian celebratory art piece to artists like Favianna Rodriguez turning the symbol of a monarch butterfly into a metaphor for a social movement for free migration. The combination of the affective qualities of the arts with the effective aims of activism moves people into awareness, interest, empathy, and action. Artistic activism, when done well, works.

Assessing the æffect of arts and activism, however, is never simple. The affect of art in the world is complicated. The effect of activism on the world is complicated. There are simply too many variables in operation to say with any definitive certitude that artistic activism universally works. Any accurate analysis of the æffect of artistic activism and any useful system of measurement and assessment need to grapple with the conditions of the field as they are, and not as one wishes they were or hopes they may be. The fact remains that there is not a unified opinion when it comes to how artistic activism works, nor on how one should measure its impact.

The honest answer to the question "does artistic activism work?" depends upon what the artistic activist sets out to do and the context in which they set out to do it. There is not, nor in my opinion should there be, a universal definition of what "working" entails when combining arts and activism, affect and effect. What does, and in my opinion should, exist are specific intentions we can compare to specific outcomes. For some artistic activists, this intent is primarily aesthetic, engaging in social issues as a means with which to maximize the affective qualities of the arts. Others skew toward the instrumental, using artistic techniques in order to maximize the effectiveness of a campaign for social change. Most artistic activists are somewhere in the middle, with an idea — however hazy it may be — of what they want to do politically, how they want to do it artistically, and why this is an appropriate approach given the audiences they hope to reach, the historical moment they inhabit, and the cultural contexts in which they are creating.

It is only relative to this particular *æffective intent* that one can answer the general question "does it work?" This should be obvious: unless you know what you want to do, you cannot answer the question of whether you've done it. This is why, in the methodology of assessment that I sketched out in chapter four, nearly half the questions posed are devoted to teasing out and clarifying the intentions of the artistic activist. Without a clear understanding of artistic aims, activist goals and concrete objectives, intended audiences and even ethical concerns, there is no way of answering the question "does it work?"

However, with intentions accounted for, it is a relatively simple operation to gauge artistic activism's æffect. Drawing from the lists generated in chapter two, if the intent is to "encourage participation," then we might look at the people engaged in a project or a cause. How many are there? Did this number increase or decrease? How did they participate? How long did their participation last? What did they do? If the intent is to "create conversation," then did we observe people talking about our piece and its concerns? Was the piece picked up by the media? Did that stimulate further discussion? What sorts of discussions ensued? Among whom? If the aim is to "shift the culture," then it makes logical sense to sample public opinion. Advertisers and politicians do this; so why not artistic activists? We can ask the intended audience what they think and feel about an issue before experiencing our intervention, and then again after. Is there a change? If the goal is some sort of material impact, then the proof is in the pudding: Did the intervention have a visible, physical result? Was a law passed? Were people mobilized to take the streets? Did more people show up at a meeting?

As a thought experiment, I want to propose a simple formula as a way of conceptualizing how this approach to assessment works. We start with our *desired* æffect: the affect and effect that we want our artistic intervention to have. I'll call this Δd. Then, after we have staged our intervention and accounted for its æffects, we have our *achieved* æffect, or Δa. By comparing Δa to Δd we can ascertain our degree of "success," or S, as in FORMULA 1.

FORM. 1

$$S = \frac{\Delta a}{\Delta d}$$

Where S = Success
And Δa= $\Delta achieved$ = Achieved Æffect
And Δd = $\Delta desired$ = Desired Æffect

This is how this formula might operate in practice. Say, like Owen Griffiths, the Welsh artistic activist introduced earlier, we are interested in increasing neighborhood participation in imagining, creating, and maintaining a community garden. The first step in building such a creative community might be getting people to show up at an organizing meeting. However, only ten people show up at the first meeting, and we want to help double attendance at the next meeting. We plan and stage an artistic activist intervention to excite, inform, and engage local people in the cause, and lo and behold, ten additional people show up at the next meeting. Plugging those values into our formula it looks like FORMULA 2.

FORM. 2

$$S = \frac{(20-10)}{(20-10)} = \frac{10}{10} = \frac{1}{1} = 100\%$$

The achieved impact matches the desired impact and so we have 100 percent success rate. Maybe, however, only five new people show up at the meeting. Plugging that achievement into our formula looks like FORMULA 3.

FORM. 3

$$S = \frac{(15-10)}{(20-10)} = \frac{5}{10} = \frac{.5}{1} = 50\%$$

It's not a bad impact, we have increased the number of people at the meeting (by 50 percent), but we have also fallen short of our goal (by the same percentage). When aiming toward multiple objectives, which is often the case in artistic activist projects, we can introduce a new value, x, which functions as a stand-in for other variables we might be measuring. The formula then becomes recursive, allowing us to measure the average rate of success of all of our objectives. Our formula now looks like FORMULA 4.

FORM. 4

$$S_x = \frac{1}{x} \sum_{i=1}^{x} \frac{\Delta a_i}{\Delta d_i}$$

And there we have it: the formula for successful artistic activism.

Is this formula serious? Yes . . . and no. The logic of the formula works, but what it can work on is very little. I offer the formula here more as metaphor than as mathematics, a heuristic tool to get us thinking about the importance of accounting for intent if measuring outcome is going to be meaningful, and thinking of the importance of measuring outcome if we are to take intent seriously. At times, with relatively straightforward objectives that can be easily measured, like increasing attendance at an organizing meeting, we might be able to use such a formula. But such easily quantifiable objectives are few and far between when it comes to artistic activism. Yes, sometimes we can observe physical effects — attendance at a meeting, participation in a project, a fruitful garden — and these can be easily measured and accounted for. But the power of artistic activism is that it also works in more affective ways. Griffiths, for example, uses his Vetch Veg project to create community gardens in the Welsh city of Swansea. But his goal isn't only having more people grow more vegetables; it's about changing their feelings about the physical place in which they live and their perception about who has a right to public space. These affective effects often occur over long periods of time and are much harder to measure, maybe even impossible. They certainly don't fit easily into the formula above.

Artistic activism is marvelously irrepressible. It is forever producing affects and effects that we did not predict or even desire; one could even argue that this is its strength. Art, if it is any good, always creates a surplus, bubbling up and slopping over the sides of whatever categories we create to contain it, spilling out on the floor, making new forms that demand new perspectives to understand and new measures to judge. As my frequent collaborator Steve Lambert is fond of saying: artistic activism is in the business of making rainbows. Think of artistic activism as a prism.

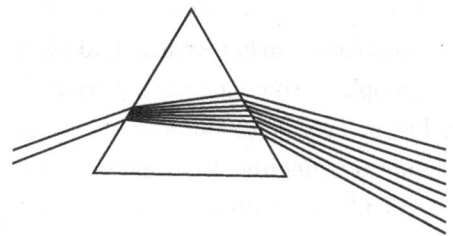

In a typical dispersive prism, a beam of white light is aimed at a certain angle at a medium, commonly a triangular chunk of glass. The white light is then refracted by the angles of the glass and broken up into its constituent spectral colors. The result is a rainbow. This is how artistic activism works as well. The artist focuses their intentions into their work, but what results when that piece is experienced by the audience is a range of output that is interpreted and acted upon in myriad ways. Simply put: the artistic activist shines their intention in, but what comes out is a spectrum of æffect, and this is something we cannot entirely control. As such, a more accurate formula for determining success might look something more like FORMULA 5.

FORM. 5

$$S_x = \frac{1}{x} \sum_{i=1}^{x} \frac{\Delta a_i}{\Delta d_i} + S_y$$

Where S_y = an æffect not intended or anticipated.

Let's return to the community garden meeting. Maybe only five of the hoped-for additional ten people show up. In terms of our original equation, the meeting is not a smashing success. But what if the people who did attend conceived of a brilliant idea that changed the entire campaign? What if two of them met and fell in love? It is not what we intended with our intervention, and we cannot account for what happened like we can count the numbers of people attending a meeting, but it is still a positive æffect. It is S_y.

The colors of the rainbow are a continuous spectrum, not the discrete categories of red, orange, yellow, green, blue, indigo, and violet we use to make sense of the gradient of color. Similarly, there is an infinite number of possible æffects of artistic activism, and thus an infinite number of ways to evaluate success: $S_y \, S_z \, S_a \, S_\beta \, S_y$, ad infinitum. Each new æffect of artistic activism can be measured only on its own axis, and what measures success in terms of bringing people to a meeting will not account for the generation of a new idea or falling in love. These multiple æffects of artistic activism — increasing attendance at a meeting, the creation of new ideas, falling in love, and so on — can add up to nothing, diverging into scattered points in empty space, each brilliant in its own way, but isolated from one another and therefore doing little to dispel the darkness. Or these different æffects can complement one another, converge into a new quality, a new force, a new light that has the potential to change everything. Some æffects of artistic activism may not be discernible to the eye or measurable by a ruler, not in the short term, nor even in our lifetimes. This is okay; we need to make our peace with the indeterminacy of art's æffect. Artistic activism, when all is said and done, is an art, not a science. There is no singular way it works and no simple formula to determine if it has worked.

Acknowledging this, however, does not allow us to retreat back into magical thinking wherein an artistic activist makes an intervention and — poof! — change happens. What artistic activists can control is their input. Think again of the prism: if light aimed at a prism is weak and diffuse, nothing much happens; no beautiful rainbows result. Similarly, if the intention of the artistic activist is muddled and their artistic aims and political objectives, audiences, and contexts are not carefully considered, then not much will happen either. This is why all the thinking and planning about affect and effect, intent and measurement, are so critical: not because one can predict exactly what will happen, but so we can make sure that *something* happens, and then, once we've determined what has happened, refocus our efforts.

In the final analysis, any methodology for assessing the affect and effect of art and activism needs to be guided by a set of principles. I offer these:

First, some sort of evaluation is necessary for socially engaged artwork. To not evaluate what artistic activism is doing is an abdication of a responsibility to those we are working with and for, and perhaps worse: it's a lost opportunity for maximizing impact.

Second, evaluation has to start with artistic activists themselves. Not only are they the ones who know what they want their work to do, but without their buy-in, they will resent the evaluation and do it badly, or not do it at all.

Third, evaluation is not something that happens after a project is done. For it to work, it needs to begin at the beginning, because...

Fourth, we may never definitively know the impact of an artistic activist project. There are simply too many variables, and part of art's power is that it can surprise us. However, the very process of thinking through intent and indicators of outcome makes for more a æffective artistic activism that has a better chance of having an impact and creating social change.

And this, in the end, is what really matters.

Acknowledgments

A BOOK LIKE THIS IS never written alone. It is composed of thousands of conversations with hundreds of people. Probably the most valuable conversations have been with my partners at the Center for Artistic Activism: Steve Lambert and Rebecca Bray. Steve has been on this journey the longest with me, beginning over a decade ago when we started interviewing artistic activists by asking them: "What works?" Steve has also been generous enough to allow me to use the term he invented as the title of this book. Three others also deserve special mention here: George Perlov, who approached Steve and me after a talk we gave to ask about the impact of artistic activism, and then stayed on as a collaborator on what we came to call The Æffect Project; Sarah Halford, C4AA's research fellow who, in addition to being a star interviewer, was a consistent sounding board for many of my ideas; and Silas Harrebye, my Danish collaborator on multiple research projects, including "The Copenhagen Experiment," testing whether artistic activism actually works. The hundred-plus interviews that generated the primary data for this book were conducted not only by myself, but by a stellar interview team that included, in addition to Sarah, George, and Steve: Emily Bellor, Fatou Kiné Diouf, Michelle Yung Hurtubise, Diana Malaj, Kelsey Murphy, Donalea Scott, Chloe Smith, Cici Sutter, and Rachael Young. Putting together the literature review for this book was also a joint enterprise, and I'd like to thank Heidi Boisvert, Andrew Boyd, Dipti Desai, Jose Falconi, Deborah Fisher, Joanna Raczkiewicz, Mark Read, TV Reed, Dorris Summer, and Nato Thompson for their suggestions of what I ought to be reading. Of specific help with suggestions on the evaluation of artistic activism were Jan Cohen-Cruz, Deborah Fisher, and Pam Korza. Marlène Ramírez-Cancio pushed me to broaden my definition of "what works," Maxwell Tremblay finally got me to understand Kant ... I think, my Gallatin School colleagues, Nina Katchadourian and Eve Meltzer, helped me figure out what is meant by artistic intent, and Matt Stanley translated my silly ideas into serious formulas (or vice versa). Special thanks also to Capri Jones, my student research assistant, who patiently read over this manuscript and responded to it with a critical intelligence far beyond his years, and Josh Knowles who helped me design and did the heavy coding for the ÆffectApp. I also learned a great deal from my students in my "How Art Works" courses at NYU, as they brought their fresh perspectives to many old texts. Salette Gressett aided my work on this project, both as an intellectual interlocutor and as a funder at the British Council USA. My research was further supported by the Open Society Foundations, the Compton Foundation, The Harmony Institute, and the Gallatin School Publications Subvention Fund and University Challenge Fund of New York University. This endeavor, from its beginnings as The Æffect Project, has benefited from the advice of an august advisory board made up of Kenneth Bailey, Luis Camnitzer, James Chung, Brett Davidson, Kathy Eldon, Deborah Fisher, Jessica George, Silas Harrebye, Rob Horowitz, John Johnson, Pam Korza, Doris Sommer, Diana Taylor, Nato Thompson, and Risë Wilson. I am very grateful to Richard Morrison, my editor at Fordham University Press, who believed in this book from the beginning and worked hard to make it a better one, and Brett Kendall for their copy-editing acumen. Andy Outis, who designed this book, outside and in, is always a joy to collaborate with. Over the course of this project, Jean Railla has been an insightful critic and steadfast supporter, and our sons Sydney and Sebastien have kept me sharp with their constant questioning. Finally, none of this would have been possible without the wisdom and generosity of all the artistic activists I have worked with and talked to over these many years. This book is for them.

Æffect Assessment Script

THE FOLLOWING IS A SCRIPT of prompts for planning and assessing the æffect of your artistic activist project. It is meant to be adapted and altered to your wants and needs, so feel free to fold, spindle, or mutilate accordingly.

Intent: what do you want to do?

What is your *activist goal*? (What Effect do you want to have?)

What is your *artistic aim*? (What Affect do you want to have?)

What is the *concrete objective(s)* of your project?

> How is your objective *Specific*? (Something that can be impacted.)
> How is your objective *Measurable*? (Something that can be evaluated.)
> How is your objective *Achievable*? (Something you can realistically do.)
> How is your objective *Relevant*? (Something in alignment with your overall goals.)
> How is your objective *Timed*? (Something with a defined deadline.)
> How is your objective *Inclusive*? (Something that engages those most impacted.)
> How is your objective *Equitable*? (Something that addresses systemic injustices.)

Audience: who do you want to engage?

Who has the *power* to realize your *concrete objective*?

Who is the *primary audience* you want to engage?

    Why do you want to engage this audience?
    What do you want this audience to *think*?
    What do you want this audience to *feel*?
    What do you want this audience to *do*?

Who is your *secondary audience*?

    Why do you want to engage this audience?
    What do you want this audience to *think*?
    What do you want this audience to *feel*?
    What do you want this audience to *do*?

Who might be an *unintended audience*?

    Why do you need to consider this audience?
    What do you want this audience to *think*?
    What do you want this audience to *feel*?
    What do you want this audience to *do*?

Ethics: how do you want to act?

What are the core values that make up your *ethical code*?

How will you apply your *ethical code* to your project?

Intervention: what do you want to create?

What is your idea for an intervention?

How will your intervention get you closer to your *activist goals*?
How will your intervention get you closer to your *artistic aims*?
How will your intervention get you closer to your *concrete objective*?
How will your intervention address your *primary audience*?
How will your intervention address your *secondary audience*?
How will your intervention address your *unintended audience*?
How will your intervention meet your *ethical code*?

Measures: how will you know if it works?

How will you know if your project is a success?

What tools can you use to know if your project is a success?
What will you learn from each of these tools?

How will you know if your intervention engaged your *primary audience* in the ways you intended?

What tools will you use?
What can you learn from these?

How will you know if your intervention engaged your *secondary audience*?

What tools can you use?
What will you learn from these?

How might you know if your intervention engaged your *unintended audience*?

What tools can you use?
What will you learn from these?

What is your overall *evaluation plan*?

Impact: did it work?

What happened? (Describe as many details as you can think of.)

What did you feel?

What surprised you?

Impact: did you engage your audiences?

Did you engage your *primary audience*?
  How do you know this?

What was this audience *thinking*?
  How do you know this?
What was this audience *feeling*?
  How do you know this?
What was this audience *doing*?
  How do you know this?

Did you engage your *secondary audience*?
  How do you know this?

What was this audience *thinking*?
  How do you know this?
What was this audience *feeling*?
  How do you know this?
What was this audience *doing*?
  How do you know this?

Was there an *unintended audience*?
  Who did it turn out to be?
  How do you know this?

What was this audience *thinking*?
  How do you know this?

What was this audience *feeling*?
    How do you know this?
What was this audience *doing*?
    How do you know this?

Impact: was it ethical?

How did your creative process and product follow your *ethical code*?

How did your creative process and product fall short of your *ethical code*?

Impact: what was its long-term impact?

What might be the long-term *æffects* of your project?

How might you evaluate these *æffects*?

Impact: did you reach your aims, goals, and objectives?

Given your *concrete objective*, how does your outcome compare to your intent?

Given your *artistic aim*, how does your outcome compare to your intent?

Given your *activist goal*, how does your outcome compare to your intent?

Iteration: what comes next?

Knowing what you now know, how might you change your project?

What do you plan to do next?

Æffect Measurement Tools

THE TYPES OF TOOLS YOU can use to measure the æffect of artistic activism are limited only by your imagination. Anything that can help you determine whether your project has done what you wanted it to do, and reached who you wanted it to reach, can be an evaluation tool. What follows are just some suggestions:

Documentation: Whatever else you do, be sure to document your process and your project. In addition to being a record, it may help you notice ways your project had an impact that you missed while you were doing it.

Observation: Standing back and observing reactions tells you something important about how your project is having an impact. Are people taking notice or passing by? Are they smiling or angry? Talking amongst themselves or lost in thought? You can observe and take notes live, or document the scene to analyze later. Creating a simple worksheet that allows observers to quickly note common responses like those above can also be helpful.

Interviews: Interviewing participants and passersby is a great way of finding out how your project is impacting your audience. Using the "think, feel, do" model, ask them what they think and feel about your project, or what they think, feel, and might do about the issue you are addressing. Interviews can be long or short; they can happen during the action to record immediate responses or take place a couple of weeks after to get a sense of what people remembered and how they might have changed their thoughts, feelings, or actions.

Surveys: Surveys are a good way to know if your project has changed public perception on the social issue you are addressing. Ideally, you will want to survey the same population before and after exposure to your project, to see if there have been any changes attributable to your intervention.

Focus Groups: Bringing together people who have interacted with your project and having a conversation with them about their experience can provide valuable information about your project's impact. Focus groups commonly occur as spoken conversations, but they can also take other forms, like an "art jam" where the audience and/or participants draw, sing, or act out their responses.

Publicity Analysis: Counting and analyzing media mentions—news stories, blog reports, social-media posts—is a way of determining how much publicity your project has gotten, and the quality and tone of that publicity. Remember, however, that media is only a means to an end and does not necessarily tell you whether your project has affected people or effected policy.

Be Creative! Artistic activists can apply their creativity to designing evaluation tools. One way to do this is by building measurements into their projects. Several examples I've seen, include:

- Concluding the intervention with a *speak-out session* with the audience...in order to gauge how people are thinking and feeling about the intervention and issue.
- Organizing vocal *call-and-responses* amongst the crowd during the intervention...to determine division or unity on an issue and whether this changes.
- Creating a *comment wall* so people can express themselves...and provide data that can be analyzed for patterns and meaning.
- Building *interactive props* like a public mural that asks people to mark the wall based upon their opinion on an issue, or a massive scale of

justice where people weigh out their position with stones in order to measure how they stand.

The brilliant thing about these types of creative evaluation tools is that they not only collect information but also engage the audience while doing it.

These are only a few of the most common evaluation tools and are provided here only as a place to start. Artistic activism is an uncommon practice and you are encouraged to explore, invent and experiment with ways of measuring æffect that work for you and your projects.

Affect and Effect

IN COMMON USAGE, *affect* AND *effect* are often used interchangeably, and given their heritage and phonetic likeness, this is understandable. Yet the words have distinct meanings, and exploring their definitions reveals something about the forces operating within and through the hybrid practice of artistic activism. Exploring the etymology of *affect* and *effect* is therefore not merely an idle academic sojourn, but provides a map to help understand the definitional ground of both art and activism, and the meanings, intentions, and impacts at play when these two practices work together.

Effect

Let's begin with *effect*. According to the *Oxford English Dictionary*, the word *effect* has multiple origins, from both the Latin *effectus* and the French *effecte* and *effect*.[1] In classical Latin, the Latin of the late Roman Republic and Empire, *effectus* means a:

> carrying out, performance, accomplishment (of something), state of completion, result, outcome, favourable result, success, mode of action or operation.

Effect then, from its inception, has a dual nature: it is both an action (*to effect*) and a result of that action: *an effect.* In postclassical Latin, the language of medieval European religion and learning, *effectus* takes on the additional, and interesting, connotation of "reality as opposed to appearance." The French roots of *effect* compliment this concern with tangible results. In the Old French of the thirteenth century, the word is used to describe *result* or *consequence*, and by 1310, when used as a plural, *effects*, describes *goods* and *movable property*. The slide from French into Anglo-Norman — and the crossing of the channel into England and, consequently, later English — brings with it the additional meanings of *legal force*, and by the fourteenth century, *purpose, end,* and *fact*. In sum, the roots of the word *effect* suggest a *carrying out* or *performance* that leads to a *result* or *outcome*. The physicality of this outcome is paramount, so much so that the word takes on the meaning of *reality* or *fact*, or even material goods and property (e.g., when we refer to one's *effects* as their personal property). While nuances of meaning abound in the definitional roots, all agree that *effect* functions as both a verb and a noun, an action and a consequence.

In usage, however, words lose such definitional clarity. One of the first written appearances of *effect* in English is also one of the first examples of English literature: Geoffrey Chaucer's *Canterbury Tales* (ca. 1390). In *Canterbury Tales*, the word is used multiple times to express an operative force, the purpose of that force, *and* its results or consequences. In "The Parson's Tale," one of the twenty-four *Canterbury Tales*, we are told that "Charmes for woundes . . . if they taken any effect, it may be parauenture that god suffreth it." A rough translation of this might be: if using charms for wounds has positive results, it may be only because God wills it. *Effect* is here both the physical action, as the use of charms (or metaphysical charms, in the case of God's will), and the material result — health.

The two primary definitions of *effect* in the *OED* capture this double character:

1.a. The state or fact of being operative or in force.
2.a. That which results from the action or properties of something or someone; results in general; the quality of producing a result, efficacy.

Again, action and consequence. But it is telling that, of all the *Canterbury Tales* told by Chaucer, *effect* appears most often in "The Parson's Tale," which deals with spiritual as well as worldly advice. It seems the materiality of *effect* slips easily into the less tangible realms of the spirit, and the ghost of *affect* haunts *effect* from its first uses in the English language.

By the eighteenth century and into the nineteenth, *effect* is found in use in the English language in reference to the arts in a manner captured by alternate *OED* definitions:

4.b.   A (pleasing or remarkable) combination of colour, form, etc., in design and the visual arts.

4.c.   A visual or acoustic device used to convey atmosphere or the illusion of reality in the production of plays, films, or broadcasts.

9.a.   The impression produced on a beholder, hearer, or reader (formerly esp. by a work of art or literature); the impression produced by a picture, building, costume, etc., viewed as a whole; the look that a collection of features has.

In 1736 the philosopher and theologian Joseph Butler refers rather tentatively to "what they call, the *Effect* in Architecture." Only a hundred years later, however, the *Times* of London writes about "theatrical *effects*" with the confidence that their readership would understand the term. Here is the *Times* of August 11, 1838: "It may be inferred, not that the mechanical ingenuity of the 17th century was superior to ours, but that the audience were less critical as to theatrical *effects*."

What is remarkable about the use of *effect* in the context of the arts is all that it encompasses. First there is the results of the artist's actions on the work of art itself: a painterly *effect*. Second, the ability of the art form to convey an illusion of material reality: special *effects*. And third, the impact, or *impression* a piece of art has on an audience: the *effect* of an artwork. The instrumental purpose of *effect* is still in operation here: it is something the artist does in order to make something happen. They might, for example, use certain brush strokes in a painting or employ a chord progression in a musical composition (*an* effect) to bring about a certain result (*the* effect). But it is the third meaning in operation here that gives *effect* a locus: impact on an audience.

Furthermore, *OED* definition 4.c. (above) suggests that *effect* may have taken on a somewhat more complicated relationship to reality than the Latin and French roots of the word imply. "Theatrical effects," or the "special effects" used in contemporary film, for example, are used purposefully to create an illusion, yet the intended *effect* on the audience is as if a real action with a real result is taking place. However, as the sentence from the London *Times* quoted proposes, this connection between tangible reality and audience *effect* gets even more complicated. The audience often knows that what they are seeing is not real, yet the experience still has a profound impact.

This is where *impression* (see definition 9.a. above) comes in. *Impression*, as it is used here, is not only a material effect. Rather, its usage suggests that *effect* can also describe an impact on the human senses as well as physical bodies. Recalling Galileo's famous distinction between the qualities that "exist in external bodies" and can be measured through size, shape, quantity, and motion, on the one side, and those like color, smell, and taste "that exist only in the sensitive body," on the other, may be helpful here. The *effect* of art, unlike that of gravity on an object dropped from a tower, is not something so easily observed and measured; it is more something sensed — internal, spiritual, emotional. On the outer reaches of the definition of *effect* is *affect*.

Affect

Affect, like *effect*, has roots in classical Latin, *affectus*, and Old French, *affect* and *affet*. In classical Latin, again according to the *OED*, *affectus* is a:

> mental or emotional state or reaction (especially a temporary one), physical state or condition (especially a pathological one), influence or impression, permanent mental or moral disposition, eagerness, zeal, devotion, love, intention, purpose.

The roots of *affect*, so it seems, are firmly grounded in the sensitive body. It is, above all, an emotional, mental, moral, or physical *reaction* that *affectus* refers to. This reaction is variable: it might be love or devotion, a sense of purpose or intention, or even, in postclassical Latin — with its ecclesiastical distrust of the sensitive body — *evil desire*. What remains constant is the sense that *affect* refers to a human *state* or *reaction*, which the twelfth- and thirteenth-century French definition delineates as one of *desire, passion*.

The primary definitions of *affect* in the *OED* are grouped under one umbrella:

I. Senses relating to the mind.

The uncomfortable pairing of *senses* and *mind* here hint that we are not talking about a purely cognitive function. Indeed, the sub definitions that follow make this clear. *Affect* is:

> I.1.a The manner in which one is inclined or disposed; (also) the capacity for willing or desiring; a mental state, mood, or emotion.
>
> I.1.b. An inner disposition or feeling (rather than an external manifestation or action).

Again it is Chaucer that provides one of the first English usages of *affect*, this time from his epic poem *Troilus and Criseyde* (ca. 1385): "And therto dronken hadde as hoot and stronge, As Crassus dide for his *affect* is wronge." Or, in a modern English translation: "And thereby had a drink as hot and strong as Crassus drank for his desires wrong."[2] How Chaucer uses *affect* here is again revealing, for it describes an emotional state, desire, that then needs qualification, *wronge*. In other words *affect* is a protofeeling of some sort but what exactly that feeling is remains open. It might be *wronge*, as it is for Chaucer, or an *evil desire*, as it meant in postclassical Latin, yet it also could describe a favorable feeling, a fondness, as when we say we have *affection* for someone or something. In fact, it is this meaning of *affect* that characterizes the second class of definitions in the *OED*:

> I.2.a Feeling towards or in favour of a person or thing; kindly feeling, affection.

Affect can be kindly or wrong, favorable or evil; it does not have a defined character. As Immanuel Kant writes in *The Metaphysics of Morals*, which, in 1799, is one of the first philosophical uses of *affect* (in German: *Affekt*): "Affects and passions are essentially distinct from one another, the former belong to feeling, so far as it, preceding reflection, renders it more difficult, or even impossible." *Affect* is the feeling one has before it is reflected upon and recognized as a defined feeling (the latter which Kant refers to as *passions*.) Sure enough, *affect*, in definition I.5.a. of the *OED*, is: "an emotional, unreflective response."

A similar distinction is at work in Kant's understanding of the beautiful and the sublime. The beautiful is bounded, tied to the object being described. One can speak, for example, of a beautiful flower or a beautiful painting and go on to describe, in a language understood by others, why and how it is beautiful. The sublime, however is boundless, it is a feeling without form and transcends the object that might stimulate the feeling.[3] Think for a moment how difficult it is to describe the majesty of a mountain or a sunset (or a dream or drug trip) and you have an idea of the sublime. *Affect* is akin to the sublime: it is something you feel, but once it is understood it passes into something recognizable, like beauty. While good art can be beautiful, great art is sublime. It moves us, but we are not quite sure how and why—it simply *affects* us.

From eighteenth-century philosophical usage, *affect* migrates in the late nineteenth century to the new fields of psychiatry and psychology, engendering a new definition:

> I.5.b. A feeling or subjective experience accompanying a
>   thought or action or occurring in response to a stimulus; an
>   emotion, a mood.

This use of *affect* extends the philosophical distinction between the subjective (and invisible) feeling and the more objective (and tangible) thought or action. Again, *affect* is imminent—it can later be recognized as a feeling, reflected upon through thought, become the driver for physical action—but the defining characteristic of *affect* is a subjective emotion, or mood. Noteworthy, however, is the highlighting of *stimulus* in this definition. The mention of stimulus above brings us back to the original definition of the Latin root *affectus* as both a state *and* a reaction. *Affect* is something that can be prompted by a stimulus. As such, we need to think of *affect* as we did *effect*: not only as a noun, as *an affect*, but also as a verb, *to affect*.

As an action word, there are two primary usages of *affect*. The first has to do with the desire *for* someone or something. As noted above, in modern usage, *affection* has largely taken the place of *affect* in this verb form. It is, however, the second general definition: "To have an effect on " (*vb.* 2, I.), that is the most useful for our purposes. Just as *affect* snuck through the back door into our definition of *effect*, here *effect* makes its entrance into *affect*. This *effect* of *affect* can be material, used most often to describe the effect of a disease upon the body, but more often than not, *affect* refers to a rather different point of human impact:

> I.2.a. To have an effect on the mind or feelings of (a person); to impress or influence emotionally; to move, touch.

It is this use of *affect* that John Milton references in *Paradise Lost* in 1667: "The trouble of thy thoughts this night in sleep *affects* me equally." Like *effect*, this refers to an action that creates an outcome. Milton's troubling thoughts have an *affect* upon him. But the impact is not something external, material, measurable, or tangible; rather, it is a troubling of his soul that touches and moves him.

There is another definition of *affect* in the *OED* that bears mention, if only for curiosity's sake:

> *n.* 4. To assume artificial or pretended manners; to put on airs.
> *v.* 5.a. To assume a false appearance of; to put on a pretence of, to counterfeit or pretend.

What to do with this definition of *affect*? The immediate temptation is to overlook it. Marginal definitions like these sneak into any language, particularly one as patchwork as English. But as with the use of *effect* to denote a category of phenomena whose aim is to give the illusion of the real, the use of *affect* as a way of describing false appearances is just too rich to ignore. While I have no intention here of recounting in full Plato's infamous attack on the arts in book 10 of *The Republic*, it is worth remembering the two primary pillars upon which his critique is built: art creates an illusion of reality, and then the audience experiences this illusion as real. Vivid scenes of war are described in the *Iliad*, but Homer knows nothing of war. He is a poet, not a soldier. Yet, the audience listening to the *Iliad* imagines they are there in Troy, witnessing the tragic duel between Achilles and Hector, smelling sweat and blood, breathing in the dust, and hearing the clash of arms. They know they are not in battle but they *feel* as if they are, and this is what really concerns Plato: the ability of the artist to generate feeling in their audience.[4] This is the *effect* of *affect*.

Æffect

At this point, I'm hoping this dry and dusty etymological exploration of *effect* and *affect* may have demonstrated some relevance for understanding the colorful and dynamic practice of contemporary artistic activism. Both words are about actions and impacts. *Effect* is used to describe material impact: something which can be measured, tested, determined as a fact. *Affect* is mainly used to describe emotional impact. These meanings graph quite well onto our understanding of activism and arts respectively. But artistic activism is a hybrid. It generates *affect* in the service of *effect*. By understanding the etymology of both words, we can recognize how they differ, where they converge, and most importantly, how they might be combined. Perhaps what is needed is a new word, one that encompases the meanings of both *affect* and *effect*, and that speaks to the need to account for both external physical transformation and fundamental transformations in feeling that is essential to artistic activism. A new word whose meaning is yet to be defined and whose etymology waits to be written. A word like *Æffect*.

Notes

Introduction: What Is Æffect?

1. I am not happy with either *assess* or *evaluate* as terms. The former has a long history (stretching back to at least the fifteenth century in the English language) of associations with the valuation of property for purposes of taxation, while the latter has a judgmental quality—determining and fixing value—that I find too instrumental and rigid. But these are the common terms we have, and so I will use them interchangeably, and somewhat unhappily, throughout this book.

2. Chantal Mouffe, "Artistic Activism and Agonistic Spaces," *Art & Research* 1, no. 2 (2007): 1–5, http://www.artandresearch.org.uk/v1n2/mouffe.html.

3. Many of the people I've interviewed for this book do not refer to themselves as *artistic activists*, sometimes because they are uncomfortable with the baggage that the words *artist* and *activist* bring with them, sometimes because they prefer another moniker, and often because they prefer not to categorize themselves at all, doing so only when circumstances demand. As one artistic activist explained when asked about his preference for terms: "It depends on who I am writing to for a grant."

4. Actipedia.org, the online database of the Center for Artistic Activism and Yes Lab, has over twenty-five hundred case studies, with more added weekly.

5. Jacques Rancière gives the example of Gustave Flaubert, who, despite being a political conformist who insisted his work had no democratic message or intent, nevertheless wrote novels like *Madame Bovary* and *Sentimental Education* that had a profound democratizing effect by valorizing the language and experiences of everyday people (*The Politics of Aesthetics* [London: Continuum, 2000], 14). In my definition, this would not be artistic activism.

6. This a useful distinction that Walter Benjamin makes in "The Author as Producer," in *Cultural Resistance Reader*, ed. Stephen Duncombe (London: Verso, 2002)

7. Potholes seem to inspire artistic activism. The CAC went on to transform a water-filled pothole in Tetovo into a fishing pond, with similar successful results. Mexican civic activists from the group Amemos Tijuana (Love Tijuana) held a birthday party for a pothole in their city in 2013. In 2015, Baadal Nanjundaswamy, an Indian artist based in Bangalore painted a large pothole green and dumped in a life-sized fiberglass crocodile to attract municipal attention. Also in 2015, an anonymous artist calling himself "Wanksy" began spray-painting large penises around potholes in Manchester, England. "I wanted to attract attention to the pothole and make it memorable. Nothing seemed to do this better than a giant comedy phallus," he told the *Manchester Evening News*. https://actipedia.org/project/birthday-party-pothole; https://actipedia.org/project/pothole-activism; https://actipedia.org/project/mystery-artist-paints-penises-around-potholes-get-them-fixed.

8. Alas, the right-wing, nationalist government was elected back into power in 2021.

9. *Oxford English Dictionary*, s.v. *affect* and *effect*, accessed June 15, 2017, http://www.oed.com/.

10. Harold Laswell, *Politics: Who Gets What, When, How* (New York: Whittlesey House, 1936).

11. Marshall Ganz, "Public Narrative, Collective Action, and Power," in *Accountability Through Public Opinion: From Inertia to Public Action*, ed. Sina Odugbemi and Taeku Lee (Washington, DC: World Bank, 2011), 273–89.

12. George Lakoff, *Moral Politics* (Chicago: University of Chicago Press, 1996). Neuroscientist Antonio Damasio even argues that "emotion and feeling are indispensable for rationality. At their best, feelings point us in the proper direction, take us to the appropriate place in a decision-making space, where we might put instruments of logic to good use" (*Descartes' Error: Emotion, Reason and the Human Brain* [New York: Penguin, 1994], xvii).

13. How to pronounce *Æffect*? My C4AA co-collaborator Steve Lambert, who came up with the term, insists that it sounds something like "I-ffect," with a long I sound. My Danish colleague Silas Harrebye, drawing on the familiar Scandinavian use of Æ, says that the pronunciation should be more like "Ehh-ffect." Pronounce it as you like. It's not the sound but the meaning that matters.

14. Fifteen years ago, the California College of the Arts began offering social practice as a concentration within its MFA program. Two years later, in 2007, Portland State University started up its Art & Social Practice program. Since then a flurry of academic concentrations and programs have opened doors across the United States. New York City, for example, holds Queens College's Art & Social Action program, the Department of Art Practice at the School of Visual Arts, and Parsons School of Design's minor in social practice. Across California, CalArts has a program titled Social Practice & Public Forms, Otis College of Art and Design has its Art and Social Practice "emphasis," and the University of California provides an "Art & Social Change Track" across its ten campuses. Elsewhere in the United States, Maryland Institute College of Art gives an MFA degree in community art, George Mason University offers a minor in "arts and social change," and the Sam Fox School of Design & Visual Arts at Washington University in St. Louis has a robust "Socially Engaged Practice" program. Even the Ivies, always late to the game, have gotten into the act. Yale University, the oldest art school in the country, launched an "Art and Social Justice Initiative" in 2017. My home institution, New York University, has *two* graduate programs devoted to the intersection of

arts and activism: Arts Politics in its performing arts school, and Art, Education, and Community Practice in its school of education and fine arts. Regardless of program and department, university courses on arts and activism abound. In the Fall of 2010 alone, NYU offered over *twenty* courses, across four schools and colleges, exploring the interconnections between arts, politics, and social activism. Looking north, an art student can minor in "social practice and community engagement" at Emily Carr University, a major Canadian art school. Across the pond, there are arts and activism programs, both applied and scholarly, at Oxford Brookes, Queen Mary, Middlesex, and Wolverhampton Universities in the United Kingdom. Further on, Universität der Künste in Berlin has an "Art in Context" MFA and one can study "global art practice" at Tokyo University of the Arts with both programs emphasizing arts and social change.

15. In recent years, in New York City alone, the Brooklyn Museum staged their monumental *AgitProp* show, the Whitney Museum offered up *An Incomplete History Of Protest*, and the Museum of the City of New York hosted *AIDS at Home, Art and Everyday Activism*. Over the past decade, the Queens Museum has centered its curatorial and educational mission around socially engaged arts, while Creative Time, the ambitious NYC-based arts institution, organizes yearly "summits" that bring together artistic activists from around the world. Even the normally stodgy Metropolitan Museum of Art launched a "Civic Practice" artist residency and seminar "committed to social change" in 2018. Around the world, from the *Disobedient Objects* show at the Victoria and Albert Museum in London to *The Art of Disruptions* at Iziko South African National Gallery, the intersection of arts and activism has become an integral part of the arts scene. No global biennale is complete these days without its "social interventions" and the requisite controversy surrounding the place of activism in the art world. In 2021, the United Kingdom's prestigious Turner Prize was awarded to the Array Collective, a group of activist artists from Belfast, Northern Ireland.

16. Large organizations like George Soros's Open Society Foundation created new initiatives like the Arts Exchange, which was institutionalized as its own program, to integrate arts into all levels of their social programming. Smaller foundations like A Blade of Grass, Compton, Rauschenberg, and Surdna have made the support of arts and activism central to their mission. Research groups such as Americans for the Art's Animating Democracy and The Culture Group produce reports and user guides for a range of actors in the field. And then there are artistic activist training institutes like The Yes Labs, Beautiful Trouble, Intelligent Mischief, Center for Story-Based Strategies, Backbone Campaign, and of course the Center for Artistic Activism, to list just a few. Perhaps most important of all is the attention paid to the practice by activists themselves. It is now common, from global activist NGOs like Greenpeace to local grassroots groups working on immigration reform such as the New Sanctuary Coalition in NYC, to develop "creative strategies" alongside more traditional legal, electoral, and mobilization approaches.

17. Doug McAdam, "The Framing Function of Movement Tactics," in *Comparative Perspectives on Social Movements*, ed. Doug McAdam, John D. McCarthy, and Mayer N Zald (Cambridge: Cambridge University Press, 1996), 348.

18. For more on this, see Stephen Duncombe and Steve Lambert, *The Art of Activism*, (New York: O/R, 2021), 87–129.

19. This includes activism's darkest "successes." The terrible truth is that the most successful artistic activists of the past century were not on the side of truth, justice, peace, and equality for all. They were the Nazis who mobilized myth, performance, design, architecture, and sartorial style in their quest for military domination and ra-

cial genocide. Lest it be forgotten, Adolf Hitler had early aspirations to be an artist. For an excellent source on the Nazi's use of arts and activism, see Frederic Spotts, *Hitler and the Power of Aesthetics* (London: Pimlico, 2003).

20. Art for art's sake, of course, did have a social function: it was a critique of the instrumentalization of nineteenth-century European capitalism and bureaucracy.

21. It is true that magic sometimes *appears* to work: spells make unfaithful lovers fall ill, but they work only because people believe they will, with that belief being the causal link.

22. Sam Hopkins, "Sam Hopkins: Leading Global Thinker of 2014," interview, Camberwell, Chelsea, Wimbledon Graduate School Blog, November 27, 2014, http://www.ccw-graduateschool.org/sam-hopkins-leading-global-thinker-of-2014/.

23. Ben Walmsley and James Oliver write: "Here's the underlying problem, the arts are rarely afforded benchmark status in their own right, but are subject to the benchmarks of other disciplines and practices" ("Assessing the Value of the Arts," in *Key Issues in the Arts and Entertainment Industry*, ed. Ben Walmsley [Oxford: Goodfellow, 2011], 2).

24. A good place to start is the excellent collection of writings brought together in *The Affect Reader*, ed. Melissa Gregg and Gregory J. Seigworth (Durham, NC: Duke University Press, 2010).

25. Nina Felshin, *But is it Art? The Spirit of Activism* (Seattle: Bay Press, 1995).

Chapter One: How Artistic Activism Works

1. See especially the chapter on "The Language of African Literature," in Ngũgĩ wa Thiong'o, *Decolonizing the Mind: The Politics of Language in African Literature* (Oxford: James Currey, 1981).

2. Judith Butler, *Gender Trouble: Feminism and the Subversion of Identity* (New York and London: Routledge, 1999), 9.

3. Men make their own history, but they do not make it just as they please; they do not make it under circumstances chosen by themselves, but under circumstances directly found, given and transmitted from the past. The tradition of all the dead generations weighs like a nightmare on the brain of the living. Karl Marx, *The Eighteenth Brumaire of Louis Bonaparte*, in *The Marx-Engels Reader*, ed. Robert C. Tucker (New York: Norton, 1972), 595.

4. John 1:1 in the King James Bible.

5. Matthew Arnold, *Dover Beach and Other Poems* (New York: Dover, 2012), 87.

6. Matthew Arnold, *Culture and Anarchy* (Cambridge: Cambridge University Press, 1990), 6.

7. In addition to its visionary role, art also has for Arnold a critical function: providing new perspectives with which to look upon our present, "turning a stream of fresh and free thought upon our stock notions and habits" (*Culture and Anarchy* 6).

8. Arnold, *Culture and Anarchy*, 69.

9. *The German Ideology* was never published in Marx's lifetime. "Abandoned…to the gnawing criticism of the mice," in Marx's own words, it did not appear in public until 1932.

10. Karl Marx and Frederick Engels, *The German Ideology* (New York: International Publishers, 1970), 39.

11. Marx and Engels, *German Ideology*, 48.

12. Marx and Engels, *German Ideology*, 47.

13. Marx's materialist theory can even explain the existence of the idealists and their faith in the power of ideas. Such a theory and its theorists can be accounted for by looking at the division of labor in a society that allows for a leisure class of priestly intellectuals who have the time, opportunity, and confidence in their own powers to put forth such "world-changing" ideas (which then justify their own worldly importance and the necessity for the continuation of this division of labor). Furthermore, the rebellious nature of these ideas can be understood as a reflection of the fissures and contradictions inherent in the conditions and relations of production of any society. Radical thinkers (and artists) are the products of the very systems they critique.

14. Robert Reich, *The Work Of Nations: Preparing Ourselves for 21st-Century Capitalism* (New York: Knopf, 1991).

15. Robert C. Solomon, "The Politics of Emotion," in *The Joy of Philosophy: Thinking Thin versus the Passionate Life* (Oxford: Oxford University Press, 2003), 39.

16. Although *emotions* and *feelings* are often used interchangeably, the former more accurately refers to the bodily, pre- or un-conscious reactions to stimuli, while the latter are the mental sensations we have as our mind, through memory, personal experience, and social conditioning, interprets these biochemical reactions.

17. Deborah Gould, "On Affect and Protest," in *Political Emotions*, ed. Janet Staiger, Ann Cvetkovich, and Ann Reynolds (New York: Routledge, 2010), 32.

18. Gustave Le Bon, *The Crowd* (Piscataway, NJ: Transaction Publishers, 1995), 55–56 (emphasis mine).

19. Le Bon, 31.

20. Silvan Tomkins, "What are Affects?," in *Shame and Its Sisters: A Silvan Tomkins Reader* (Dunham, NC: Duke University Press, 1995), 34.

21. William James, "The Physical Basis of Emotion," *Psychological Review* 101, no. 2 (1994): 207.

22. Brian Massumi, "The Autonomy of Affect," *Cultural Critique*, no. 31 (*The Politics of Systems and Environments*), Part II (Autumn 1995): 83–109.

23. Max Weber, "Objectivity in Social Science and Social Policy," in *The Methodology of the Social Sciences* (Glencoe, IL: Free Press, 1949). More recently, the promise and problems of using *ideal types* is raised by Kieran Healy in "Fuck Nuance," *Sociological*

Theory 35, no. 2 (2017): 118–27; and John Durham Peters "'You Mean My Whole Fallacy Is Wrong': On Technological Determinism," *Representations* 140 (2017): 10–26.

24. Marx, *Capital*, vol. 1, in *The Marx-Engels Reader*, ed. Robert C. Tucker (New York: Norton, 1972), 344.

25. Silvan Tomkins, "What are Affects?," in *Shame and Its Sisters: A Silvan Tomkins Reader* (Durham, NC: Duke University Press, 1995), 37.

26. The Culture Group, *Making Waves: A Guide to Cultural Strategy* (n.p.: Air Traffic Control Education Fund, 2014), 49.

27. Culture Group, *Making Waves*, 5.

28. Favianna Rodriguez is also a member of The Culture Group.

29. Sade Lythcott, "Theater Artists Respond to the Trump Era" panel discussion with Rachel Chavkin, Ari Edelson, Margaret R. Lalley, and Stephen Duncombe at The University Seminars, Columbia University, New York, March 20, 2017.

30. Raymond Williams, *Marxism and Literature* (Oxford: Oxford University Press, 1977), 132.

31. Pierre Bourdieu uses the term "structuring structure" to describe the social systems with which we make sense of the world. For Bourdieu this *habitus*, as he calls it, is primarily mental, but I think it works well for the emotional as well (see his *Distinction: A Social Critique of the Judgement of Taste* [Cambridge, MA: Harvard University Press, 1984]).

32. "Emotions give ideas, ideologies, identities, and even interests their power to motivate," writes social movement theorist James M. Jasper, concluding that, "without them there might be no social action at all" ("The Emotions of Protest: Affective and Reactive Emotions in and around Social Movements," *Sociological Forum* 13, no. 3 [1998]: 420 and 398, respectively).

33. Stuart Hall, "Cultural Studies and the Centre: Some Problematics and Problems," in *Culture, Media, Language: Working Papers in Cultural Studies,1972–79* (London: Routledge; Centre for Contemporary Cultural Studies, University of Birmingham, 1992); Raymond Williams, "Culture," in *Keywords: A Vocabulary of Culture and Society* (Oxford: Oxford University Press, 1976). Both Hall and Williams, in turn, were influenced by Antonio Gramsci's writings on culture, especially in *Selections from the Prison Notebooks* (New York: International Publishers, 1971).

34. As Clifford Geertz writes: "Man is an animal suspended in webs of significance he himself has spun" (*The Interpretation of Cultures* [New York: Basic, 1973], 5).

35. Peter Schjeldahl, the late *New Yorker* art critic, explains the crystallization that art does: "The aesthetic isn't bounded by art, which merely concentrates it for efficient consumption" ("The Art of Dying," *The New Yorker*, December 16, 2019, n.p.).

Chapter Two: What Artistic Activism Does

1. The Bible, see Gen. 1:1, Exod. 20:4, Isa. 40:6–18; The Qur'an, see 21:51–66.

2. Plato, *The Republic*, bk. 10, ed. and trans. Desmond Lee (New York: Penguin, 1955).

3. Aristotle, *Poetics*, trans. S. H. Butcher (New York: Hill and Wang, 1961).

4. Ching Hao, "A Conversation on Method," in *The Chinese Theory of Art*, trans. and ed. Lin Yutang (New York: Putnam's Sons, 1967), 65. The emphasis on capturing the spirit, or *chi*, of what is represented is essential to the six techniques of painting which set the contemporary standards for the evaluation of Chinese art in the Imperial Period and beyond.

5. Matthew Arnold, *Culture and Anarchy* (Cambridge: Cambridge University Press, 1990); Mahatma Gandhi, *Hind Swaraj*, in *Cultural Resistance Reader*, ed. Stephen Duncombe (London: Verso, 2002), 200–204; John Berger, *Ways of Seeing* (London: Penguin and British Broadcasting Company, 1972); Karl Marx and Frederick Engels, *The German Ideology* (New York: International Publishers, 1970); Ngũgĩ wa Thiong'o, *Decolonizing the Mind: The Politics of Language in African Literature* (Oxford: James Currey, 1981).

6. W. E. B. DuBois, "Criteria of Negro Art," *The Crises*, October, 1926; Frantz Fanon, *On National Culture*, in *The Wretched of the Earth* (New York: Grove, 1963); Antonio Gramsci, *Selections from the Prison Notebooks*, trans. Quintin Hoare and Geoffrey Nowell Smith (New York: International Publishers, 1971); Thiong'o, *Decolonizing the Mind*; Jacques Rancière, *The Politics of Aesthetics*, trans. Gabriel Rockhill (London: Continuum, 2004).

7. Immanuel Kant, *The Critique of Judgement*, trans. James Creed Meredith (Oxford: Clarendon, 1952);

8. Bertolt Brecht, "A Short Organum for the Theatre," in *Brecht on Theatre*, trans. John Willet (New York: Hill and Wang, 1964)

9. Claire Bishop, "The Social Turn: Collaboration and its Discontents," *Artforum*, Winter 2001; Boris Groys, "On Art Activism," *E-Flux Journal* 56, no. 6 (2014); Chantal Mouffe, "Artistic Activism and Agonistic Spaces," *Art & Research* 1, no. 2 (2007).

10. Oswalde de Andrade, "Cannibalist Manifesto," trans. Leslie Bary, *Latin America Literary Review* 19, no. 38 (1991): 35–37; André Breton, *Manifesto of Surrealism*, in *Manifestoes of Surrealism*, trans. Richard Seaver and Helen R. Lane (Ann Arbor: University of Michigan Press and Ann Arbor Paperbacks, 1972); Audre Lorde, *Poetry Is Not a Luxury*, in *Sister Outsider* (Berkeley, CA: Crossing, 1984); José Muñoz, *Disidentifications: Queers of Color and the Performance of Politics* (Minneapolis: University Of Minnesota Press, 1999).

11. Walter Benjamin, "The Author as Producer," in Duncombe, *Cultural Resistance Reader*, 67–81.

12. Grant Kester, *Conversation Pieces: Community and Communication in Modern Art* (Berkeley: University of California, 2004).

13. Augusto Boal, *Theatre of the Oppressed*, trans. Charles A. and Maria-Odilia Leal McBride (New York: Theatre Communications Group, 1979).

14. Theodor Adorno, *Aesthetic Theory*, trans. R. Hullot-Kentor (Minneapolis: University of Minnesota Press, 1997); Herbert Marcuse, *The Aesthetic Dimension*, Beacon Press (1979).

15. John Dewey, *Art as Experience* (New York: Perigree and Penguin, 2005).

16. For instance, see discussion of Victor Cousins in John Wilcox, "The Beginnings of l'Art Pour l'Art," *The Journal of Aesthetics and Art Criticism* 11, no. 4 (1953): 368; see also Théophile Gautier, *Mademoiselle de Paupin* (London: Penguin, 2005). It should be noted that Cousins and Guatier were making a case for a nonutilitarian art at a time of the ascendance of rational science, capitalist industry, and planned bureaucracy. As such, a defense of art's lack of utility was a form of social critique. To "do nothing," in this social and historical context, was doing something.

17. Eleonora Belfiore and Oliver Bennett, "Rethinking the Social Impact of the Arts," *International Journal of Cultural Policy* 13, no. 2 (2007): 135–51; Belfiore and Bennett, *The Social Impact of the Arts: An Intellectual History* (New York: Palgrave Macmillan, 2008).

18. The affective power of story-telling and the ability of the arts to stimulate emotions was, of course, one of the things that convinced Plato that arts were a threat to the republic see *Republic* 10).

19. The alienation of art from everyday life through esotericism was of concern to John Dewey (see *Art as Experience* [New York: Perigee and Penguin, 2005]). Dewey's mission was to bring art back home by understanding it not as a thing in itself, but as something embedded in webs of social experience. Indeed, it was this connectedness to common experience, Dewey thought, that enabled art to communicate.

20. In this sort of approach to artistic activism, Grant Kester explains "Conversation becomes an integral part of the work itself. It is reframed as an active, generative process that can help us speak and imagine beyond the limits of fixed identities, official discourse, and the perceived inevitability of partisan political conflict" (*Conversation Pieces*, 8).

21. Suzanne Lacy's *Roof Is on Fire* project is probably the best-known example of this staple of "social practice" art. In 1994 Lacy choreographed a scene where teenagers had frank conversations about drugs, sex, school, and family in parked cars on a rooftop garage in Oakland, California—with Oakland residents listening in.

22. In his emphasis on power dynamics expressed through the physical body and movement, and the limitations of language as a tool of communication and connection, Leonardo's approach is analogous to that of Boal in *Theatre of the Oppressed*.

23. While the emphasis here is on giving opportunities for those who are silenced socially and culturally, a platform to express themselves and tell their stories, it also calls into question the very words and concepts and sensibilities that can, and cannot be spoken and "make sense." Thiong'o, as a playwright and theorist, raises this in the context of the alienation of natives from their own experience when forced to express themselves through the colonizer's language (see *Decolonizing the Mind*), while the philosopher Rancière explores this through what he calls "the distribution of the sensible," the regime of sensing and sense-making through which expression is valorized or silenced (see *Politics of Aesthetics*).

24. This capacity of arts for change is at the heart of Walter Benjamin's critique of con-

ventional political arts. Art can be *about* radical political contents, yet not necessarily function radically insofar as it reinforces the division of labor between worker and thinker, producer and consumer, artist and audience. Radical art, in Benjamin's estimation, "is better the more consumers it can turn into producers, that is, readers or spectators into collaborators" ("Author as Producer," 78).

25. Boal, explaining the importance of retraining the body from passivity to activity, transforming the spectator to the "spec-actor," writes: "The liberated spectator, as a whole person, launches into action. No matter that the action is fictional; what matters is that it is action!" (*Theatre of the Oppressed*, 134).

26. One of the earliest accounts of art making the invisible visible I've come across is the classic "six techniques" of Chinese painting, outlined by Hsieh Ho in the fifth century CE. The most important, and hardest to master of the techniques is capturing in a painting the invisible spirit, or *chi*, that animates the visible form of reality ("The Six Techniques of Painting," in *The Chinese Theory of Art*, trans. and ed. Lin Yutang [New York: Putnam's Sons, 1967]).

27. In very different ways, of course: King was interested in a documentary representation of white supremacy in order to communicate to those who refused to believe it; Picasso was invested in an expressive representation of the horrors of war for those who refused to feel it.

28. This relationship between the real and illusion is one of the other powers of art that drove Plato to despair. Art, for Plato, was an imitation, not a representation of reality. Worse, it was an imitation of an imitation (the *real* real existing in a world of forms, accessible only through rational philosophical inquiry). Worse yet, art created the illusion of reality through its performance or exhibition. Yet another reason to ban it from his ideal Republic (*Republic* 10).

29. John Cook and Sander van der Linden, "Facts Versus Feelings Isn't the Way to Think About Communicating Science," *The Conversation*, Summer 2017, https://theconversation.com/facts-versus-feelings-isnt-the-way-to-think-about-communicating-science-80555; Gerald L. Clore and Jeffrey R. Huntsinger, "How Emotions Inform Judgment and Regulate Thought," *Trends in Cognitive Science* 11, no. 9 (2007): 393–99; Antonio Damasio, *The Strange Order of Things: Life, Feeling, and the Making of Cultures* (New York: Pantheon, 2018); Damasio, *Descartes' Error: Emotion, Reason and the Human Brain,* (New York: Penguin, 1994).

30. What Ari is restating here is, of course, Aristotle's theories of identification from the *Poetics*.

31. The circumvention of barriers through artistic practices was critical to theorists and artists like André Breton and the Surrealists. The barriers, for Breton, were Western rationality itself: "The realistic attitude" and "the reign of logic" which stood in the way of meaningful (or perhaps meaningless) social change. André Breton (*Manifesto of Surrealism*, 6–9).

32. Andrew Ross, a prominent activist academic and member of Gulf Labor, was banned from the United Arab Emirates—but for his scholarly research into labor issues, not his creative work with the artistic activist group.

33. https://improveverywhere.com/about/. This is not to say that Improv Everywhere are purists. They do "commercial" surprises for individuals and corporations, but there is

a firewall between these and their more "artistic" performances.

34. Implicitly understanding the problem of the hegemonologue, advertising since the "creative revolution" in the field in the 1960s has made surprise into a routine practice: calling the VW Bug a "lemon" or using self-parody in making outlandish promises to sell deodorant. This "oddvertising," as it is sometimes called, truncates the moment of surprise by inevitably introducing the product as an answer to the question of "what is this?"

35. See, for example, the theories in Bishop, "Social Turn," Groys, "Art Activism," and Mouffe, "Artistic Activism and Agonistic Spaces."

36. In the grand tradition of the twentieth-century, Avant-Garde Political Beauty's founder, Phillip Ruch, even issued his own politico-aesthetic manifesto in *Wer, Wenn Nicht Wir?* (Munich: Ludwig, 2015).

37. Wafaa's words also call to mind Bertolt Brecht's *Verfremdungseffekt*, or "alienation effect" ("The Street Scene: A Basic Model for an Epic Theatre," in *Brecht on Theatre*, trans. John Willet [New York: Hill and Wang], 125).

38. Ann Markusen and Anne Gadwa, *Creative Placemaking* (Washington, DC: National Endowment for the Arts, 2010), 3.

39. Markusen and Gadwa, *Creative Placemaking*, 3.

40. In a classic scene from Virginia Woolf's groundbreaking essay *A Room of One's Own* (1929; repr. New York: Harcourt, 2005), the author juxtaposes the mean, dark, and cramped place of a women's college with the rich and comforting atmosphere of a luncheon at the nearby men's college. In the women's college, thoughts are guarded and opinions shrill, whereas amongst the men, the creativity that comes with confidence is nurtured: "No need to hurry. No need to sparkle. No need to be anybody but oneself. We are all going to heaven and Vandyck is of the company" (11).

41. Muñoz, *Disidentifications*.

42. These are pockets of resistance in Gramsci's "war of position" in, *Selections from the Prison Notebooks*.

43. As Audre Lorde writes: "Poetry is the way we give name to the nameless so it can be thought." Audre Lorde, ("Poetry Is Not a Luxury," in *Sister Outsider* [Berkeley, CA: Crossing, 1984], 37).

44. "Fired my imagination" was how Leon Trotsky critically assessed the æffect of Tatlin's tower, and the other contributions of the early Soviet avant-garde (*Literature and Revolution* [New York: Russell and Russell, 1957]).

45. As Lorde reminds us, dreams, like art, are places in which to imagine the unimaginable: "I could name at least ten ideas I would have found intolerable or incomprehensible and frightening, except as they came after dreams and poems" ("Poetry Is Not a Luxury," 37).

46. This is very much the relationship of the artist to the movement imagined by Frantz Fanon, in his essay "On National Culture" (in *The Wretched of the Earth* [New York: Grove Press, 1963]). The artist is less an independent visionary than an embedded

scribe for Fanon, and art does not lead the struggle for (Algerian) independence as much as give it support.

47. Théophile Gautier, who once wrote that "the only things that are really beautiful are those which have no use (*Mademoiselle de Paupin* [London: Penguin, 2005], 23), would have applauded the young artist.

48. For the genesis and early history of the concept of *l'art pour l'art*, see John Wilcox, "Beginnings of l'Art Pour l'Art."

49. Nato Thompson, "Living as Form," in *Living as Form: Socially Engaged Art from 1991–2011*, ed. Nato Thompson (Cambridge, MA: MIT Press and Creative Time, 2012), 18–33; Christine Dwyer, "Time-Tested Tools for Evaluation," *ArtsBlog* (Americans for the Arts), May 2, 2012, http://blog.artsusa.org/2012/05/02/time-tested-tools-for-evaluation/; Animating Democracy, *Introduction: A Values Guide to Evaluating Arts & Social Justice Work* (New York and Washington, DC: Americans for the Arts, 2015), 4; Beverly Naidus, *Arts for Change: Teaching Outside the Frame* (New York: New Village, 2009), 5.

50. Indeed, in a prior article entitled "Does it Work? The Æffect of Activist Art," I identified fourteen ways that artistic activism worked (*Social Research* 83, no. 1 [Spring 2016]: 115–34).

51. For example, in the article, I came up with four themes to describe how artistic activism works:

Imminent cultural shift: artistic activism can have an immediate impact on the way people think about an issue, for example "moving the needle" on public opinion.

Ultimate cultural change: artistic activism can have a profound, long-term effect on the way people think and perceive reality.

Imminent material impact: artistic activism can have an immediate, visible material impact.

Ultimate material outcome: artistic activism can produce deep, long-term structural or material change.

Susan C. Seifert and Mark J. Stern, in their *Civic Engagement and the Arts: Issues of Conceptualization and Measurement* (New York and Washington, DC: Animating Democracy and Americans for the Arts, 2009), usefully outline three ways in which art works as a form of activism:

Didactic theories of action: "the ability of the arts and culture to instruct or persuade the population."

Discursive theories of action: "the use of the arts to provide settings in which people can discuss issues, form conceptions and take action."

Ecological theories of action: "cultural participation as a form of civic engagement… that increase social capital and community capacity."

And in their *Continuum of Impact*" guide (2010, repr. New York and Washington, DC: Animating Democracy and Americans for the Arts, 2017), Pam Korza and Barbara Schaffer Bacon of Animating Democracy offer another useful breakdown of how arts can impact society, at the level of:

Knowledge: what people know—awareness and understanding;

Discourse: how people communicate—deliberation, dialogue, and media;

Attitudes: what people think and feel—values, motivation, and vision;

Capacity: know-how and resources—social capital, leadership, creative skills, and civic engagement;

Action: what people do—participation and mobilization

Conditions: change that is lasting—systems, physical, conditions, access, and equity.

52. In a comprehensive study of studies on "Social Impacts of Participation in the Arts and Cultural Activities" commissioned by Australian governments, the researchers came to a damning conclusion concluded that: "There is much anecdotal and otherwise informal evidence of positive impact(s) from participation in the arts and cultural activity but little data to support the hypotheses," primarily because the research results reviewed "provide evidence of diversity and complexity rather than of clear lines of causality or even associations between arts and cultural programs or activities and their impacts in the multiple arenas of the social domain" (Australian Expert Group in Industry Studies [AEGIS], *Social Impacts of Participation in the Arts and Cultural Activities, Stage Two Report: Evidence, Issues and Recommendations* [Canberra: Cultural Ministers Council Statistics Working Group, 2004], 10–11). While artistic activism is a more pointed practice than merely "arts participation," here, too, complexity and diversity are easier to ascertain than clear causality.

Chapter Three: Does Artistic Activism Work?

1. Galileo Galilei, cited in Lewis Mumford, *Technics and Civilization* (New York: Harcourt Brace, 1934), 48.

2. As a recent report prepared for the Ford Foundation, on *Evaluation Frameworks for Social Justice Philanthropy* argues, evaluation is key for (1) determining concrete *results*, and progress toward, or away, from the project's stated goal; (2) generating *enthusiasm* amongst participants, as they can observe real progress and results; (3) course *correction*, as project organizers reflect upon the project in process; (4) accelerated *learning*, by testing assumptions and strategies and generating new insights and practices; (5) demanding *accountability*, as good intentions are checked against empirically verified results (Max Niedzwiecki, *Evaluation Frameworks for Social Justice Philanthropy: A Review of Available Resources* [New York: Ford Foundation Working Group on Philanthropy for Social Justice, 2011], 5).

3. AndACTION, *Pop Culture Works for Social Change* (Washington, DC: Spitfire Strategies, 2017), http://andaction.org/wp-content/uploads/2017/03/Pop-Culture-Works-for-Social-Change_FINAL.pdf; Animating Democracy, *Introduction: A Values Guide to Evaluating Arts & Social Justice Work* (New York and Washington, DC: Americans for the Arts, 2015), http://animatingdemocracy.org/sites/default/files/INTRO%20A%20 Values%20Guide.pdf; John Borstal and Pam Korza, *Aesthetic Perspectives: Attributes of Excellence in Arts for Change*, Animating Democracy (New York and Washington,

DC: Americans for the Arts, 2017); The Australian Expert Group in Industry Studies (AEGIS), *Social Impacts of Participation in the Arts and Cultural Activities, Stage Two Report: Evidence, Issues and Recommendations* (Canberra, Australia: The Cultural Ministers Council Statistics Working Group, 2004); Eleonora Belfiore and Oliver Bennett, "Determinants of Impact: Towards a Better Understanding of Encounters with the Arts," *Cultural Trends* 16, no. 3 (2007): 225–75; BYP Group, *The Basics of Social Impact Evaluation, Resource 1*, Creative Victoria Social Impact Program, (New South Wales and Victoria, Australia: BYP Group, 2018); Suzanne Callahan, *Moments of Transformation: Rha Goddess's LOW and Understanding Social Change* (New York and Washington, DC: Americans for the Arts, 2009); Jan Cohen-Cruz, "The Imagination and Beyond: Toward a Method of Evaluating Socially Engaged Art," in *Future Imperfect: A Blade of Grass 2014–15*, ed. Elizabeth M. Grady (New York: A Blade of Grass Books, 2016), 144–53; Geoffrey Crossick and Patrycja Kaszynska, "Understanding the Value of Arts and Culture," The AHRC (Advocacy Humanity Reimagination Change) Cultural Value Project (London: Arts and Humanities Research Council, 2016); The Culture Group, *Making Waves: A Guide to Cultural Strategy* (n.p.: Air Traffic Control Education Fund, 2014); Christine Dwyer, "Time Tested Tools for Evaluation," *ArtsBlog*, May 2, 2012, http://blog.artsusa.org/2012/05/02/time-tested-tools-for-evaluation/; Christine Dwyer, Pam Korza, and Barbara Schaffer Bacon, "Arts and Civic Engagement: Briefing Paper for Working Group of the Arts & Civic Engagement Impact Initiative," *Animating Democracy* (blog), April 2008, http://animatingdemocracy.org/sites/default/files/dwyer_531.pdf; Fenton Communications, *See, Say, Feel, Do: Social Media Metrics That Matter* (Los Angeles: Fenton Communications, 2012); Alexis Frasz and Holly Sidford, *Mapping the Landscape of Socially Engaged Artistic Practice* (New York: Helicon Collaborative, 2017); Susan Galloway, "Theory-Based Evaluation and the Social Impact of the Arts," *Cultural Trends* 18, no. 2 (2009): 125–48; The Harmony Institute, *Impact Playbook: Best Practices for Understanding the Impact of Media* (North Potomic, MD: Harmony Institute, 2013); Y. Raj Isar, Kristina Hellqvist, and Dacia Viejo Rose, *Artistic Activism in Situations of Extreme Conflict: The Challenge of Evaluation* (Brussels: IETM [Interactive Electronic Technical Manuals], 2004); Maria-Rosario Jackson, Joaquín Herranz, and Florence Kabwasa-Green, *Art and Culture in Communities: A Framework for Measurement*, Policy Brief No. 1 of the Culture, Creativity, and Communities Program (Washington, DC: Urban Institute, 2003); Helen Klebesadel, "Features of Effective Activist Art," *Helen Klebesadel: A Muse and Her Artist* (blog), May 2, 2011, https://klebesadel.wordpress.com/2011/05/02/activist-art-art-that-works/; Pam Korza and Barbara Schaffer Bacon, *Continuum of Impact*, Animating Democracy (2010; repr. New York and Washington, DC: Americans for the Arts, 2017); Korza and Schaffer Bacon, "Evaluating Impact/Appreciating Evaluation," in *A Working Guide to the Landscape of Arts for Change*, Animating Democracy (New York and Washington, DC: Americans for the Arts, 2012); Lachlan MacDowall, Martin Mulligan, Frank Panucci, and Marnie Badham, *Spectres of Evaluation*, Centre for Cultural Partnerships (Melbourne, Australia: Melbourne University Press, 2013); Francoise Matarasso, "Use or Ornament: The Social Impact of Participation in the Arts," *Comedia*, Autumn 1997, https://www.culturenet.cz/coKmv4d994Swax/uploads/2014/11/1997-Matarasso-Use-or-Ornament-The-Social-Impact-of-Participation-in-the-Arts-1.pdf; Kevin McCarthy, Elizabeth Heneghan Ondaatje, Laura Zakaras, and Arthur Brooks, *Gifts of the Muse: Reframing the Debate about the Benefits of the Arts* (Santa Monica, CA: RAND Corporation, 2004); Ian David Moss, *Theory of Change and Evaluation Frameworks*, Evaluation Exchange Workshop 1 (New South Wales and Victoria, Australia: BYP Group, 2018; Philip M. Napoli, *Measuring Media Impact: An Overview of the Field*, Media Impact Project of the Lear Center at University of Southern California, December 1, 2014, https://mediaimpact.issuelab.org/resource/measuring-media-impact-an-overview-of-the-field.html; National Endowment for the Arts, *How Art Works: The National Endowment for the Arts' Five-Year Research Agenda, with a System Map and Mea-*

surement Model, based on a manuscript prepared by Monitor Institute (Washington, DC: National Endowment for the Arts, 2012); Andrew Newman, "Imagining the Social Impact of Museums and Galleries: Interrogating Cultural Policy through an Empirical Study," *International Journal of Cultural Policy* 19, no. 1 (2013): 120–37; Max Niedzwiecki, *Evaluation Frameworks for Social Justice Philanthropy: A Review of Available Resources* (New York: Ford Foundation Working Group on Philanthropy for Social Justice, 2011); Tanya Notley, Andrew Lowenthal, and Sam Gregory, *Video for Change: Creating and Measuring Social Impact*, working paper by the Video4Change Network, 2015 (repr. *Journal of Human Rights Practice* 9, no. 2 [2017]: 223–46); Alex Parkinson, *Framing Social Impact Measurement, Research Report R-1567-14-RR* (New York: The Conference Board, 2014); Nick Rabkin, *Hearts & Minds: Arts and Civic Engagement* (San Francisco: James Irvine Foundation, 2017); Teresa Sanz and Beatriz Rodriguez-Labajos, "Does Artistic Activism Change Anything? Strategic and Transformative effects of Arts in Anti-Coal Struggles in Oakland, CA," *Geoforum* 122 (2021): 41–54; Marilyn Smith, Rebecca Fisher, and Joelle Maderm, *Social Impacts and Benefits of Arts and Culture: A Literature Review* (Gatineau, Quebec: Department of Canadian Heritage, 2016); Mark J. Stern, "Measuring the Outcomes of Creative Placemaking," in *The Role of Artists & The Arts in Creative Placemaking* (Baltimore, MD: Goethe-Institut, 2014); Mark J. Stern and Susan C. Seifert, *Civic Engagement and the Arts: Issues of Conceptualization and Measurement*, Animating Democracy (New York and Washington, DC: Americans for the Arts, 2009); Stern and Seifert, *The Arts and Civic Engagement: A Field Guide for Practice, Research, and Policy*, Social Impact of the Arts Project (Philadelphia: University of Pennsylvania Press, 2009); Deirdre Williams, *How the Arts Measure Up*, Working Paper no. 8, The Social Impact of Arts Programs (Philadelphia: University of Pennsylvania Press, 1997); Ben Walmsey and James Oliver, "Assessing the Value of the Arts," in *Key Issues in the Arts and Entertainment Industry* (Oxford: Goodfellow, 2011); Walmsey, "Towards a Balanced Scorecard: A Critical Analysis of the Culture and Sport Evidence (CASE) Programme," *Cultural Trends* 21, no. 4 (2012): 325–34; Ricardo Wilson-Grau and Heather Britt, *Outcome Harvesting* (New York: New York: Middle East and North Africa [MENA] Office and the Ford Foundation, 2012).

4. V. S. Ramachandran and William Hirstein, "The Science of Art: A Neurological Theory of Aesthetic Experience," *Journal of Consciousness Studies* 6, no. 6–7 (1999): 15–51. For a critical view, see John Hyman, "Art and Neuroscience," in *Beyond Mimesis and Convention*, ed. Roman Frigg and Matthew C. Hunter, Boston Studies in the Philosophy of Science 262 (Dordrecht: Springer, 2010), 245–61.

5. "Our assessment is artist-driven," Deborah Fisher, Executive Director of A Blade of Grass, proclaims, "we don't look for anything the artist isn't asking us to look at ("Evolving the Institution," in Grady, *Future Imperfect*, 15).

6. This is what Mark Stern and Susan Seifert call "becoming a learning organization" (*Civic Engagement and the Arts*, 37; see also *Arts and Civic Engagement*).

7. In full disclosure, my organization, the Center for Artistic Activism, has received funding from A Blade of Grass and I have evaluated grantees for ABOG.

8. Christine Dwyer, *Evaluation Plan: Arts and Equity Initiative*, January, 2009, 2, https://animatingdemocracy.org/sites/default/files/Portland_A%26EI%20EvalPlan.pdf.

9. Dwyer, *Evaluation Plan*, 2.

10. To convince community stakeholders, for instance, of "improved Community Relationship w/ Police Department," Dwyer recommended pre- and post-intervention surveys

of community members as to the "perception that police are fair/act fairly, especially on part of communities of color/immigrant communities" (*Evaluation Plan*, 5–9).

11. Korza and Schaffer Bacon, *Continuum of Impact*, 37.

12. Borstal and Korza, *Aesthetic Perspectives*, 25.

13. These distinctions are "ideal types," useful for analysis. In messy reality, however, all three methodologies get mixed together. Cohen-Cruz spends a great deal of time working with artistic activists up front clarifying their intent; Dwyer engages one-on-one with them, facilitating their creative process; Korza carefully crafts the frameworks for others to "Do-It-Yourself." All three have worked with one another on evaluation projects and research.

14. Ricardo Wilson-Grau and Heather Britt, "Outcome Harvesting" (New York: Middle East and North Africa [MENA] Office and the Ford Foundation, 2012).

15. "Pulling it Off," can be marked not only as the success of a project, but the ability to be in a place to make projects. In a striking moment in conversation with the esteemed artistic activist Coco Fusco, she reminds us that being a Black, middle-aged, woman artist "who hasn't disappeared" and is still making art and making a living and working to change the world was, for her, a clear marker of success.

16. While Dow never changed their policies regarding ethical accountability, there was an immediate impact of the Yes Men's action: the stock price of Dow Chemical plummeted (alas, only to shoot back up almost as rapidly when people realized that Dow had no intention of acting responsibly).

17. Recently, someone told me of a version of *Journal Rappé* in Russia. When I asked Keyti about it, he said he had never heard of it and took the fact that he hadn't as a marker of his project's success.

18. As Ben Walmsley and James Oliver conclude when critically assessing the models for arts assessment: "This is not to devalue evaluation or outcomes per se, which can play an important role in terms of maintaining and developing good arts practice. But evaluation that is based on the needs or expectations of the paymaster does not necessarily adequately reflect the performance of an artist or arts organization in terms of their own practice, needs and expectations (let's say creativity)" ("Assessing the Value of the Arts," 4).

19. Audre Lorde, "The Master's Tools Will Never Dismantle the Master's House," *Sister Outsider* (Berkley, CA: Crossing, 1984).

20. Eleonora Belfiore and Oliver Bennett, who have done extensive work on reviewing both historical and contemporary, as well as philosophical and empirical, studies of the impact of the arts, conclude: "From the investigations we have undertaken, we know enough of the complexities involved to conclude safely that it is not possible to develop a rigorous protocol for the assessment of the impacts of the aesthetic experience that can be boiled down to a handful of bullet-points and a user-friendly 'evaluation toolkit,' to be easily applied to any art form in any setting and replicated whenever the need for impact evaluation arises" ("Determinants of Impact," 262–63).

21. Paulo Freire, *Pedagogy of the Oppressed*, trans. Mya Bergman Ramos (New York: Continuum, 1986), 58.

22. Freire, *Pedagogy of the Oppressed*, 24.

23. Freire, *Pedagogy of the Oppressed*, 101.

24. Freire, *Pedagogy of the Oppressed*, 67–68.

25. Freire, *Pedagogy of the Oppressed*, 101.

26. As Oliver and Walmsley write in their influential work on "Assessing the Value of the Arts": "In terms of public value, reflexivity is about not taking the so-called objective or subjective measures of value for granted, of imagining one or the other to be real or true, but in seeking out greater objectivity, recognizing that it can only be approached from various inter-subjectivities (including institutional) with a central reference point being practice, its conditions and situation. A consequence of this praxis should be to challenge a predetermined value that is imagined as the real goal or achievement, and thereby challenge a conception of value based on a single or linear reality of practice and its productions. In other words, value is emergent, not fixed and given; but as a dialectic of practice and its productions (the spaces of social relations), it is always under negotiation and in-the-making, and contingent on the multiple experiences and expressions of inter-subjectivity" (4–5).

27. Suzanne Callahan's in-depth evaluation (bolstered by a university research team) of the social impact of a performance piece by Rha Goddess on mental health, concludes with a "lessons learned" for future evaluation. The first lesson: "Begin with the artist's vision and intention for their work. Evaluation should honor that vision, follow its intent, and attempt to measure the degree to which that vision is realized" (*Moments of Transformation*, 19).

28. Rather late in this study, Greg Burbidge, the research and policy specialist of Calgary Arts Development, introduced me to the "developmental evaluation" models of Michael Quinn Patton. While I developed my method of assessment independently, I have since learned to appreciate Quinn's emphasis on contextuality and collaboration, and above all, the idea that evaluation, when done well, is an integral part of *developing* the project rather than merely judging after the fact. See Irene Guijt, Cecile Kusters, Hotze Lont, and Irene Visser, *Developmental Evaluation: Applying Complexity Concepts to Enhance Innovation and Use,* report from an expert seminar with Dr. Michael Quinn Patton (Wageningen, The Netherlands: Wageningen University and Research Centre for Development Innovation, in collaboration with Learning by Design and Context, 2012); Elizabeth Dozois, Marc Langlois, and Natasha Blanchet-Cohen, *DE 201: A Practitioner's Guide to Developmental Evaluation* (Victoria, British Columbia: University of Victoria: International Institute for Child Rights and Development, 2010).

Chapter Four: Assessing Æffect

1. For example, the staff at the ActionAid platform in Ghana, with input from regional artistic activists, reformulated the method so that it emphasizes an exploration of values and feelings of the participants.

2. Ibou Niang and Ummi Yakubu were particularly helpful in constructing this hypothetical example, and the idea for cleaning up a beach through the construction of a trash elephant came from a group of West African artistic activists I, and the Center for Artistic Activism, worked with in Guinea-Conakry in the Winter of 2017.

Appendix Æ: Affect and Effect

1. Unless otherwise specified, all definitions and historical quotations are from the *Oxford English Dictionary*, s.v. *affect* and *effect*, accessed June 15, 2017, http://www.oed.com/.

2. Geoffrey Chaucer, *Troilus & Cressida*, modernization by A. S. Kline (London: Poetry in Translation, 2001), 230.

3. Immanuel Kant, *The Critique of Judgement*, trans. James Creed Meredith (Oxford: Clarendon, 1952).

4. Plato, *The Republic*, ed. and trans. Desmond Lee (New York: Penguin, 1955).

Index

To help with assessing the æffect of artistic activism, these tools were created by the Center for Artistic Activism and are provided to you, for free.

The Æffect App: An online, digital mentor for æffective artistic activist interventions built upon a series of prompts and reflections to help you develop stronger projects, evaluate their impact, and plan next steps. The app provides helpful examples and useful resources, and can generate a report of your process at the end. https://aeffectapp.org/

The Æffect Planning and Assessment Toolset: A complete toolset for helping you plan and assess your artistic activism. It includes the Æffect Assessment Script, the Æffect App, a downloadable and fillable worksheet, basic measurements, examples of adaptations, and more. https://c4aa.org/assessment-toolset

Stephen Duncombe is Professor of Media and Culture at New York University and author and editor of nine books and numerous articles on the intersection of culture and politics. These include *Dream: Re-Imagining Progressive Politics in an Age of Fantasy* (New Press, 2007; O/R Books, 2019), the *Cultural Resistance Reader* (Verso, 2002), and, with Steve Lambert, *The Art of Activism* (O/R Books, 2021). He is the creator of the Open Utopia, an open-access, open-source, web-based edition of Thomas More's *Utopia*, and co-creator of Actipedia.org, a user-generated digital database of artistic activism case studies. A life-long activist, Duncombe is the co-founder and Research Director of the Center for Artistic Activism, a research and training organization that helps activists create more like artists and artists strategize more like activists.